sculpture parks in europe
a guide to art and nature

created & edited by valeria varas and raul rispa

introduction by jimena blázquez abascal

Birkhäuser
Basel

sculpture parks in europe
a guide to art and nature

created by   valeria varas and raul rispa, editors

from an idea by   jimena blázquez abascal & documenta artes

concept, project, and design   the editors + documenta artes y ciencias visuales
assistant editors   manuel garcía ,alba castillón, elisabetta domènech, irene molina

credited texts   the authors
non-credited texts   paul harsh, raul rispa, editorial team, jimena blázquez, ana morales
iconographic material, data   parks, museums and respective individuals (see p. 254)

graphic design and layout   eva r. jular + paco márquez + alessia guerzoni
documentation   maya velkova, fundación nmac, paula llull, ana morales, laura lópez, documenta artes' editorial staff
maps   arancha otero, manuel garcía
cover design   muriel comby

international editions   paul harsh, teresa santiago
english version   david cohn, aisha prigann, paul brykczynski, samantha lyle, keith absalom

library of congress cataloging-in-publication data. a CIP catalog record for this book has been applied for at the library of congress.
bibliographic information published by the german national library.
the german national library lists this publication in the deutsche national-bibliografie; detailed bibliographic data are available on the Internet at http://dnb.dnb.de.

this publication is also available in a german language edition
(isbn 978-3-0356-1115-1)

©   2017, 2006 for the english edition
birkhäuser
p.o. box 44, 4009 basel, switzerland
part of walter de gruyter gmbh, berlin/boston
©   **documenta artsDiffusion**, s.l., madrid 2016, 2017
©   editorial@documenta-arts-diff.com
©   documenta artes y ciencias visuales, madrid 2006
fundación nmac, vejer de la frontera 2006
©   artworks reproductions: their **copyright holders**
all rights reserved
printing and binding   gráficas irudi s.l, vitoria gasteiz
printed on acid-free paper produced from chlorine-free pulp. TCF ∞
d.l.   m-29925-2016, 2017   printed in spain

ISBN   978-3-0356-1116-8

9 8 7 6 5 4 3 2 1   www.birkhauser.com

This book is about sculpture parks, which form part of a wider field: art and nature. On page 6, the editors provide notes and clarify important terms regarding the nature, scope, attributes and developmental process of the work featured within this book. The reader will notice that the book has two main functions and purposes: firstly, to serve as a reference, reading or study material with which to learn more, take pleasure in knowledge, investigate, etc. and secondly, to serve as a travel guide for cultural trips, providing information on where to go and what to see. Therefore, there are two kinds of reading material – one consisting of continuous, project-related text; the other of concise reference sections – which has resulted in the inevitable repetition of certain ideas. To best serve these dual purposes, the book has been structured in three parts: an introduction, a main body and a final section with useful tools.

The Editor's Note in the first section is essential reading for any demanding or professional reader. The Note is not just a listing; it explains the selective character of the book: the 177 parks, gardens, centres, etc. are outlined in descriptions that vary in length and content according to their assessment on 10 levels – from a brief mention in the text to specific entries of up to 6 pages. It includes a borderless, European map, which illustrates the vast territory covered. The introduction by Jimena Blázquez provides the reader with some basic insight into the subject and the selected "art and nature projects."

The second section is organised alphabetically, first by country, then by the towns where the parks are located, although it begins with a route that runs through two countries, Germany and Holland. All are listed according to their original language toponym. Each country's chapter begins with an introduction – synthetic but rich in information and focused on the subject at hand – aimed in three principal directions: the environment, historical milestones and key artistic references, particularly contemporary ones. In addition, information on other centres and events as well as sites that are somehow related to the guide's core material is provided in boxes or as captions. As for the parks, a column at the top of each entry provides practical information and facts compiled by the editorial team based on questionnaires supplied ad hoc by each park. Depending on the assessment given, each centre with an individual entry will be described in 1 to 6 pages.

Each description contains two types of interrelated content: visual and written material. The former contains photographs of the sculptures or other important works; the main entries also include maps of the area and/or park. The photographs were selected from material provided by the museums or parks (also responsible for all details relating to authorship, titles and dates of the artwork), and the maps were prepared by the Documenta editorial team from materials provided by each entity; everything was selected and coordinated into a visual discourse by the editor, Valeria Varas. The written material is editorial, unless indicated otherwise or directly quoted, supervised by the editor, Raul Rispa, and based on texts provided by the museums and the NMAC Foundation, in-house production and the vast amount of documentation managed by the editorial team.

The third section includes an alphabetical vale to the parks; a selected bibliography to deepen the reader's knowledge of artists, themes, art movements and specific art centres; acknowledgement of the long list of contributors who made this project possible.

The Editors appreciate any and all suggestions that might improve or update the content of this publication.

We are made of stardust. We are Nature and yet we harm Mother Earth. These are self-evident truths that some choose to ignore and others forget. At the dawn of the 21st c. climate change and a loss in biodiversity are the correlates of a consumerist society governed by a media empire that touts banal-ity, spectacle and fleeting events.

In February 2004, we met Jimena Blázquez and Paula Llull from the NMAC Foundation to talk about art and nature. They had an idea for a directory about European sculpture parks; we had plans for the subject matter. We decided to merge their idea with one of our programmes. We developed the concept and created the project for the book and its publication – all very innovative. The following notes, along with the information on page 5 are there to facilitate the use and enjoyment of this book.

At the very beginning everything had been One, a fact upheld by both modern science and ancient myths of creation: Egyptians, Sumerians, Hindus, Hebrews, Greeks, Chinese and Americans. The Big Bang is estimated to have occurred 15 billion years ago. Plato established the dualism of opposites that via Descartes has governed western civilisation until today: good and evil, matter and spirit, body and soul, art and nature. Meanwhile, a non-dual view of the world lies at the core of Hinduism: *Vedas* (1500 BC), *Advaita Vedanta* (9th c.), Taoism: universe, nature, yin and yang, Buddhism, Spinoza, Hegel's system, Lukács' aesthetic, the non-separation of subject and object in Heisenberg's uncertainty principle, the "everything has a bearing on everything" in deep ecology. The ending of Wittgenstein's *Tractatus* and the beginning of Lao Zi's *Dao De King* (5th c. BC) coincide.

The origins of the arts lie in fertility rituals. In the introduction to each country we cite primordial artworks such as goddess statuettes and megaliths, which embody the inextricable connection between art and nature. These objects also bear a formal similarity to contemporary work that has been emphasised by current theory and criticism.

Sculpture stood apart from nature for thousands of years as a servant to architecture, a decorative and figurative element until a scant 90 years ago. Heidegger traced the origins of artwork to the way man clears the earth to make it habitable ("das Roden" in German), trimming plants and draining swamps. A thousand years before, China's highest art form the garden, was created by excavating the earth. Nothing remains of the earth as it was prior to the arrival of man[1], no untouched nature is left in Europe. Both in theory and practice, the environment is a product of human technology, of *techne* – meaning knowing how to do something, a shared origin with the arts.

The Egyptians had gardens 4,600 years ago; legend shrouds the hanging gardens of Babylon, the time in which the Bible tells of God creating the Garden of Eden and placing Adam and Eve in it. The Persian parks and "paradises" fascinated the Ancient Greeks to such an extent that their thinkers philosophised and taught in the garden, the supreme place of knowledge Plato's Academy, Aristotle's Lyceum, the Garden of Epicurus – brought to Rome by Lucullus, they became places of power – Nero's Domus Aurea, Hadrian's Villa – intellectual havens – the villas of Varro, Cicero, Pliny the Younger, Horace – and fused with science – the automatons of Alexandria. They are all imitations of nature, architectural spaces with sculptures and artworks, which in their essence are still important today – Italian Renaissance gardens, French geometry, English landscaping, German public parks – modulated by the exquisite variations.

Found in the air and water gardens of Moorish Spain, the sinuous stone and ponds of China, the abstract bareness of the Japanese Zen garden. Artifact, that which is done with art – be it park or sculpture.

On the most basic level is the garden as pleasant backdrop for harmoniously placed sculptures, a cultured locus amoenus. Since the book deals with the 20th c., the first were the Brookgreen Gardens (ca. 1930) and De Cordova (1950) in the USA and the Kröller-Müller (1961) in Europe. Moving to the next level, a whole panorama unfolds: projects for site-specific sculptural works; art in nature centres based on a plan and design; gardens that are in themselves works of art – such as those of Isamu Noguchi or Derek Jarman. During the mid-20th c. however, sculpture was an expanding field[2]; in other words, the boundaries between disciplines were dissolving. Moving beyond Duchamp's found object, assemblage, installation, process art are shifting from the sculpture's centre to that which surrounds it. At the same time, architecture and the art of creating landscapes, gardens and urban areas are not only returning to the prehistoric cromlechs – as Morris states with regards to his *Observatory*: a type of para-architectural complex – but also transforming industrial wasteland into habitats.

In capturing this rich diversity, the book focuses on sculpture parks and art in nature centres, but also provides examples of these artistic practices. Included are the most far-reaching and radical varieties to emerge under the banner of art in nature: land art, environmental art, earthworks, introduced in the USA in the 1960s by Robert Morris, Nancy Holt and Dennis Oppenheim, following the first two laws of thermodynamics, specifically entropy as theorised by Robert Smithson[3] and put into practice by Smithson, Michael Heizer and Walter De María; the artistic realisation of the aforementioned non-dual view of the world.

You have in your hands a guide operating on two levels of critical assessment – selection, evaluation – both an explicit and implicit orientation for the reader on which to direct their gaze or their steps as well as a practical manual: a tool with which to chart a crucial field in contemporary art without getting lost amidst the many languages. It is a collective work in every sense of the word, far removed from the subjective tastes of a single author: the 1855 Burckhardt travel guide about Italy, Oer Cicerone, has little in common with our 18 countries and 2006, the 670th anniversary of Petrarch's account of ascending Mont Ventoux.

It is a modern day palimpsest: many hands at work, sharing a single voice. A complex structure is used to build the discourse, both in the overall book and on each page: different kinds of text, data, maps, photographs. The main texts – 9/10ths factual, descriptive and at times intersecting; 1/10th subjective assess-

Alberto, *El pueblo español tiene un camino que conduce a una estrella*, 1937, Paris, demolished, later reproduced in front of the Museo Nacional Centro de Arte Reina Sofia, Madrid, 2002

ments – avoid the abuse of pseudo-jargon used by the agraphic "pack of cultural managers": site-specific has therefore been left as a (polysemous) mark.

The information design translates into a layout that is not only pleasant but expressive, heuristic and follows a pattern that seeks an interaction with the reader. The guide, in provoking and awaiting your answer is more important because of the meanings and functions that each reader obtains from using its structural network than for what is is on its own.

The whole is different from and superior to its parts; it is content and discourse in and of itself. Therefore, it does not shy away from being highbrow, assuming that the reader already possesses certain knowledge, a thirst for information or a desire for aestheic pleasure.

1 Maderuelo 1996
2 Krauss 1979
3 Smithson 1967 and 1968

norge

ireland   nederland

            united kingdom

                                belgique/
                                belgië

                                            luxembourg

                        france

                                    españa

            portugal

sverige

finland

latvija

danmark

lietuva

deutschland

polska

slovakia

svizzera/
suisse/schweiz

austria/
österreich

hungary

românia

italia

croatia

bulgaria

albania

Many things have changed in Art and in Europe in the second half of the second decade of the 21st c. with respect to the start of the century. In 2006, this was a seminal and innovative work, published at the same time in five international co-editions, in English, Spanish, German, Italian and Dutch: it was the first in the field, covering from the north of Europe to the extreme south of the sub-tropical Canary islands. All the editions sold out earlier than expected.

We set ourselves a term of ten years for issuing the second revised, updated and extended edition. For many, the period seemed too long. But in our view, it was just right, for reasons of both historical and art critical rigour and because it is a serious (although attractive) publication in book format. In the empire of the banal and ephemeral, we would not want to be like a yearbook or gastronomic guide that changes its ratings every year. This is a time of the scientific disciplines of History and Criticism.

When the first edition appeared it seemed we had "to fight for what is obvious" (Dürrenmatt). Now, the parks and sculptures attract visitors in growing numbers, at a greater rate than enclosed museums. They are no longer second-class, at least in the most advanced countries. In 2015 the Art Fund Prize for Museum of the Year 2014 was given to a sculpture park: the YSP Yorkshire Sculpture Park (p. 236). And in 2016, among the five finalists was a new private and not institutional venture: Jupiter Artland, close to Edinburgh (p. 218). Before this, the market, which always has an eye for business opportunities, had already initiated its sculpture park in London in 2005 at the Frieze art fair, with free access for the public.

Everything has its history. We all know of the relationship between sculpture and gardens, art and nature (see p. 6–7). From Ancient Greece we recall the rustic sanctuaries where statues and trees coexisted in a spontaneous rather than planned way (Ridgway 1981). We know how Cicero asked his editor, the great Atticus, to send him Greek sculptures that would be integrated in the gardens of his villas on an equal footing with trees and plants. And there was the legendary sculpture garden of Lorenzo de Médicis in Renaissance Florence.

That history has its contemporary chapter in the 1960s, when sculptors emerged from the studio to install works all'aperto. In 1968 the indispensable Robert Smithson showed his "Earthworks" in the Dwan New York gallery. Five years later Lucy R. Lippard recorded without possible doubt the "dematerialisation of the art object" (1973). And six years after that, the often-quoted article by Krauss "Sculpture in the Expanded Field" (1979) set up a theoretical structure for the phenomenon. Before sculpture parks had been created in the United States (in the 1930s) and in Europe – the Middleheim 1950 and the Kröller-Muller 1961. In other words, artists and the other members of the art system were ahead of art theory and criticism.

In the 1st edition of 2006 of this guidebook most of the parks selected responded in the final instance to the classical Roman concept of *hortus conclusus*, the garden of a closed villa with an access gate.

Over these 10 years, the concept has been extended towars open spaces. And the idea of sculpture has "expanded": here, we use the term "sculpture parks" to simplify the title of the book. This generic name includes sculpture gardens, sculpture trails including sculptures and art installations, earthworks, site-specific art (coined by Robert Irwin, c. 1968), land art, arte povera, environmental art with environmental concerns and a connection between the artist and nature using natural materials, ecological art, EcoArt, environmental sculpture, sustainable art, landscape art, landscape architecture, etc. The borders between the traditional fields of art have become blurred, if not completely erased.

The writings of Robert Smithson are fundamental and valid today. But unlike half a century ago, today historical study, theoretical reflection and the exercise of criticism cover various fields, keeping pace with and even triggering new artistic practices.

In the field of History, Soviet culture, meaning the USSR and the countries of the Eastern Bloc with democratic or popular republics, has been revisited and re-appreciated with a less ideological and Manichean approach, in particular since the 1990s. At the First Congress of Soviet Artists it was recognised that "the character of Soviet man, who is emancipated from explotation [...] has not yet been represented in works of art":

the self-criticism dates back to 1957 at the height of the Khrushchev thaw, which brought to light the false rigid homogeneity of the institutional practice of "Stalin's World". Twenty-four years earlier what Gorky in 1932 called "Socialist Realism" was implemented as the official aesthetic of the Party and the USSR. Gorky was building on his magisterial revolutionary novel The Mother (1906), which was based on the Russian realism of the 19th century. The key role of the body was initially advocated by Lunacharsky before Stalin, and reinforced by the cultural doctrine of Zhdanov, the Secretary of the Central Committee of the Communist Party since 1946.

In 2012 an international conference at Moderna Museet in Stockholm reviewed socialist realism, its production and consumption as an Aesthetic of Power, with major panellists such as Daniel Birnbaum, Boris Groys, Evgeny Dobrenko, Jerome Bazin, etc. The response to the question raised there by Mirela Tanta: "State propaganda or sites of resistance?" today appears very clear. That same year, Andrea Fraser highlighted in the text contributed to the Whitney Biennial of 2012, that "the art world [Western] has been a direct beneficiary of the inequality and concentration of the wealth of exacerbated capitalism": 1% of the increase in the wealth of the super-rich (0.1% of the population) involves a rise of more than 14% in the price of art. Galleries, fairs, biennials, museums, show works of political art. And nothing changes.

Now without the a priori ideas fostered by the respective hegemon, we know that there are important works of socialist realism (created under communism) and social realism (created under capitalism). A whole new thematic and transnational section (following the chapter on the United Kingdom) presents a highly selective review of the former communist block, from Lithuania to Albania and Bulgaria.

Rapid climate change through human action that threatens life on the planet has led to a reaction from artists and art theorists. There is an "Ökologische Naturästhetik" (Böhme 1989), an "Ökologische Ästhetik" (Strelow / David 2004) and an Ecology of Sculpture, in which the praxis and theory of Prigann (unfinished) (pp. 49, 58) and Llull 2012, propose the recovery of industrial ruins for new uses and site-specific works designed not for timeless permanence, but to be returned to Earth, to be dissolved back into it: this is something that various artists represented in this book had begun. The first congress of the IAA International Aesthetics Association was held in Berlin 1913. For its centenary the 19th ICA International Congress of Aesthetics (2013, Krakow, Poland), with the remarkable title and slogan "Naturalising Aesthetics", dedicated three of its ten themes to the field of art and nature. And at the 20th ICA in Seoul (July 2016) the Aesthetics of the Environment and Ecology are once more major themes and new concepts for designed space.

More radical by making explicit its focus on climate change and suggesting what art can bring to the table are Eco-Aesthetics by Miles (2014), along the lines of the Araeen manifesto (2009) or the Demos (2009) sustainability policies. The Aesthetics of Landscape is attracting growing interest, and thus the prize from the British Landscape Research Group for the best international thesis in 2016 has been awarded to the interdisciplinary: a New Geophilosophy by Menatti.

Our aim is to overcome dualism in favour of a "culture of complexity" (Kagan 2011). But without falling into the "anoixism" extended from Asia by Weilin Fang and others, which is worthy in terms of its opening up to nature, but whose acceptance of any doctrine may be read as neo-neo-liberalism in a new Chinese version of retrograde post-modernism.

In a historical period of an unprecedented invasion by the technification of what is human, the mass entertainment industry is eager to offer virtual reality everywhere as "experiences that are more real than the real world." We do not believe that this path is that of the natural evolution of Humanity, which is obviously still continuing. Maybe because we are something of an "artful species" (Davies 2013), or from an innate "art instinct" (Dutton 2010), it is Art and Nature which can still win us a future in which to believe.

For all these reasons, and to reflect on-site investigations and documentary critical analyses, this 2nd edition has been revised quantitatively and qualitatively, updated and extended. It has eliminated 16 parks or sites, including some destroyed, others re-evaluated. Now it contains 171 sites, compared with 133 in the 1st edition, of a greater variety of types and in seven more countries. Readers of the text and viewers of the reproductions of the artworks have at their disposal what the wisdom of Cicero once advised: sculpture, nature and books.

an introduction   Jimena Blázquez Abascal

Over the course of European history, the relationship between art and nature has acquired a complex character, which has been studied time and again in fields as diverse as philosophy, art history, aesthetics, psychology, sociology and the semiotics of art. According to the most traditional school of thought, art is not natural, but rather its exact opposite. Art is artifice, the antonym of nature. The paradigm of "art imitating nature" originated in Ancient Greece and essentially means that an artwork reproduces the tangible physical world, the visible reality. This was exemplified by the pictorial genre and its meticulous representations of landscapes or still lifes in which the detailed copy or reflection of what has been observed are paramount.

Menhir, Champ Dolent, Bretagne, France

The Ancient Greeks saw this faithful representation not only in the material world, but also in the processes that occur within it: "When we knit, we imitate the spider; when we build, the swallow; when we sing, the swan and the mockingbird."[1] In his Theogony (7th c. BC), Hesiod perceived art as an imitation of truth; a theory that was further developed by Socrates, later consolidated by Plato and Aristotle and presented art as the pure mimesis of nature, as the same reality, which eventually led to the idea that copying the universe was an innate tendency of humankind.

Since our very beginnings, we have not only formed part of the earth like flora and fauna do, but have also used it as a source of artistic inspiration throughout our history. Through the mimesis of the natural world, we have expressed our fears, our beliefs, our desires and emotions as well the aesthetic values of each era.

The relationship between art and nature has thus marked our artistic practices and theories throughout time. During the Renaissance, the writings of Leon Battista Alberti and the paintings of Leonardo da Vinci once again reaffirmed the paradigm of art as an imitation of reality. In the mid-19th and early 20th c., the Romantic movement arose in response to the neoclassic academic rigidity and rationalism, thus countering a way of thought that had governed Europe for countless centuries before. Romanticism was full of emotion, exalting nature and the picturesque and seeking the sublime. The natural world was transformed into myth, an unknown force that became one of the primary artistic subjects of the century, as seen in the landscapes of Constable, Friedrich, and Turner, in which the artists explored the most hidden and incalculable depths of nature.

A short time later, the legacy of Romanticism and the advent of photography contributed to the inrush of impressionist painting – a new way of approaching nature, in which colour and light played the most significant roles. "But the most dramatic shift, the most radical in thousands of years, took place in the early 20th c. when a handful of truly revolutionary artists from different parts of Europe began to push art towards abstraction, abandoning the canon that equated beauty with a harmonious reproduction of the world be it earthly and biological or imagined and ideal. Instead, these artists created new forms, which were abstract rather than realistic, describing no thing or being in particular." Some were influenced by Paul Cézanne, others looked to primitivism, Pablo Picasso and George Braque introduced cubism, the futurists and Malevich, Kandinsky, Mondrian, to name just a few pioneers of the avant-garde, inaugurated a whole new era; an era that contributed to the development of the European sculpture parks included in this book.

Artists like Umberto Boccioni and his "States of Mind," Pablo Gargallo and his transposition of concave and convex surfaces, Wladimir Tatlin and his "counter-reliefs" revolutionised sculpture, whereas Jean Arp (his own experiments and Dada activities), Naum Gabo (pure geometric constructions), Constantin Brâncuși (ovoid forms), El Lissitzky (his Proun, "positioned between art and architecture") and the Soviet constructivists broke new, fertile ground from which the modern masters would emerge. After Marcel Duchamp and his ready-mades (1913), art would never be the same again, moving away from the "work of art"and towards the "object".

These groundbreaking ideas paved the way, half a century later, for environments and assemblages, minimalism, conceptual art and Arte Povera, land art, earthworks or earth art, radically formulated by Smithson and Turrell and often collectively described, as is customary in Italy, as "environmental art." These movements profoundly altered the traditional dialectic between the earth and the artifact (*arte factum*).

Since then, this interrelationship has become the subject of an increasing number of investigations by theorists and artists, using a wide array of expressive media: painting, photography, video, poetry, literature, and, of course, sculpture, "understood here as moving beyond the traditional statue to encompass new typologies like installations and pervious and habitable objects or quasi-architecture." Europe has a long tradition of art in nature, especially as far as sculpture and installation are concerned, which dates back to the early dolmens and menhirs of prehistoric times. Thousands of years later, the tradition continued with the Italian gardens of the Renaissance with statues and grottos, the baroque French gardens with labyrinths and parterres, the landscaping of the 18th c. English gardens and the introduction of figurative sculpture as an element of garden decor throughout the continent. Embodied in these examples is a repeated and close exchange between the artificial and the natural, between the creator and the fantasy, in a constant search for the link between the landscape and artistic creation.

During the last few years,[2] there has been a notable rise in the number of centres dedicated to sculptural projects in natural settings. Artwork of this kind, which reflects on or relates to nature, is usually realized in parks, gardens, forests, wetlands, valleys, coasts; and shores. These enclaves are not urban, but they have been touched by human intervention. The artworks located within them do not alter

the substance of the original environment, thus expressing a new nexus between the artificial and the natural.

This publication, currently the only one of its kind, provides an extensive look at the European continent, which has always stood out for its interest in culture and the arts. Its incredibly diverse natural landscape is home to some of the most beautiful and remote places, which embody both the similarities and contrasts between the countries that make up the continent.

Europe is already home to several sculpture parks, but their immense public appeal has led to many new initiatives and a yearly increase in their number. At the same time, several public art projects of dubious quality, realised in both urban and green spaces, cropped up during the late 20th c. Overall, these are characterised by doubtful or low quality work or a debatable integration into the environment. Projects like these have been omitted from this guide, which has followed rigorous selection criteria based on certain characteristics. Firstly, we have opted for spaces and centres with a coherent and permanent collection and have based our selection on the artistic quality of the work and the relevance of the artists. The natural setting of the centres and the protection and respect given to the environment also played an important role in the selection process. The variety of the different centres allows the reader to understand the immense cultural and natural diversity of the European continent.

Constantin Brâncuși, *Endless Column*, 1938, Târgu-Jiu, Romania

During the past century, the natural environment has been abused, its resources exploited for individual gain. We have distanced ourselves from nature and in doing so have lost our respect for it, decimating and modifying the earth to suit our new ways of life. Urban sprawl has encroached on nature, highways and motorways have divided it, pollution, deforestation, fires, and the misuse of its resources have made us lose our connection to the earth, forgetting the fact that it is our most important asset, whence we came from and without which we could not survive. Conscious of the damage inflicted, an increased collective awareness is fostering a more cordial dialogue and respectful approach towards nature. A new understanding has emerged through artistic expression that aims to improve our relationship with the environment, promoting increased awareness and direct contact with nature, both far too neglected in the shadow of unbridled industrialisation and modern technology.

Richard Serra, *Château La Mormaire*, 1994, Grosrouvre, France

Cultural forms of expression, previously concentrated in urban areas, have been largely decentralised, contributing to an increase over the past few years of art centres in outlying, natural settings.[3] Both private and public initiatives have founded centres dedicated to a respectful dialogue with the environment and the spreading of modern and contemporary culture. At the same time, these centres encourage the public to consider and understand art from a different perspective, one that might strike visitors as quite unfamiliar when compared to a traditional museum experience.

The act of seeing sculptures in nature is a consistently different and often surprising experience, depending on the artist's conception of the piece and the dialogue that exists between the artwork and the site. Some pieces are of a more intimate nature, others are more visual or monumental or play with pre-existing elements in the landscape, such as sounds, smells, climate, or light. In other cases, the pieces blend into the landscape and thus force the viewer to look at the work in a different way. By focusing on minute details, for example, the environment can be perceived in a more discerning manner.

Sculpture parks, most of which are located in outlying areas, have benefited significantly from the increase in cultural tourism since the end of the 20th c. Most of the parks attract both a local clientele as well as foreign visitors, who all share a common love for art and nature. Artworks by internationally renowned artists, accompanied by an appealing educational and cultural programme, often revitalise the areas in which they are located.

Stimulating the economy via cultural means, which often involves turning previously unrelated sites into artistic projects – quarries, mines, forests, wetlands, former industrial sites, etc., can aid in the recuperation of degraded environments. This socio-economic improvement is unique to these sites, which are located outside of the common circuits.

Another key element of the sculptural parks as well as an important draw for the public is the protection of the environment. As the reader will see, artistic intervention in these spaces always occurs within an environmentally friendly context, ensuring that the landscape is never harmed by the creative process. Some pieces go even further, their goal being a return to nature and a new way for mankind to approach the universe. The aim is not just to show the work of sculptors or to establish a dialectic relationship between art and nature, but also to foster contact with and respect for the earth.

The book features several places that are located within nature protection areas. National parks, nature reserves and natural parks are places of public interest and protected to varying degrees. Due to their immense ecological value, national parks enjoy the highest level of protection.

In Holland, a museum and an outdoor sculptural collection were combined with a preserved landscape and opened to the public, as can be seen at the Kröller-Müller, located in the De Hoge Veluwe National Park. Another very different example is the Kielder Water and Forest Park in Scotland, where the richness of the landscape coexists with sculptures, installations, tourism, and the lumber industry, all organised within the framework of a sustainable development programme.

The reader is given insight into the different educational policies and varying conduct of park visitors with regards to the environment. The general public in Nordic countries like Sweden and Denmark and others like Holland and Belgium is conscientious and very involved in the protection of their natural heritage, exhibiting a profound respect for the environment. For example, some parks can be explored on bicycle and many allow picnics. In southern European countries like Spain, Italy, or Portugal, these practices are not allowed due to countless experiences with the public's ill conduct and lack of respect.

In the Nordic countries, the parks are generally open between the months of May and September due to the harsh climatic conditions and limited daylight during the winter. In southern Europe, activities run throughout the year and public attendance is more consistent, although there is a notable increase during the summer holidays.

A common denominator amongst all European sculpture parks is that the most frequent visitors are families. This is the reason why most visits are recreational in character, seeking not just enrichment in contemporary culture, but also the direct contact with nature.

The selected projects in this publication feature the work of both young, emerging talents and acclaimed, established artists who have worked or created pieces at several of these centres, including Sol LeWitt, Richard Long, Ian Hamilton Finlay, Richard Serra, Dan Graham, Henry Moore, Magdalena Abakanowicz, Antony Gormley, Ulrich Rückriem and Marina Abramovic. The range of artists whose work has fostered a respectful approach towards nature is incredibly diverse. The artworks help us to observe nature from a new vantage point, in which the ephemeral becomes an important trait and fragility an element to be protected.

Much of the work is defined by its site-specific character, meaning that the artist took the location into account while planning and creating the artwork. Most of the pieces are per-manent fixtures in the landscape and have been realised in situ. The site-specificity expresses the artwork's integration into the environment, the history and traditions of the place. The work blends in, adapts or occasionally even alters or distorts its context. The meaning of these sculptural works is completed or complemented by the environment in which they are located. They originate from the site, and their scale, size, and placement are determined by the topography of the space. The artwork forms an integral part of the landscape, becoming inseparable from and dependent on its surroundings.

The final "object" is what remains, what we can contemplate and appreciate. However, the artist's thought process with regards to the placement of the piece also plays an important role in the meaning of a site-specific installation. Upon grasping the vast number and diversity of these artworks in Europe, we find that the interrelationship of art and nature is becoming increasingly inseparable, taking on such power that it is often difficult to imagine certain natural settings or gardens without the sculptures contained within them.

This guide is a journey to unexpected places and remote sites in search of meaningful and profound artistic creation, providing insight into the work of well-known artists and those still awaiting discovery, exploring new places, and meeting the people who inhabit them and revealing that Europe's greatest treasure lies in the respect and tolerance of our shared interest in nature and culture.

1 Tatarkiewicz 1976
2-3 Late 20th and early 21st c.

"The limits of my language mean the limits of my world"
Ludwig Wittgenstein

Robert Morris, *Observatory,* 1971–77, Lelystad,
courtesy of the Province of Flevoland

Opposite page:
Julian Opie, *Imagine you can order these I & II,*
1994, Caldic Collection, Rotterdam, courtesy
of the artist and the Lisson Gallery

sculpture parks

art route germany – the netherlands:

Since 2000
Kunstwegen
Städtische Galerie Nordhorn
Vechteaue 2   D-48529 Nordhorn
Tel. +49 (0)5921971100
kontakt@kunstwegen.org
www.kunstwegen.org
Dir. Thomas Niemeyer

Opening hours: permanently
Admission: free
• Access for the disabled
• Pets allowed
• Photographs allowed
• Guided tours (booking required)
• Temporary exhibitions in Städtische
  Galerie Nordhorn
• Educational programmes
• Library
• Publications: leaflet, guide, video
• Coffee shop
• Picnic area
• Car park

How to get there:
• By car, walking or by bike
• Airport: Münster / Osnabrück

Accommodation & Eating out:
  Tel. +49 (0)5921961196
  www.vechtdaloverijssel.nl
  www.grafschaft-bentheim-
  tourismus.de

Kunstwegen (meaning art path or art route in Dutch) is the title of an outdoor sculptural project that has one of the longest trajectories in all of Europe. It covers a distance of 145 km between the towns of Ohne (Lower Saxony, Germany) and Zwolle (Holland) – or between Zwolle (pop. 125,000) and Ohne (pop. 572), depending on one's direction or point of view.

The route follows the river Vechte – as it is known in German – or Overijsselse Vecht – as it is known in Dutch. The Vechte is a small waterway measuring only 167 km in length, which originates close to Munster and flows into the Zwarte Water (Black Water) after Zwolle, in the vicinity of Hassett. By the year 2006, about 75 sculptures and installations by an equal number of artists had been placed along the Kunstwegen and the Vechte between Nordhorn – located 75 km NW of Munster and only 25 km from the Dutch town of Enschede – and Zwolle – located 80 km NE of Amsterdam.

Half of the represented artists are well-established and internationally renowned names in the contemporary art scene, whereas the other half are sculptors, many of them German and some Dutch, who tend to work on a predominantly national level. The majority of the work is concentrated around Nordhorn and the neighbouring town of Frenswegen, and the remaining pieces are distributed throughout a dozen towns. Kunstwegen was officially inaugurated in the year 2000, but the placing of the sculptures had started years earlier; due to the fact that the Nordhorn area has been developing public art projects since the late 1970s.

The project's basic concept is for "the artistic works to refer directly and concretely to the places of realisation." The organisers hope that the "works' integration into specific historical, regional, aesthetic, and landscape contexts" will "re-sharpen perspectives on the environment in which we live and evolve."

Experienced organisers in the field of art exhibitions were recruited for the project and given the task of selecting the artists for each section of the route. A group of historians put together reference mate-

rials for each area, and a landscape planning office compiled characteristics of the local environment so that the artists had in-depth know-ledge about the sites where they would intervene. More importantly, each piece had to meet a clearly defined goal: the creation of an "open cultural space" in which the "artistic contributions serve to unite landscape and natural phenomena, historical events, and re-gional peculiarities into a multi-faceted cultural space."

Two of the most famous pieces are Dan Graham's parabolic pavilion in steel and mirrored glass above the river and Jenny Holzer's conceptual and unsettling *Black Garden*, which measures 3,447 m² The 10.5-m *Pappelturm* is the work of Nils-Udo, and the solid, heavy, 7-m-tall *Nordhornstengel*, located next to the Nordhorn-Aimelo canal, is by Bernhard Luginbühl. All of the aforementioned pieces are located in Nordhorn. In the nearby Frenswegen, Ulrich Rückriem planted two of his characteristic but somehow always unique granite stelas. Marin Kasimir built a 60-m-long wall entitled *No Peep Hole*, and Tobias Rehberger authored the ironic and suggestive *Caprimoon'99*: a lamp illuminating a fluorescent white cement bench, placed in a romantic, bucolic setting. Both of these pieces are located in the Lage area. Luciano Fabro's installation at Spöllberg consists of a 240-m-long chain; its rusty colour creates a striking contrast to the verdant fields around it. Mark Dion assembled two small houses about 4 m in height in Brunas Heide. Ann-Sofi Sidén created a complex installation entitled *Turf Cupola*, consisting of a 28-m tower and a 6 x 4-m structure with 16 monitors and 16 cameras in Neugnadenfeld. Two installations, one 10-m piece by Olafur Eliasson, *Der drehende Park*, and another measuring 12 x 13 m by Suchan Kinoshita, are located in Emlichheim. Joseph Kosuth created the delicately conceptual piece *Taxonomy Applied n° 2*, located in Ommen.

The list continues to include up more than five dozen pieces located along this artistic route by Cai Guo-Quiang, Richard Deacon, Fischli&Weiss, Ilya and Emilia Kabakov, Lawrence Weiner, etc.

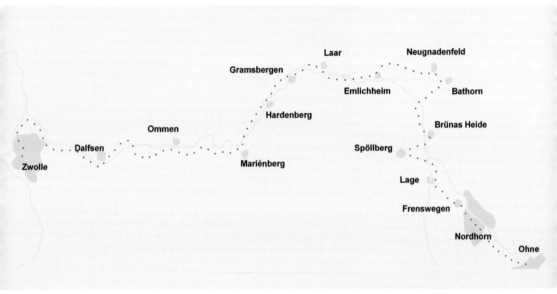

Cai Guo-Qiang, *Skylight*, 1999,
Gramsbergen
Peter Fischli / David Weiss, *Ein Weg durch das Moor*, 1999, Bathorn
Ilya and Emilia Kabakov, *Wortlos*, 2000, Laar

Opposite page:
Karl Prantl, *Kreuzweg*, 1979, Frenswegen – Nordhorn

Hans van den Ban   Herbert Baumann   Hede Bühl   Reinhard Buxel   Cai Guo-Qiang
Eugène Dodeigne   Jeroen Doorenweerd   Olafur Eliasson   Luciano Fabro   Fischli / We
Georg Herold   Jenny Holzer   Franka Hörnschemeyer   Nan Hoover   Olav Christopher J
Kaltwasser   Paul de Kort   Joseph Kosuth   Till Krause   Kubach-Wilmsen-Team   Herr
Christiane Möbus   Rien Monshouwer   Jan van Munster   Louis Niebuhr   Nils-Udo
Cornelius Rogge Willem de Rooij Peter Rübsam   Ulrich Rückriem   Hans Schabus   R
Timm Ulrichs   Henk Visch   Lawrence Weiner   Tine van de Weyer

Ernst Caramelle   Bonnie Collura   Stephen Craig   Christiaan Paul Damsté   Richard Deacon   Braco Dimitrijevic   Mark Dion
Makoto Fujiwara   Hamish Fulton   Wolf Gloßner   Dan Graham   Tamara Grcic   Eva Grubinger   Erich Hauser   Hawoli
Ilya and Emilia Kabakov   Andreas Kaiser   Marin Kasimir   David Kessler   Kinoshita / Boeyen   Folke Köbberling/Martin
Lamers   Paul Etienne Lincoln   Peter van de Locht   Bernhard Luginbühl   Marko Lulic   Bert Meinen   Gerhard Merz
Alwie Oude Aarninkhof   Rudi Pabel   Ralf Peters   Uwe Poth   Karl Prantl   Tobias Rehberger   Thomas Rentmeister
Schad   Christoph Schäfer   Antje Schiffers   Michael   Schoenholtz   Martijn Schoots   Ann-Sofi Sidén   Andreas Slominski

austria österreich

Austria is one of the birthplaces of art. About 27,000 years ago, humans created the *Venus of Willendorf*, a small, female statue with round curves and pronounced sexual organs, a fertility symbol perhaps linking female gender, Mother Earth, sculptural art, primordial goddesses and creative fruitfulness. Two-thirds of this central European nation, which borders eight countries, is in the Alps, which stretch from west to east with high peaks reaching 3,797 m and several glaciers. The flatland is limited to the Danube Valley, which cuts across the northern part of the country. The climate is continental and the flora varies according to the altitude and orientation of the mountains. Due to abundant rain and snowfall, the southern slopes have been shaped by antropic action, with cultivated land and even vineyards at up to 1,500 m. Meanwhile, the northern slopes and areas between 1,500 and 2,200 m are covered in thick, conifer forests: red fir, larch, cembran pine, black Austrian pine.

Here human activity began in prehistoric times and resulted in a cultural milestone: the Hallstatt civilisation. Today this small town with a population of 1,130 next to a beautiful lake has been declared a World Heritage Cultural Landscape. Between 1000 and 500 BC this area was the focal point for the development of the Iron Age in Europe. If the Venus expressed a profound interrelationship between art and nature, then there is an equally strong connection between the telluric condition of the metals and the man-made artifacts crafted to exploit the salt deposits – ca. 3000 BC – and the many metal objects, such as fibulas, plates and friezes, adorned with geometric and figurative motifs.

The Celts arrived in the 4th c. BC, then the Germanic tribes (2nd c. BC) and finally the Romans, who consolidated their limes along the Danube and built Vindobona, which would eventually become Vienna, the capital, a thousand years later in 1142. Even today, this fusion between the tribal north and the Greco-Roman south exerts its influence on the area's cultural legacy. In 803, Charlemagne established the Ostmark or Ostarrichi – the Eastern March, origin of Österreich, Austria in English, then the eastern border of Europe, which would forever turn the country into a link between east and west.

The country was unified by the House of Babenberg (976), then taken over by the Habsburgs, or House of Austria, in the 13th c., who halted the Turkish advance onto Vienna in 1529 and headed the imperial families of Spain (16th–17th c.) and Austria. Empress Maria Theresa (1740–80) created Austria's modern state, which under Franz Joseph I (1848–1916) expanded into the Austro-Hungarian Empire. The Empire collapsed following its defeat in World War I and was replaced by the First Republic. Annexed by Hitler's Germany in 1938 and occupied by the Allies in 1945, Austria did not become a sovereign and independent nation again until 1955. The Second Republic is a federal system with nine states.

Vienna (pop. 1,741,000) has been the world capital of music since the 18th c. At the turn of the 20th c., the city experienced a magnificent cultural era, lending its name to schools in diverse disciplines and pro-

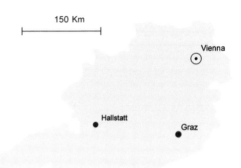

150 Km

Vienna

Hallstatt

Graz

83,871 km², 8.6 million inhabitants, member of the European Union since 1995

ducing universally recognised authors such as Freud, Wittgenstein and Schönberg. Of particular interest to the arts and the radical shift from the mimesis of nature to abstraction, from historicism to the new language of the 20th c., is the Vienna Secession, founded by Gustav Klimt (1897), which broke new ground with its namesake pavilion, designed by the architect Joseph Maria Olbrich. "To Every Age Its Art, To Art Its Freedom" reads the motto over the building's entrance. Then came the work of Otto Wagner and later Hoffman – pieces of all kinds, from jewelry to fashion, the Wiener Werkstätten and the seminal written – *Ornament and Crime*, 1908 – and built work of Adolf Loos. Sculpture did not reach comparable heights, but after World War II a few key artists emerged: Friedensreich Hundertwasser and his peculiar hybrids, the building on Vienna's Kegelgasse, Hoflehner, Wotruba's formal cubism, Franz West's minimal and monochrome work.

Graz (pop. 310,000), the second largest city – capital of Styria – lies in the south-eastern valley of the Mur River, which connects Vienna and Venice. Known as the "garden city" for its green hills and parks – the Schlossberg, the Stadtpark – and home to several universities and thousands of students, the city fosters a continuous dialogue between tradition and the avant-garde. In architecture, the Graz School brought the work of the Werkgruppe Graz – Pichler and others – and the Team A Graz in contact with the radicalism and the visions of Abraham, Domenig, St. Florian or Kada, all of them paving the way for the European Capital of Culture 2003 to present the first building of an Archigram member, the biomorphic Kunsthalle with its shifting skin, or *The Thing and The Wing*, a sculpture-installation-architecture, which can only be seen as a unified entity if driving past it at high speed (later moved to a different town) or Vito Acconci's installation-architecture-engineering-urban design.

From top to bottom and left to right:
Peter Cook, Kunsthalle, 2003
ORTLOS architects – Andreas Schrötter / Ivan Redi, *The Thing*, 2003
Vito Acconci, Mur Island, 2003
Volker Giencke, Botanical Garden, 2003–04, all in Graz

Since 1981 / new setting in 2003
Österreichischer Skulpturenpark
Park: Thalerhofstr 85
A-8141 Unterpremstätten,
Offices: Mariahilferstraße 2–4, 8020 Graz
Tel: +43 31680179704
skulpturenpark@museum-joanneum.at
office@skulpturenpark.at
www.skulpturenpark.at
Dir. Nikolaus Breisach

Opening hours:
Apr.–May, Sept.–Oct.: 10am–6pm
June–Aug.: 10am–8:30pm
Admission: fee charged
• Access for the disabled
• Pets allowed
• Photographs allowed
• Guided tours (booking required)
• Temporary exhibitions
• Educational programmes
• Leaflet
• Picnic area
• Car park

How to get there:
• By car: 20 minutes
• By bus: line 630 from Jakominiplatz
• By taxi or arranged shuttle service
• Airport: Graz

Accommodation & Eating out:
Graz has plenty of facilities from high-
quality hotels to rooms for students,
from formal restaurants to fast food.
The Schwarzl Leisure Centre also
offers some restaurants and hotels
nearby. www.graztourismus.at

Austrian Sculpture Park was originally established on the property of
the regional ORF Radio and Television station in Styria.
In 1981, the head of the Austrian Radio (ORF) studios in Styria
ordered that works of art should be placed on the land that belongs
to them, thus making this Art Park a point of encounter with contemporary art. This was the birth of the idea of looking for the right
sites for sculptural creations around the world. In 2000, the Swiss
landscape architect Dieter Kienast prepared 7 ha of land for the
International Garden Fair Unterpremstätten. The design of the space
was ideal for setting up a great open-air sculpture park. Cooperation
between the private foundation Österreichischer Skulpturenpark, created specifically for this purpose, PORR AG and the federal state of
Styria laid the foundations for the creation of an international sculp-

ture park, which was officially opened in 2003.
In 2007 the government of Styria, in an agreement with the foundation, transferred management to the Universalmuseum Joanneum.
This integrated the Austrian Sculpture Park into a solid scientific,
artistic and cultural context, while making it better known and opening its doors to a broader range of the general public. The park exhibits more than 70 Austrian and international sculptures that interact
with nature. In turn, the carefully moulded and always changing nature
enters into dialogue with the works of art, which are subjected to
the weather conditions and either become integrated into the landscape or react to it. The vocabulary of contemporary sculpture
extends from the abstract to everyday objects, from anthropomorphic figurations to articles of everyday use. Through this dialogue
with the environment, the works tell us of art and society, their conflicts and dreams, but also create spaces for encounter.
The dancing trees (Tanzende Bäume) of Timm Ulrichs and the ark of

Opposite page:
Tobias Rehberger, *Asoziale Tochter*,
2004

On this page:
Above:
Nancy Rubins,
Airplane Parts and Hills, 2003

Bottom:
Mario Terzic, *Arche aus lebenden
Bäumen*, 2011

living trees (Arche aus lebenden Bäumen) by Mario Terzic, for example, are directly related to the processes of growth and death that
surround them. The basket (Korb) by Oswald Oberhuber demon-
strates that a sculpture can also hang on a wall; in other words, it can
dialogue with an image. The conversation between the image and
space may also be extended to a dialogue between art and nature,
as can be seen in the confrontation of the sculptures by Fritz
Hartlauer and Jörg Schlick, inspired by the rules of form and growth.
The works of the so-called "old masters" such as Hans Aeschbacher,
Joannis Avramidis and Wotruba are in a terraced landscape open to
the sky, while the moving machines, such as a car (Erwin Wurm), a
ship (Michael Schuster), a plane (Nancy Rubins), or sails (Martin
Walde), deal with the destiny of machines, of social and technical
dreams and transform the landscape according to their own definition.
Jeppe Hein, Tobias Rehberger, Susana Solano, Peter Weibel, Matt
Mullican, Yoko Ono, Boris Podrecca are other artist on the park.
These above-mentioned works are just some of the examples that
illustrate the way in which the Austrian Sculpture Park extends the
horizon of dialogue and works towards a better understanding of the
language of contemporary sculpture.

belgique belgië

"Le plat pays qui est le mien," Jacques Brel sang in the middle of the 20th c. "Le plat pays" are the plains, coastal dunes and low plateaus of the north, and the plateaus of the Ardennes in the south, with forests, a continental climate of mists, "avec un ciel si bas / avec un ciel si gris," and two navigable rivers, connected by canals, that empty into the North Sea.

This is the former province of Gallia Belgica, conquered by Julius Caesar in 57 BC. The Romans, settling in the centre and south of the territory, established the linguistic frontier that still exists today. It was part of the Carolingian empire, and between the 16th and 18th c. it formed part of the Habsburgs' Spanish empire – origins that make it the heart of the European Union. Some of its territories were integrated at times in the Netherlands and others in France, while a nationalist movement re-emerged at the end of the 18th c. Invaded and occupied in the two World Wars, small in size, densely populated, and with a high quality of life, today it is a country where tradition and avant-garde modernity are singularly combined.

The Kingdom of Belgium was founded in 1831. It is a parliamentary monarchy, which in 1958 joined with Holland and Luxembourg to form the Benelux countries, an economic union that reflected the strong ties of civil society among the three countries. The Constitution, reformed at the end of the 20th c., articulates the state in a federal form, with the territorial regions and linguistic communities of Flanders, Wallonia, and Brussels.

The Flemish community suffered an economic crisis in 1981–92, which was reflected in cuts in the public spending, but at the beginning of the 21st c. there was a considerable increase in funds for art, artistic patrimony, and socio-cultural activities. The region's cultural capital is Antwerp (pop. 503,000), an important port, cradle and home of Peter Paul Rubens and today the birthplace or home of artists such as Panamarenko, Guillaume Bijl, Luc Deleu, etc. What are perhaps the most avant-garde galleries and the most cosmopolitan Belgian museums can be found here, such as the Middelheim, where art and nature co-exist in harmony, and it is one of the international capitals of fashion design, with avant-garde creators such as Martin Margiela, Dries van Noten or Anne Demeulemeester.

Hugo Voeten Art Centre, Geel, Antwerp displays about 20 sculptures by hitlerian, controversial Arno Breker

Left: *The Wounded*, 1938
Henk Visch, *Morgen is alles anders*, 1996, Middelheimmuseum, Antwerpen

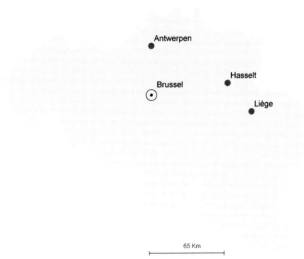

● Antwerpen

Hasselt
Brussel ●
⊙

Liège
●

30,528 km², 11.3 million inhabitants,
member of the European Union since
1957

⊢————————⊣ 65 Km

In the 1960s, the French community established a democratic cultural and educational policy, with support for creative and artistic expression. Its capital, Liège (pop. 185,000), has a Museum of Modern and Contemporary Art, and the new campus of its university is the setting for the Sart-Tilman outdoor museum.

For the German-speaking community, numbering 700,000, the priorities in cultural policy are the support of education for both adults and children, and to stimulate creative and artistic quality through aide dedicated to the improvement of the cultural professions.

Brussels, the capital of the country and headquarters of the European Union's government (pop. 965,000), is a multilingual city where the three communities co-exist under the motto of multiculturism. The city is also home to most of the country's French-speaking cultural institutions. The Museum of Modern Art is found here, and the installations of Mauro Staccioli – a large triangle of red concrete in the Tournay-Solvay Park (1996), a large red square in the Rond-Point de l'Europe (1998) in Boitsfort, and a large arch at the entry to Park Lane in Zaventem (2001) – and the International Fair of Contemporary Art is celebrated every April, attracting the best-known galleries and collectors of a country with a strong collecting tradition, known for its avant-garde and transgressive spirit in the acquisition of contemporary art.

Its internationally recognised artists – those cited and others such as Rik Wouters, Eugene Dodeigne, Pol Bury and his kinetic art, Jeff Geys and, among those under the age of 40 at the turn of the century and the millenium, Wim Delvoye, who uses every possible technique and support, architects such as Stephane Beel, comics artists and fashion designers – those already mentioned and others of Antwerp – correspond to a creativity sustained through liberty, imagination without measure, and the use of forms and materials without limitations.

The modern relation between art and nature in related fields such as sculpture had its first episode in the Art Nouveau of Victor Horta, continued with the application of Ebenezer Howard's concept of the Garden City (1898) by Louis van der Swaelman in the garden suburbs of Brussels – Kapelleveld (1922, Woluwe), Le Logis and Cite Floreal (Watermael-Boitsfort) – and extends into the 21st c. with the gardens and classical-modern landscape architecture of Jacques Wirtz in Hasselt (1976) and the Kontich Park (1988) of Antwerp.

Since 1950
Middelheim Museum
Middelheimlaan 61   2020 Antwerpen
Tel. +32 (0) 2883360
middelheimmuseum@stad.antwerpen.be
www.middelheimmuseum.be
Dir. Sara Weyns

Opening hours:
Oct.–Mar.: 10am–5pm
Apr.–Sept.: 10am–7pm
May.–Aug.: 10am–8pm
Jun.–Jul.: 10am–9pm
Admission: free
• Access for the disabled
• Pets allowed
• Photographs allowed, mind the artists'
  copyrights
• Guided tours: fee charged
• Exhibition pavilions
• Educational programmes
• Library: see Documentation Centre
  below
• Documentation Centre Burgomaster
  Lode Craeybeckx: publications,
  prints, drawings, slides, photographs,
  CD-ROMs, videos, etc. Appointment
  only
• Publications: catalogues and
  exhibition brochures
• Bookshop & Reception
• Café
• Picnic area
• Car park

How to get there:
• By car: exit Berchem-Wilrijk off the
  "Ring" round Antwerp
• By bus: lines 32, 190, 21
• By trams: 7, 15
• Airport: Antwerp

The outdoor museum is located in a neighbourhood on the southern outskirts of the city, on grounds probably used for summering in the 14th c., when they were already known as Middelheim. This private property was acquired by the city in 1910 to prevent its subdivision, and its gardens were opened to the public. The museum was born after the first international sculpture exhibition was held in the park in 1950, when it was decided to convert 20 of its hectares into a permanent open-air museum – other areas of the park were later used for the University and other facilities. Since 1950, 20 biennials have been held here, and in 1993, coinciding with Antwerp's designation as European Cultural Capital, the museum took a new direction,

focusing on the acquisition of international contemporary art, and interpreting the concept of "outdoor sculpture" in its widest sense, so as to include the most contemporary artistic tendencies. For this purpose, in 2000 the museum was enlarged to 27 ha and reorganised, and a new storage facility was built by architect Stephane Beel.
The permanent collection includes some 300 works that virtually trace the history of modern and contemporary sculpture. It begins with what Brancusi called "the starting point of modern sculpture" in

the 19th c. works of Auguste Rodin – the equivalent in sculpture of his contemporaries Paul Cézanne, Paul Gauguin, or Vincent van Gogh; his works here include a *Balzac* of 1892–97. The collection continues with works by Antoine Bourdelle, Aristide Maillol, Georg Kolbe, and Raymond Duchamp-Villon (a piece from 1914); and by members of generations fully of the 20th c., such as Wouters, Pablo Gargallo, Henri Laurens, Ossip Zadkine, and Lipchitz. It continues with works by Henry Moore, Alexander Calder, Louise Nevelson, Marino Marini, Barbara Hepworth, Giacomo Manzu, Max Bill, etc.; others by Lynn Chadwick, Jesus Rafael Soto (a piece from 1969), Phillip King, Jef Geys, Per Kirkeby, Panamarenko, Laurence Weiner, and Dan Graham; and

artists proper to the last third of the century, such as Franz West, Bijl, Matt Mullican, Thomas Schütte, Harald Klingelhöller, Pedro Cabrita Reis, Jessica Stockholder, etc. It closes the century with pieces by figures such as Julien Opie (see p. 17), Tony Cragg – Envelope, 1996 – or Henk Visch (see p. 26). From the 21st c. there are works by Carl Andre, Timm Ulrichs, Joep van Lieshout and others.

Middelheim also has pavilions for temporary exhibitions, such as the 2005 show of Boy & Erik Stappaerts (B), Yutaka Sone (J), Corey

Opposite page:
Juan Muñoz, *Two figures for Middelheim*, 1993

This page:
Auguste Rodin, *Balzac*, 1897

McCorkel (USA), Mark Lewis (C), Donckers (B), Lee Bul (K), Balka (PL), Augustijnen (B) and Knut Asdam (N).

It offers entertainment and cultural activities for a variety of audiences from outdoor concerts and theatre in the summer to guided tours, work groups, and children's workshops. Its Documentation Centre, named after the major under whose mandate the museum was created, contains 50,000 publications and documents on the Fine Arts from Rodin to the present, and is open for visits and book loans. Finally, a new entrygate (2006) on the corner of Middelheimlaan and Lidendreef streets, designed by achitect-sculptor-installation artist John Körmerling, is an example of the blurred lines between disciplines, as were in their time the constructions of Van Lieshout and Luc Deleu.

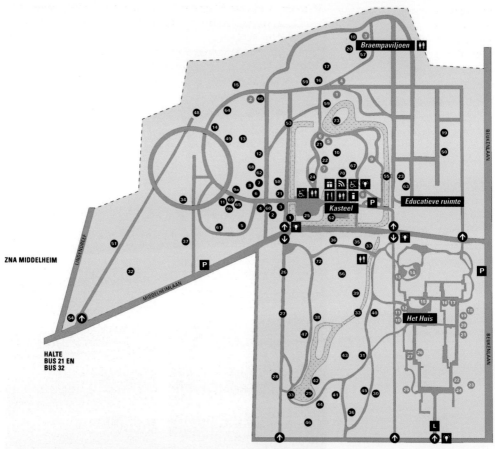

1 Lode Craeybeckx 2 Henry Moore 3 Rik Wouters 4 Auguste Rodin 5 Auguste Rodin 6 Bourdelle 7 Constantin Meunier 8 Jean Arp 9a Artistide Maillol 9b Artistide Maillol 10 Max Bill 11 Giacomo Manzù 12 Pablo Gargallo 13 Henri Laurens 14 Raymond Duchamp-Villon 15 Eugène Dodeigne 16 Carl Milles 17 Camiel van Breedam 18 Albert Szukalski 19 Jesús Rafael Soto 20 Alexander Calder 21 Marino Marini 22 Barbara Hepworth 23 Constant Permeke 24 François Pompon 25 Lawrence Weiner 26 Carl Andre 27 Juan Muñoz 28 Thomas Schütte 29 Luciano Fabro 30 Guillaume Bijl 31 Per Kirkeby 32 Franz West 33 Matt Mullican 34 Henk Visch 35 Panamarenko 36 Isa Genzken 37 Atelier Van Lieshout 38 Charles Vandenhove 39 Tony Cragg 40 Joachim Bandau 41 Harald Klingelhöller 42 Bernd Lohaus 43 Honoré d'O 44 Jessica Stockholder 45 Timm Ulrichs 46 Didier Vermeiren 47 Franz West 48 Luc Deleu 49 Dan Graham 50 Chris Burden 51 Pedro Cabrita Reis 52 Erwin Wurm 53 Corey McCorkle 54 John Körmeling 55 Ai Weiwei 56 Roman Signer 57 Philippe Van Snick 58 Antony Gormley 59 Johan Muyle 60 Jef Geys Muyle 61 Rudolf Belling 62 Johan Creten 63 Selçuk Mutlu 64 Mari Andriessen 65 Germaine Richier 66 Pablo Serrano 67 Ossip Zadkine 69 Oscar Jespers 70 Rik Wouters 71 Leon Vranken 72 Daniel Dewar and Grégory Gicquel 73 Kati Heck

Since 1977
Domaine de l'Université de Liège
Château de Colonster   B-4000 Liège
Tel. +32 (0)43662220
musee.pleinair@ulg.ac.be
www.museepla.vlg.ac.be
Cur. Pierre Henrion
    Jean Housen
    Edith Schurgers

Opening hours: permanently
Admission: free
• Access for the disabled
• Pets allowed
• Photographs allowed
• Guided tours: fee charged
• Exhibition halls with changing shows
• Educational programmes
• Coffee shop: university cafeteria
• Restaurant: university restaurant
• Picnic area
• Car park

How to get there:
• By car: Liège – Sart-Tilman
• By bus: from Liège centre lines 48, 58
• By train: arrival at Liège Guillemins
  Station, then by bus
• Airport: Liège (15 km)
  Brussels (80 km)

Accommodation & Eating out:
  In the city of Liège

The open-air museum is a collaboration between the University of Liège and the Ministry of Culture. A policy of conservation and investigation has resulted in the development of a collection that in 2016 comprised more than 100 works installed on the university campus. The idea for an outdoor museum in Sart-Tilman was born with the first designs for the university campus in 1961, and inaugurated in 1967 with the first of its sculptures, Pierre Culot's *Mur de pierre d'âge viseen*. Various other sculptures by Francis Andre, Jean-Paul Laenen and Léon Wuidar were also installed before the museum was created. Two kinds of projects are found in Sart-Tilman: site-specific art, in which the works are integrated in the site for which they were conceived; and works installed in a space without having been especially conceived for it.

Of the first type, six interventions beside the plaza of the Rectorate stand out; and of the second, works such as *Souvenir* and *L'aigle,* by Andre Willequet, *Relâche,* by Paul Machiels, George Grard's *La Caille,* or Olivier Strebelle's *L'endormie n° 5,* among others.

But sometimes a surprise comes after the installation, as in the case of the work *Jeune fille agenouillée*, by Charles Leplae, which establishes an intimate and tender dialogue with its surroundings, making it one of the most seductive pieces of the collection.

In addition to the permanent collection and an intensive acquisitions programme that began in 1991, the Outdoor Museum of Sart-Tilman organises a prize for young sculptors from Belgium's French community. Besides a cash award, a temporary exhibition of work is organised.

Clockwise from above left:
Lambert Rocour, *Untitled*, 1999
Rik Wouters, *La Joie de vivre*, 1912
Léon Wuidar, *Labyrinthe*, 1987

danmark

Denmark spreads out across the Jutland peninsula, an extension of Germany's northern plain, and 406 islands of which the largest and most populated are Seeland, with the capital Copenhagen (pop. 501,000; Greater Copenhagen, 1.8 million), Fionia, and Lolland.

During an earlier geological period, Denmark and the Scandinavian Peninsula were connected, but a rise in sea level separated them and created the Skagerrak and Kattegat straits and a series of channels such as the Sund, the Big Belt, and the Little Belt. As a result, the country is now flanked by the North Sea in the west and the Baltic Sea in the east, Copenhagen lies across from Swedish Malmö, and Danish Helsingør – site of Elsinor Castle, the setting for *Hamlet* – and the neighbouring Helsingborg are divided by just 4 km of water.

The glaciers formed a landscape of plains and small, gentle hills, none higher than 200 m. It is a cyclist's paradise, a sport that is widespread, facilitated and well-regarded here. A mildly cold, seaside climate marks this landscape, where forests are few and 70% of the land is cultivated by the active and very productive agricultural and cattle industries, which form the basis for one of the world's most highly developed economies.

In the 9th c., the border was established along the Eider against the Franconian empire; the Viking (Norman) expeditions began, ransacking the English coasts and the continent as far as Paris and Seville. In 911 they finally settled in Normandy, from where they would sail a century and a half later to conquer England. By 980 the Christianisation, unification, and incorporation of Denmark into the western world was complete. Copenhagen was founded in 1165, and the Kalmar Union (1389) brought Denmark, Norway, and Sweden under one rule. Sweden seceded in 1523, but Norway and Denmark remained united until 1814. Following the defeat of Napoleon, Denmark ceded Norway to Sweden. With renewed energy, Denmark began to take advantage of the enthusiasm for commercial expansion that had commenced in the previous century.

Throughout the 19th c. the country made significant advances in education, agriculture, and democracy, and it entered the 20th c. as one of the most socially progressive nations in Europe. During World War II, Denmark was invaded by Germany, and since 1945 the country has been ruled by socially democratic governments. During this time, the country, which is ruled by a constitutional monarchy and has a population that is 90% urban and liberal, became one of the most advanced, prosperous, and open societies in Europe.

The gold-covered, bronze disc Solvognen (Sun Cart) dates back to the early Danish Bronze Age, ca. 1600 BC. The piece is adorned with spiral motifs and a boat – a religious symbol – both indicative of a Nordic style. The pieces from the Iron Age show Celtic, and later Roman, influences, whereas in the Germanic period and after the year 400 the most notable pieces are golden jewels. The *Jelling* stone is a 10th c. "sculpture" or stela, with the runic inscription "King Harald had this monument made Gorm his father and Thyra his mother, this Harald who conquered all Denmark and Norway and

43,094 km² (excluding the Faroe Islands and Groenland; the latter measures more than 2 million km² in size, making it the largest island in the world), 5.6 million inhabitants, member of the European Union since 1973

made the Danes Christians." Bertel Thorvaldsen was the first Danish artist to enter the annals of international art history for his 19th c. neo-classic sculptures, mostly created in Rome and exhibited at his museum in Copenhagen. The 20th c. began with Kai Nielsen and his Rodin-influenced, monumental sculptures, followed by Henry Heerup's surrealist explorations and Sonja Ferlov's body of work. The most internationally acclaimed, however, is Robert Jacobsen, the foremost Danish sculptor of post-war Europe, who lived in Paris and created highly personal and abstract pieces in metal. His fame on the international scene was only briefly contested by the multifaceted, experimental pop-artist Per Kirkeby – the second half of the 20th c. showed a significant U.S. American influence on the Danish visual arts –, a student of the Eks-skolen (School for Experimental Art, 1961) who championed socially responsible art, artistic versatility and a critical view of reality. In the 1980s, Willy Ørskov approached art from a more intellectual standpoint. Finally, the generation to emerge at the turn of this century and succeed in a borderless Europe and an interconnected world includes artists like Joachim Køster and his video-art, Eliasson and his installations and the very young, ironic and playful Jeppe Heim.

In Denmark the limits between different disciplines began to blur very early on. In 1917, it passed its first law to protect the environment. "Urban development provided new possibilities for working with nature," remarked Salto, citing Earl T. Sørensen and his landscape architecture at the University of Aarhus (1931–47), whose buildings were designed by Kay Fisker, as one example. A different approach is reflected in his allotment gardens – small, lawn quadrants surrounded by oval hedges – in Nærum (1948). Swedish artist Andersson has worked on gardens, landscape, art and urban development in the Scanpark (Copenhagen, 1996) and elsewhere. Even bridges and motorways are the subject of landscape design and aesthetics, such as the Lingby motorway by Edith and Ole Nørgaard (1965–74). Last but not least, the work of the incomparable Arne Jacobsen exemplified not only outstanding modernist architecture, but also the best in Danish industrial and furniture design.

himmelhøj

Since 2004
Naturlagepladsen Himmelhøj
Kalvebod Faelled
Miljøministeriet
Skov-og Naturstyrelsen
(Danish Forest and Nature Agency)
Haraldsgade 53   2100 Copenhagen
Tel. +45 39472000
sns@sns.dk
www.skovognatur.dk

Opening hours: permanently
Admission: free
• Picnic area

How to get there:
• By bus: 31, 32, 33, 34
• By subway: Vestamager Station

The Ministry of the Environment commissioned Alfio Bonanno to convert an area of the natural habitat in Kalvebod Fælled – Kalvebod Fælled is now a part of the new nature park Amager, just outside Copenhagen, – reached by metro – into an open-air recreational area for the general public, that would also promote respect for and knowledge about the natural world. It comprises some 30,000 m² of largely swampy terrain, with a varied flora – orchids, willows, birches, pines – and fauna. The artist has made four site-specific installations between land art and landscaping, using tree trunks, branches, stones, and earth. *Amogerorken* is the flagship of the project (55 × 18 × 5 m). Vito Bonanno remarks, "with its organic form and size it creates an exceptional contrast with the 'floating' and mechanical metro station." At *Rævehulen*, visitors are asked to "gather feathers from the area and insert them in the ceiling." *Ildstedet* is a work 15 m in diameter; and Insektskoven is a labyrinthine circular forest of 260 burned oaks (24 m). In the distance, a gigantic coal-burning power plant can be seen, as well as the skyline of the capital, the futuristic skyscrapers of Ørestad and the largest shopping centre in Scandinavia. Bonanno exclaims, "it's a 'borderland' full of contrasts between nature and culture!"

Alfio Bonanno,
Amagerarken (Amager Ark), 2004

Rævehulen (Giant Birds Nest), 2004
The *Rævehulen* does not exist any longer. All Alfio's installations are made of natural material, and therefore they will descompose

farum international sculpture park

Since 1999
Farum International Sculpture Park
Farum Kulturhus
Stavnsholtvej 3 3520 Farum
Tel. +45 72354575
farumkulturhus@furesoe.dk
www.farumkulturhus.dk
Dir. Zanne Jahn

Opening hours: permanently
Admission: free
• Access for the disabled
• Pets allowed
• Guided tours: fee charged
• Publications: guide, leaflet
• Picnic area
• Car park

How to get there:
• By car, bus, and train
• Airport: Copenhagen

Accommodation:
  In Farum: Farum Park Sports- and
  Conference Center, tel. +45 44342500
  (1.5 km). Bregnerød Kro,
  tel. +45 44950057 (3 km).
  In Vaerløse (4 km): KolleKolle Hotel,
  Courses and Conference Center,
  tel. +45 44984222

Located some 20 km northwest of Copenhagen, the Farum International Sculpture Park began as a singular cultural event held in one of the town's green spaces.

During the month of August 1999, eight Danish and international artists were invited to create sculptures in marble: the promoter of the project, the Moroccan-Israeli-Parisian artist Yaël Artsi, Jun-Ichi Inoue, Cynthia Sah, Nicolas Bertoux, Pal Svensson, Jesper Nergaard, Kemal Tufan, and Tetsuo Harada. Each worked personally and intensively on the production of their respective works. During the weeks of planning and execution, Farum's citizens could study the small models exhibited in the park, talk with the artists, observe the hard labour of sculpting the marble, etc.

The resulting works were later exhibited on a green. They did not leave Farum, becoming a permanent part of the garden. Sited close together, they form a sculptural group unified by the condition and colouring of their material and the conventional space of trees and grass that is their setting.

Jun-Ichi Inoue, *Meditative Place*, 1999

Yaël Artsi, *The cloud*, 1999

herning & birk centerpark

Herning offers all kinds of services
activities, entertainment, etc.
www.visitherning.com

Herning (pop. 46,000), on the Jutland peninsula, 91 km by road west
of Aarhus and 309 km from Copenhagen, was established at the start
of the 19th c., and experienced a boom following the Second World
War. It now plays host to trade fairs, with the biggest facilities in
Scandinavia, concerts, a university campus, and three buildings by
Jorn Utzon.
An art museum was set up in what had been a textile factory in the
1960s, and became the HEART Herning Museum of Contemporary
Art, a luminous minimalist project by Steven Holl, with a sculpted

volume that houses works by Vasarely, Manzoni, Asger Jorn, Beuys,
Merz, Cronhammar and other Danish artists. The monumental *Elia*
(2001) is a work by Cronhammar that is almost a building in itself,
with a diameter of 60 m and a height of 41 m. It can be climbed via
the groove in the semi-sphere made by the steel stairs.
The Carl-Henning Pedersen & Else Alfelts Museum is a peculiar triple
hybrid. It was designed (1976) by the architect C. F. Møller
(1898–1988) with work by Pedersen, a Danish painter in the CoBrA
group. After crossing the irregular pyramid you enter the "interior"
space, which in reality is open-air. To the side, visitors pass through
a corridor that is the work *Allotment* (1998) by Antony Gormley.
Birk is an unusual neighbourhood in its harmonious coexistence,
or interpenetration, of nature, the visual arts, architecture, sculpture,

HEART Herning Museum of Contemporary Art, Steven Holl, 2009

Carl-Henning Pedersen & Else Alfelts Museum, C.F. Moller, 1976

Opposite page:
Elia, Ingvar Cronhammar, 2001
Below, *Geometrical Gardens,*
designed by C.Th. Sørensen

This page, below:
Sculpture Park designed
by C.Th. Sørensen

gardens, landscape art and architecture and urban planning, in an environment that blurs the traditional borders between these disciplines. C. Th. Sørensen (1893–1979), a Danish garden and landscape architect of international fame, designed a circular space next to the geometric gardens museum, De Geomestrike Haver, with modular rooms that express a "complexity of simplicity" not visible to visitors. At a tangent to the Geometric Gardens and also circular, the Skulpturparken is a park of 36 framed sculptures by various Danish artists, including Robert Jacobsen (1912–93) and Søren Jensen (1917–82), and the Dutch constructivist Carel Visser (1928–2015), etc. "Experience art in nature with the whole family" is the fitting municipal slogan.

humlebaek louisiana museum

Since 1958
Louisiana Museum of Modern Art
Gl. Strandvej 13   3050 Humlebæk
Tel. +45 49190719
arrangement@louisiana.dk
www.louisiana.dk
Dir. Poul Erik Tøjner

Opening hours:
Tue.–Fri.: 11am–10pm
Sat.–Sun. and public holidays11am–6pm
Mon.: closed
Admission: fee charged
• Access for the disabled
• Pets not allowed
• Photographs allowed in permanent
  collection
• Guided tours (booking required):
  fee charged
• Indoor galleries
• Temporary exhibitions
• Educational programmes
• Children's wing
• Publications
• Shop
• Concerts
• Workshop
• Lectures
• Artlive festival
• Café
• Car park

How to get there:
• By car: E47 / E45 motor road
• By bus: line 388
• By train: from Copenhagen or
  Helsingor to Humlebæk Station
• Airport: Kastrup / Copenhagen

Set amidst an impressively beautiful, natural landscape, the park surrounding this old villa is one of many dotting the coastal road alongside the narrow sound which simultaneously separates and unites Denmark and Sweden. The view from here looks out towards the sea, framed by the tops of tall trees. This is where, in 1958, the Danish merchant Knud W. Jensen founded the Louisiana Museum of Modern Art. It is one of the most outstanding international collections of contemporary art in Europe, particularly as far as sculpture is concerned. Located 35 km north of Copenhagen, Louisiana was a 19th c. manor belonging to one of the owner's ancestors, a man who married three times, each time to a woman named Louise. On the eastern side, the terraced slope leads down to the sea, whereas on the north-western side it meets the Humlebæk Lake. The view and the water are two key elements in this 1.2-ha space, characterised by an interrelationship of art, architecture and landscape that is particularly noteworthy. Upon constructing the new buildings, the Danish architects took great care to keep most of the garden areas open and uncluttered. There are three major exhibition halls located to the west, south and east (underground).

"The collection includes significant chapters in 20th-c. art," says Poul Erik Tøjner, the museum's director, who summarises the collection's content thusly: "The art of Alberto Giacometti is one of the museum's distinct fields of strength – as is the art of Alexander Calder, whose sculptures have almost become a symbol for Louisiana, and Henry Moore, who has contributed unmistakably to the character of the park with its view of the sound. Not to mention Pablo Picasso, Jean Dubuffet, Morris Louis, Andy Warhol, Robert Rauschenberg, Yves Klein, Anselm Kiefer, Sigmar Polke, Georg Baselitz, Per Kirkeby [...]." Approximately 60 pieces of the sizeable collection are located throughout the park. The gently sloped terrain has been re-designed and cultivated since the opening. The dialogue between the neat, manicured areas and the wild, natural spaces sets the stage for the placement of the sculptures. A series of sculptures are visible from

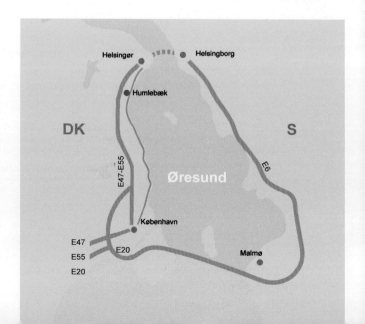

Alexander Calder, *Little Janey-Waney*, 1964–76

inside the museum or the corridors through enormous windows. Some sculptures stand at specific, carefully chosen places in the patios, whereas others required more space around them and have therefore been placed "in the park in relation to trees, grass, or water."

Every piece benefits from having its particular serene environment. Several sculptures were created specifically for the museum or were acquired with a concrete location in mind. Finally, several site-specific works were created in the 1980s: a piece by Joel Shapiro, *The Gate in the Gorge* by Richard Serra; *Self-Passage* by Trakas, which is accessible by way of several, narrow paths; and a 12-m-long piece by Enzo Cucchi (see map p. 40). The work covers a wide range of pieces, from five by Jean Arp to one by Dan Graham, from approximately 20 by Heerup to one by Ørskov, from one each by Joan Miró, Isamu Noguchi, and Max Bill to three by Sekine and Max Ernst.

The Lousiana Museum is an important modern and contemporary art destination: 724,580 visitors in 2015.

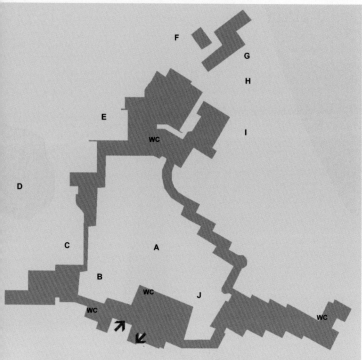

A The Sculpture Garden
B The Old Villa
C Children's Wing
D The Lake Garden
E Museum Café
F Concert Hall
G Boathouse/Guesthouse
H Conference Room
I The Big Hall
J Museum Shop

Some of the artists and artworks in
the permanent collection:
Jean Arp, *Coupes superposées*;
Concrétion humaine sur coupe ovale;
Vénus de Meudon; *Seuil aux créneaux*
végéttaux; *Seuil-réflection*
Max Bill, *Construction*
Alexander Calder, *Nervures minces*;
Little Janey-Waney;
Almost Snow Plough
César, *La Victoire de Villetaneuse*
Enzo Cucchi, *Scultura Africa*
Jean Dubuffet, *Manoir d'essor*
Max Ernst, *Le Grand assistant*;
La Grenouille; *La Tortue*
Svend Wiig Hansen, *Stående kvinde*;
Siddende kvinde
Henry Heerup, *Frueform*; *Nanna figur*;
Mor og barn; *Mand og kvinde*;
Untitled; *Maske*; *Fugl*; *Nisse*;
Kumme; *Pjerrotpigen*; *Hoved*;
Rødodovremanden; *Portrætbuste*;
Tumling; *Thors kat*; *Vædderstele*;
Solbarn; *Troldkaellinger*; *Maske*
Brian Hunt, *Daphne II*
Dani Karavan, *Square*
Per Kirkeby, *Tor II*; *Untitled*
Harry Kivijärvi, *Viisasten kivi*;
Pieni monumentti
Henri Laurens, *Grande femme debout à*
la draperie
Joan Miró, *Personnage*
Henry Moore, *Relief no. 1*;
Reclining Figure no. 5;
Reclining Figure;
Three Piece Reclining Figure
Isamu Noguchi, *Queen of Spades*
George Rickey, *One Up One Down*;
Oblique Variant IV
Nobuo Sekine, *Phases of Nothingness*;
Phases of Nothingness – Cone;
Phases of Nothingness – Nine Pieces
Richard Serra, *The Gate in the Gorge*
Joel Saphiro, *Untitled*
George Trakas, *Self Passage*
Willy Ørskov, *Untitled*

A work by Max Ernst and visitors gateway

Top:
Jean Arp & Henry Moore

Right:
Richard Serra, *The Gate in the Gorge*, 1983–96

kolding **trapholt**

Since 1988
Trapholt Museum of Art & Design
Kunsthanvaerk, Design og Mobeldesign
Aeblehaven 23   DK 6000 Kolding
Tel. +45 76300530
kunstmusem@trapholt.dk
www.trapholt.dk
Dir. Karen Grøn

Opening hours:
Tue.–Sun. 10am–5pm, Wed. 10am–8pm
(free admission from 5pm)
Mondays closed
Admission:
  Park: free. Museum: fee charged
• Access for the disabled
• Pets not allowed
• Photographs allowed, no flash
  indoors
• Guided tours: fee charged
• Exhibition halls with changing shows
• Educational programme
• Library for research purposes
• Bookstore & Shop
• Coffee shop & Restaurant: Café
  Medina, open terrace in summer
• Picnic area
• Car park: free

With views of the Kolding Fjord, the Trapholt Sculpture Garden surrounds the Museum of Art & Design, Applied Arts, Design, and Furniture Design, one of Denmark's largest and most popular museums outside Copenhagen, located 132 km away.

In the early 1930s Dr. Lind acquired 2.75 ha of land here and commissioned Carl Th. Sørensen to prepare a landscape architecture design. The garden was finished by 1934, and its design features many of the characteristics of the prestigious architect's approach to landscaping. He believed that a garden should never imitate nature. What he wanted was to create an art of the garden, so that in itself it would be a work of art. Gardens, he maintained, should be spaces generated by plants, in which people can relax and stroll. The sources that nurture this vision in his projects come from both nature and art: on the one hand, the Danish countryside – grassy fields, clumps of forest, a bed of flowers over a green pasture – and on the other, the visual vanguard of his time – the abstract, geometric forms of Soviet Constructivism, and the dynamic lines and forms of Italian and Russian Futurism. His gardens are very stylised landscapes in which curving, oval and spiral lines underlie a work that appears to have grown naturally.

The starting point for the lay-out of the park is the spectacular view of the fjord. The space is defined by a line of trees that frame the extensive area of grass. Towards the south, views of the fjord and the countryside are framed by groups of trees; to the west, a path gradually disappears into a natural pergola, etc. 13 sculptures by Danish artists are arranged in this setting – see plan on the opposite page including works by Lars Ravn. But the key piece is the handsome and functional *Trapholtmuren* by artist Finn Reinbothe and architect Boye Lundgaard, which divides the terrain into two sections: the area to

How to get there:

Trapholt is located, approx. 4 km east of the Kolding town centre

- By car: from the Kolding town centre, take the ring road that runs right round the town – towards E20 / E45 Odense/Vejle – along Fynsvej – turn right onto Lyshøj Allé – follow the signs for "Kunstmuseum"
- By bus: line 7 or 9 to Lyshøj Allé
- By train: to Kolding Station, then by bus, 7 or 9 to Lyshøj Allé
- On foot or by bike: take Fynsvej, Jens Holms Vej, Strandvejen, Gl. Strandvej, Fjordvej, Skolebakken and Lyshøj Allé to Æblehaven.
- Airport: Billund

Accommodation:

Kolding Fjord Hotel
Comwell Kolding (3 km)
First Hotel Kolding (4 km)
Hotel Byparken (4 km)
Scandic Kolding (4 km)

the east of the wall remains unaltered, while the new buildings for the museum have been built to the west. Inspired by Christo's *Running Fence* project (1972–76), Trapholt's wall goes further, becoming a habitable sculpture, a sculptural architecture, or an artistic-architectonic installation, given that its interior is a vestibule, a pedestrian route to the museum.

Another singular work in this setting is the summer house of Arne Jacobsen, a radical project of 1970 consisting of cubic modules of 10 m^2 which can be modulated in different ways to meet differing needs. The museum offers an ample collection of Danish visual art, including the Franciska Clausen Collection, the donations of Richard Mortensen, designer furniture, craft works, ceramics, textiles, and an interesting shop.

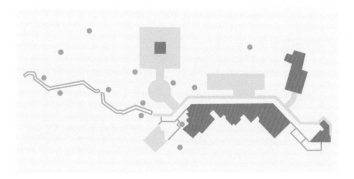

Finn Reinbothe, Boye Lundgaard,
Trapholtmuren,
(3 partial views), 1996

Since 1993
Tranekær International Centre for Art
and Nature
Tranekær Castle Park, Tranekær
Langeland
Slotsgade 84
5953 Tranekær
Tel. + 45 62513505
teamlangland@vip.cybercity.dk
Dir. Alfio Bonano
mail@alfiobonanno.dk

Opening hours: permanently
Admission: fee charged
• Access for the disabled: only the path
  around the lake
• Pets allowed only if on leash
• Photographs allowed for private use
• Guided tours can sometimes be
  arranged
• Publications: guide, leaflet
• Picnic area
• Car park

How to get there:
• By car: Highway E20 Copenhagen to
  Odense, then Highway A9 from
  Odense to Rudkøbing, and Road 305
  from Rudkøbing to Trankær.
• By train and bus: IC train from
  Copenhagen Airport or Copenhagen
  Central Station to Nyborg, then by
  bus 910 to Rudkøbing – Tranekær.
• Airport: Kastrup / Copenhagen

Accommodation & Eating out:
  In Tranekær, Rudkøbing, Tulleboelle,
  Lohals: contact Langeland Tourism,
  tel. +45 62513505, fax +45 62514335
  info@langeland.dk

Gertrud Købke Sutton writes: "Tranekær, Castle and village are situated on Langeland, the beautiful island between Funen and Lolland in
southern Denmark. Once the centre of a baroque garden, the Castle
is now surronded by a 19th c. park modelled in the English taste with
a lake and splendid exotic trees. In 1990 at the initiative of the
Danish-Italian artist Alfio Bonanno in collaboration with the art historian Gertrud Købke Sutton and Poet Vagn Lundbye, the Count
agreed to open the park to artists working in nature. [...]
TICKON, i.e. Tranekær International Centre for Art and Nature, is not
an institution in the usual sense, but a non-profit-making project that
with support from varying foundations invites artists to stay and
work in the park – and neighbouring counties. It was opened with an
International conference in 1993 and 16 works by artists such as
Andy Goldsworthy, Chris Drury, Alan Sonfist, David Nash, Lars Vilks,
and Nils-Udo. The criterion for participation is sensibility and an
artistic expression based on a dialogue with a particular place. A sine
quo non is the artists' ability to listen and observe. [...] For most of
them the dialogue with nature's eternal cycle is of greater importance than the survival of their works. Thus many interventions are
short-lived or symbolic. [...] TICKON is not a sculpture park but a living organism.
To this day more than 30 artists from different countries have been
invited to work. [...] They all bear witness to the vitality of a symbiosis
of nature and artists as commentators and collaborators. In addition,
contributions by people of a more scientific approach such as biolo-
gists, botanists, etc. are welcomed."

Above:
Alfio Bonanno, *Between Copper Beech
and Oak*, 2001

Opposite page:
Mikael Hansen,
Organic Highway,1995

deutschland

Inhabited since the Paleolithic – the Heidelberg and the Neanderthal man – Germany was settled by the Celts in the 5th c. BC and Germanic tribes in 200 BC, halting the northern expansion of imperial Rome at the 550 km *limes* established between the Rhine and the Danube, which lasted until Odoacer put an end to the Western Roman Empire in 476 AD. Today Germany lies at the centre of Europe and belongs to the five largest economies in the world; its contributions to music, philosophy, science, and technology shape western culture.

The southern areas are pre-Alpine and varied in character. The centre is mountainous and bisected by enormous rivers – the Rhine, Weser, and Elbe flowing into the North Sea and the Oder into the Baltic Sea. The coal-mining region of the lower Ruhr Valley has been one of the world's most important industrial complexes and most densely populated areas since the mid-19th c. The north, a vast plain shaped by glaciers, has low hills (200 m), navigable estuaries and the Bremen and Hamburg harbours. A temperate maritime climate in the southwest and harsher continental conditions in the northeast, marked by rain and snowfall, nourish the southern conifer forests and central mountains, the northern flatlands and beech, oak, and spruce forests, cattle pastures, and fields on old, deforested plains.

The first Christian bishopric (314) was in the Roman Treveris. The division of Charlemagne's empire in 843 consolidated feudal power and the dukedoms (Bavaria, Saxony, etc.), German art emerged under Otto I and in 962 the Holy Roman Empire of the German Nation was established, reaching its height under Emperor Charles V. Prussia rose to power under Frederick II the Great (1740–86), and Napoleon dissolved the remaining empire in 1806, followed by the industrial revolution of 1840, economic unity and a new state governed by Bismarck that reinforced Prussian hegemony. After the French defeat at Sedan (1870), Prussian rule brought about unification, economic prosperity (Gründerzeit) and World War I. Following Germany's defeat, the Weimar Republic (1919–33) provided social advances but could not withstand economic disaster. The horrors of Hitler and Nazism resulted in millions of casualties and a destroyed and later divided post-war Germany. During the 20th c. latter half, the European Union and the country's reunification heralded a new era.

The English garden first appeared in Germany at Wörlitz-Dessau (Anhalt-Dessau,1773). Its popularity spread through Hirschfeld's books, a theorist and promoter of the public park as a place of leisure and moral improvement for all social classes. The first public park was the English Garden in Munich by Sckell and Rumford (1789). Pückler-Muskau, another theorist, followed Repton and created his own in Muskau (1816). However, the most important landscape architect was Peter Joseph Lenné, often collaborating (1816–41) with the acclaimed German architect Karl Friedrich Schinkel: Sanssouci and Charlottenhof, Potsdam; Charlottenburg and the Tiergarten renovation, Berlin. Sculpture during the late 19th c. was predominantly Greek classical (Hildebrand's nudes) or

357,868 km², 81.3 million inhabitants, member of the European Union

Hamburg

Neuenkirchen

Berlin

Nordhorn Münster Hannover Potsdam Muskau

Nieheim Dessau

Marl Paderborn

Borken Willebadessen Dresden

Duisburg Dortmund Kassel Weimar

Düsseldorf Bottrop

Neuss-Holzhein

Köln

Bad Homburg

Frankfurt

Saarbrücken

München

150 Km

Previous page:
Nils-Udo, *Habitat*, 2000, Kunstweg
Menschen Spuren, Neandertal

Below:
Peter Eisenman, *Memorial to the Murdered Jewish of Europe*, 2005, Berlin

Jugendstil (Max Klinger's work). Lehmbruck worked in a similar vein to Rodin and Brâncuşi. Kirchner's expressionism (*Die Brücke*, Dresden 1905) took on unexpected forms in the figures of Barlach. The road to abstraction was paved by *Der Blaue Reiter* (Munich 1911) by Kandinsky and Marc, etc. Equally crucial to surrealism and modern-day performance were the provocative upheavals of Dada and Jean Arp, Max Ernst (Cologne 1919), Kurt Schwitters and his *"Merzbau"* (Hanover), Hausmann's photographic experiments (Berlin) – encouraging the New Objectivity that would later emerge in Dresden and Berlin (1923). Another decisive factor was the Bauhaus, founded by Gropius (Weimar 1919) and later led by Meyer and Mies van der Rohe (Dessau 1925). The advent of Nazism forced these artists into exile and branded their work as "degenerate art" (1938). The post-war period began with Marcks and references to Hildebrand and Uhlmann and Soviet constructivism. The Zero Group (1957, Mack, Piene, Uecker) developed a new interest in nature and technology (outdoor light art). The 1960s saw the rise of Kricke, and Joseph Beuys' groundbreaking, critical artwork, and actions began to play an international role. Ideas such as his utopia on earth, the relationship between art-ecology were included in his installation *7,000 Oaks* (documenta 7, 1982). This nexus of art-nature continued in the generation of Haacke, Rückriem, and Vostell, followed in the late 1970s by Lüpertz and neo-expressionism, in the 1980s–90s by Kippenberger's versatility and in the 21st c. by younger artists like Rehberger and artists, landscape architects, urban planners and gardeners (Latz, Prigann) with aesthetic and social answers to a world of industrial ruins, exemplified by the preserved ironworks at Völklingen.

documenta Kassel

Kassel (pop. 210,000) is home to the enormous Wilhelmshohe Park (350 ha), designed by Guarniero in 1701, later remodelled as an English garden and site of the city's emblem, the statue of Hercules, a copy (1717) of the *Hercules Farnesio* that stands in Naples. Nowadays, however, it is better known for its quadrennial or quinquennial exhibition, created in 1955 by Arnold Bode, painter and professor at the city's academy, in a city still showing traces of the devastation and horror inflicted by World War II. The event began with a structure by Frei Otto and parallel to the Bundesgartenschau (federal garden show) with the aim of exhibiting international art, encouraging a new appreciation of abstract art, which had been persecuted by the Nazis as "degenerate," and expressing the superiority of western values over those of communism. Since 1972 the event has generally taken place between June and September and has become one of the most important international events for the visual arts, showcasing the most current tendencies in contemporary art, oftentimes within a thematic framework. For example, the 4th edition in 1968 was dominated by minimalism and pop art; the 5th, under Harald Szeeman, centred on the consumption of images; the 11th in 2002 examined globalisation and true democracy as something yet to be realised.

documenta GmbH
Friedrichsplatz 18   D-34117 Kassel
Tel.: +49 (0)561707270
office@documenta.de
www.documenta.de

Landschaftpark Duisburg Nord Duisburg

The intervention by Peter Latz, a landscape architect specialised in revitalising industrial wastelands and author of the Bürgerpark Hafeninsel, Saarbrücken (1979–91), is an example of parks that are environmental artworks in their own right and expresses the now blurred boundaries between art, architecture, landscape design, and gardening or between the words garden, park, and urban development. At Duisburg Nord (1991–99), Latz created a "narrative park", recycling forgotten buildings and materials and giving them new value as both historical remembrance and plastic object. Working with plants, gardens, and design elements, he generated a new kind of recreational space, which functions as both a statement and a public space with social uses; a world with a particular dialectic between industrial artifice and nature.

Quadrat. Josef Albers Museum Bottrop

In the Ruhr Valley, Duisburg – Essen – Dortmund form a continuous metropolitan area (pop. 6 million). During the 1980s the coal region's heavy industry suffered a severe crisis, followed by a transformation of the old industrial sites into museums, cultural centres and new service sector companies. In Bottrop (pop. 120,000) this cultural complex includes the work of Josef Albers, a Bauhaus professor and investigator of the relationship between colour and geometry – *Homage to the Square*, crucial to both abstract art and a deeper understanding of perception. His small sculptural park features artwork by Max Bill, Donald Judd, Bernar Venet, George Rickey, Norbert Kricke, and half a dozen German artists.

Im Stadtgarten 20, D-46236 Bottrop,
Tel.: +49 (0)204129716
www.quadrat-bottrop.de

Skulptur Projekte Münster

This contemporary public art competition – not to be confused with the Münsterland Biennale – includes the participation of sculptors from around the world and has been celebrated every ten years 1977–2007. Artists like Buren, Turrell, Beuys, Cattelan, Judd, Hirchshorn, Sol LeWitt, Kirkeby, Richard Long, Huang Yong Ping – pictured, *The 100 Arms of Guan Yin*, temporary installation, 1997 –, and Rosemarie Trockel (2007) have taken part in this important event. About 100 projects are kept on as permanent pieces.

www.skulptur-projekte.de

Insel Hombroich Neuss

"Kunst parallel zur Natur."
Located 10 km from Dusseldorf (pop.
590,000) in the valley where the
Neandertal man lived 60,000 years ago,
this Roman encampment from the 1st c.
BC is now, 20 c. later, a dynamic city (pop.
150,000) with a well preserved 13th c. col-
legiate church. In this heavily exploited
agricultural and industrial region, some 20
ha of former farmland have been turned
into an "island" of parkland and wild
meadows, designed by the landscape
architect Bernhard Korte. Here one finds
11 pavilions for activities by artist-architect
Erwin Heerich, working artists (Anatol
Herzfeld, a disciple of Beuys; Gotthard
Graubner) and the Museum Insel
Hombroich, with its singular collection of
Persian, Khmer and Chinese (Han Dynasty)
sculpture as well as works by Arp,
Brâncuși, Calder, Chillida, Fautrier,
Schwitters. Some of them are housed in
the High Gallery (1983), the Labyrinth
(1986), the Tower (1989, pictured below),
the Snail (1993, pictured at centre), the
Tadeusz pavilion, IIB and Archive and the
Rocket Station (2000, pictured above). Karl
Heinrich Muller was the driving force
behind the project's even more ambitious
step: the Hombroich RaumOrtlabor (2008),
a long-term "open experiment" in which
artists and architects like Raimund
Abraham, Ando, Ban, Fehn, Finsterwalder,
Heerich, Thomas Herzog, Hoidn I. Wang,
Kirkeby, Krischanitz, Kruse, Libeskind,
Nishikawa, Frei Otto and Siza work on
devising "new modes of living." Few rules

apply – 90% landscape and 10% construction (10% communal facilities, 90%
for living, working, cultural creation); coexistence of vegetation, fauna, and humans;
"making spaces for different forms of
life and ideas in Hombroich" where
"culture is an integral part of life";
"forms of architecture which produce
and permit change themselves"; paths
that emerge from use, rather than paved,
marked and lit streets; land without fences
and walls; without advertising; self-gener-
ated energy. In the words of Wilfried
Wang, a "countermodel," the search
for forms [...] and the respect for nature."
Stiftung Insel Hombroich, Minkel 2,
D-41472, Neuss
www.inselhombroich.de

Since 1997
Blickachsen – Sculpture Biennale in
Bad Homburg and Frankfurt RheinMain
Organised by Blickachsen Foundation
Ferdinandstr 19
61348 Bad Homburg v. d. Höhe
Tel. +49 (0)617228907
info@stiftungblickachsen.de
www.blickachsen.com
Curator Christian K. Scheffel

Opening hours: permanently
Admission: free
• Access for the disabled
• Pets allowed
• Photographs allowed
• Guided tours: fee charged
• Educational programmes
• Publications: guides, catalogues,
  leaflets
• Coffee shop
• Restaurant
• Car park

How to get there:
• By car from Frankfurt or Kassel: from
  A5 at Bad Homburger Kreuz intersec-
  tion, turn onto A661 signposted Bad
  Homburg / Oberursel. Take the first
  exit signposted Bad Homburg and
  follow major road. At second traffic
  light, turn right into Marienbader Platz
  which merges into Ferdinandstraße.
  At the end of Ferdinandstraße, turn
  left into Kaiser-Friedrich-Promenade.
  The Kurpark is on the right.
• By train: from Frankfurt Hauptbahnhof
  on suburban line S5 to Bad Homburg
  station,15-min walking distance to
  the Kurpark.
• Airport: Frankfurt

Accommodation & Eating out:
  A wide range of hotels and restaurants is available

Blickachsen is a biennial series of sculptural exhibitions which has its
centre in Bad Homburg's Kurpark and castle gardens. This town (pop.
52,000), famous during the 19th c. for its healing baths and casino,
served as a popular leisure spot for the international nobility and roy-
alty of the time. Nowadays, it is one of the wealthiest districts in
Germany, home to bankers and financiers working in nearby
Frankfurt. Its Kurpark was designed in the mid 19th c. by Germany's
then foremost landscape architect, Peter Joseph Lenné – a passionate
promoter of the English lanscape garden. The spa's neoclassic buildings have been preserved within the park's approximately 48 prime

locations throughout the Rhine-Main region. The name Blickachsen or
"axes of view" refers to the axes that constitute the gardens' principal
design element. During the exhibitions, the sculptures are placed
along these axes, giving rise to new perspectives of both the art and
the landscape. The artwork enters into dialogue with the natural and
historical context, an exchange that is especially pronounced when
the artist has created a piece with a specific location in mind.
Blickachsen was the idea of Christian K. Scheffel. Since 1997, the exhibition has been showing the work of renowned, established artists
as well as young, emerging talents. The event has grown continually
and has now expanded beyond Bad Homburg to include other

prime locations throughout the Rhine-Main region, thus adding new perspectives that are linked to the original idea of the project. The pieces are exhibited from May to October. Some of them are then acquired and installed permanently on sites throughout Bad Homburg. Each Blickachsen exhibition is jointly curated with a different partner museum, some of which have been Wilhelm Lehmbruck Museum in Duisburg or the Skulpturenmuseum Glaskasten in Marl – see pp. 52 and 56, respectively – the Beyeler Foundation in Riehen (Basel) and the Kunsthalle in Mannheim, the Beyeler Foundation (Switzerland), the Yorkshire Sculpture Park (UK), the Frederik Meijer

Opposite page:
Jaume Plensa, *Poets*, 2011

Above:
Sui Jianguo, *Legacy Mantle*, 1997

Sculpture Park (USA), or the Maeght Foundation (France). Each of these noteworthy events is complemented by a published catalogue as well as guided tours of the events. Some of the renowned artists to participate so far are listed below.

Magdalena Abakanowicz, Amador, Carl Andre, Arman, Jean Arp, Max Bill, Louise Bourgeois, Bard Breivik, Alexander Calder, Anthony Caro, Eduardo Chillida, Richard Deacon, Anthony Gormley, Nigel Hall, Jörg Immendorff, Per Kirkeby, Joseph Kosuth, Markus Lüppertz, Joan Miró, David Nash, Miquel Navarro, Jaume Plensa, Sui Jianguo, Mark di Suvero, Jean Tinguely, Timm Ulrichs, Joana Vasconcelos, Bernar Venet, Erwin Wurm.

Neue Nationalgalerie
Potsdamer Straße 50
10785 Berlin

Berlin is a city with a great tradition of public gardens (the Tiergarten dates back to 1527) and wooded areas, as well as important Modern Movement architecture, though the two aspects have remained somewhat separate. The courtyard and surroundings of the Neue Nationalgalerie, a masterpiece by Mies van der Rohe, 1968, is the site for more than 40 pieces by international sculptors such as Laurens, Calder, Chillida, Marino Marini, Henry Moore, Barnett Newman, George Rickey, and Richard Serra, Bernhard Luginbühl, Karl Prantl, as well as German ones, including Bernhard Heiliger, Heinz Mack, and Ulrich Rückriem.

The collection is called Skulpturenpark der Neuen Nationalgalerie und die Skulpturen am Kulturforum, after the prime urban space on the edge of East Berlin, close to the Potsdamer Platz. It hosts a dozen cultural institutions and two major buildings by the exponent of organic architecture Hans Scharoun: the Berlin Philharmonic and the Berlin State Library.

Top left to right and below:
Works by Alexander Calder, Richard Serra, and Ulrich Rückriem

Since 1994
About 90 km to Hamburg and
about 129 km to Hanover

www.skulpturengartendamnatz.de

Temporary exhibitions, conferences,
concerts, workshops

In contrast to the powerful state-run Neue Nationalgalerie of Berlin, there are examples that show how aesthetic quality and commitment to the planet are not related to power and money. Two individuals, Monika Müller-Klug and Klaus Müller-Klug have established a delicate, advanced and subtle sculpture garden of 10,000 m² without any major stars from the international art circuit.

In a village with a population of 314, Damnatz, on the banks of the river Elbe in the district of Lüchow-Dannenberg, Lower Saxony, the two artists born in the 1930s have set their sculptures in non-ornamental nature. They have also played host to other colleagues, mostly German sculptors born between the end of the 1920s and the 1950s, many with established careers in Germany. There are some 30 site-specific works by artists including Gerson Fehrenbach, Otto Almstadt, Hartmut Stielow, Hannes Meinhard, Georg Seibert, Erich Reischke, Hans Schohl, Ilja Heinig, as well as some other European artists.

Klaus Müller-Klug, *Quader
im Lichthof*, 2000

Monika Müller-Klug, *Welle
über Land*, 2002

Since 1990 (current sculpture park)
Stiftung Wilhelm Lehmbruck Museum –
Centre for International Sculpture
Friedrich-Wilhelm-Straße 40
47051 Duisburg
Tel. +49 (0)2032833172
info@lehmbruckmuseum.de
www.lehmbruckmuseum.de
Dir. Dr. Söke Dinkla

Opening hours:
Tue.–Fri.: 12am–5pm
Sat.–Sun.: 11am–5pm
Admission: free
• Access for the disabled
• Pets allowed
• Photographs allowed
• Guided tour
• Public guided tour, Sunday 11.30am
• Temporary exhibitions
• Educational programmes
• Library
• Publications

How to get there:
• By car, by train (10 min. from Central
  Station)
• Airport: Dusseldorf (20 km)

The Wilhelm Lehmbruck Museum and Foundation – Centre for International Sculpture is one of the most important in Europe and home to a collection that includes some of the most significant German and international artists since the early 20th c.
Duisburg, in the industrial heart of the Ruhr Valley, is the world's largest port and an important centre for the iron and steel industry inland. "In December 1905, a group of twelve socially conscious Duisburg citizens issued a public call for the creation of a permanent art institution," according to the official history of the museum. Among them was Wilhelm Lehmbruck, a Duisburg native and the son of a miner, who was then studying at the Academy of Fine Arts in the neighbouring town of Dusseldorf. He would later achieve great success in both Paris and Cologne during the 1910s and eventually be considered the most important German expressionist sculptor. This

distinction made him the obvious choice for the task of acquiring pieces for the museum's collection, for which the patron was the family of the industrialist Eduard Böninger.
In 1931 the museum was established as the Duisburg Museum of Art. In 1959 it underwent large-scale remodelling when a new building – a project designed by Manfred Lehmbruck, architect and son of the famous sculptor – was added in Kant Park, on a plot of land belonging to the Boninger family. Along with the new building – a concrete and glass structure that was to serve as a model for future museum design – the museum also opened a sculptural park, which has become one of its defining characteristics. It seems appropriate that this mix of sculpture and park should be created in a place that bears Kant's name; after all, the Königsberg philosopher made an essential, theoretical contribution to the subject of art and nature in

his work *Kritik der Urteilskraft (Critique of Judgement,* 1790).
Manfred Lehmbruck's design contained one essential concept and a concrete, formal application: the relationship between art and nature in general, and the interaction between the museum's building and the park's biology in particular. The location of the outdoor objects – many of them large in scale and commissioned specifically for this site – has been changed on several occasions, a decision based on a variety of museum-related criteria and the wish to maintain a certain pattern of dispersal to their arrangement. The 1990 lay-out included more than 40 pieces by a variety of artists, such as Wilhelm Lehmbruck, Henri Laurens, Henry Moore, Meret Oppenheim, Eduardo Paolozzi, Richard Serra, Alan Sonfist, Bogomir Ecker, George Rickey and Norbert Radermacher.
The outdoor sculptures are not limited to the collection in Kant Park.

André Volten, *Sculpture for a plane,*
1979
Magdalena Abakanowicz, *Nine figures room,* 1990

They continue in the adjoining pedestrian zone, heading south and towards the downtown area. Duisburg initiated a programme in 1950 that included public art in their urban planning strategy; this has led to the acquisition of artwork by a variety of artists, including Marta Pan, Fabrizio Plessi and Menashe Kadishman.
Heading towards the inner harbour, one comes to the so-called "Fountain Mile." Here, along the entire Königstraße, a 15-year effort has brought together seven spectacular fountains designed by artists such as Ottmar Alt, Ulf Hegewald, Niki de Saint Phalle and Jean Tinguely, Wasa Marjanov, among others. Another example of urban art is the work that artists like Isa Genzken, Gerhard Richter, Manfred Vogel, and Eberhard Bosslet have completed in five underground stations since 1980. Where the Rhine and the Ruhr meet, stands the *Rheinorange* monument, a 25-m-high work by Lutz Fritsch. The city

has more to offer in terms of art: the *Garden of Memories* by Dani Karavan and the Landschaftspark Duisburg-Nord by Peter Latz – see p. 48.

The city and the foundation, both sharing such a keen interest in sculpture, lend their joint support to the Wilhelm Lehmbruck Prize, an award aimed at supporting artistic talent and reinforcing international, cultural relations. An independent panel of judges chooses the winner of this award, which the city bestows every five years on an artist for their cumulative career and artistic body of work. The museum also organises an exhibition of the winner's work. Among those honoured with this distinction are Eduardo Chillida (1966), Norbert Kricke (1971), Jean Tinguely (1976), Claes Oldenburg (1981), Joseph Beuys (1986), Richard Serra (1991), Richard Long (1996), Nam June Paik (2001), Reiner Ruthenbeck (2006), etc.

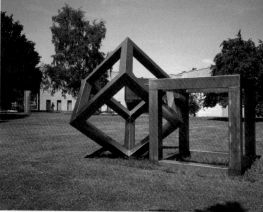

Klaus Simon, *Sculpture for a tree*, 1989
Alf Lechner, *Dice-construction*, 1973
Dani Karavan, *Dialogue*, 1989, looking into the Sculpture Court of Lehmbruck Museum

Since 2007
Naturparkverein Fläming e.V.
Naturparkzentrum
Mon.–Sun. 9am–5pm
Tel: +49 (0)3384860004
info@flaeming.net
www.kunst-land-hoher-flaeming.de

Fläming is a region and a hill chain that runs over 100 km from the Elbe river to the Dahme river in the German states of Saxony-Anhalt and Brandenburg. Brandenburg is 100 km from Berlin, an hour's train ride south of Berlin, between the railway stations at Bad Belzig and Wiesenburg/Mark. There are two routes in the sculpture trail in the Hoher Fläming Nature Park: the North Route, 17 km long, opened in August 2007, and the South Route opened in May 2010. Each has works selected in a public competition and chosen by a jury chaired by professor Rolf Kuhn of the famous IBA Internationale Bauausstellung. This is an international architectural exhibition originally held in Germany starting in 1901, with the current one (2012–2020) hosted by the region of Parkstad Limburg, Holland. IBA aims to develop new cultural, environmental and social concepts in architecture and urban planning. The North Route shows 10 prize-winning works in a federal competition; the South Route 12 works in competition for artists from Flanders and Fläming.

Josefine Günschel and Roland Albrecht, *Von Liebe und Sinnen*

Sebastian David, *Weltentür im Hohen Fläming*

Sculptors North Route: Susken Rosenthal, Susanne Ruoffe, Joerg Schlinke, Wolfgang Buntrock/Frank Nordiek, Jahna Dahms, Sebastian David, Walter Gramming, Josefine Günschel/Roland Albrecht, Jens Kanitz, Hartmut Renner.
Sculptors South Route: Silke De Bolle, Guy van Tendeloo, Marion Burghouwt, Johan Walraevens, Barbara Vandecauter, Marie-Christine Blomme, etc.

Gelsenkirchen-Uckendorf
North of the Ruhr
North Rhine-Westphalia
Admission: free
www.hermanprigann.com

Herman Prigann (1942–2008) is a singular and unique creative force of the last third of the 20th c. and the start of the 21st c. Rather than being in our era of hyper-specialisation and hyper-fragmentation of content and audiences, he appears to emerge from the glorious Renaissance: artist, architect, landscape designer, painter, sculptor, draughtsman, creator of land art, author and theoretician (Ecological Aesthetics), urban planner, landscape artist, active in the recovery of industrial areas from ruins; sometime his works are bound to be diluted on earth. This guidebook also presents other works in other areas (see p. 63). IBA International Bauausstelung Emscher Park was a regional government programme of structural changes in the landscape and abandoned industrial buildings in the "rust belt" of the German Ruhr mining basin, designed to generate a green, modern, rich and restored metropolitan area (1989–1999). During the work, Prigann created his now-famous *Stairway to Heaven* (Himmelstreppe) on the mound piling up the tailings from the old Rheinelbe mine, which blurs the borders between traditionally separate disciplines.

skulpturenpark heidelberg

Since 1995
Orthopädische Universitätsklinik
Schlierbacher Landstraße 200
Tel.: +49 (0)638021101
www.skulpturenpark-heidelberg.de

Opening hours: permanently
Admission: free
Monograph annual exhibition of
an artist in the halls and corridors of the
hospital, as David Nash in 2009, Werner
Pokorny in 2016

The Garten- und Landschaftspark der Orthopädischen Universitätsklinik Heidelberg, in the gardens and landscape park of the University
Orthopaedic Hospital, is located in the district of Schlierbach, and is
easily accessible by urban train or car. Its creation was sponsored in
1995 by the non-profit cultural association Friends and Sponsors of
the Heidelberg e.V. Sculpture Park.

The park offers visitors a compact, quiet and lyrical space with more
than 25 abstract artworks by German artists and international artists
of the 20th and 21st c. making up a permanent exhibition. The works
date from between 1957 and 2015, and include well-known artists
such as Bernhard Heiliger, Hans-Michael Kissel, Hartmut Stielow, Hans
Steinbrenner, Werner Pokorny, Friedrich Gräsel, Hannes Meinhard,

Hannes Meinhard, *3 Stelen*,
2003
Werner Pokorny, *Haus und
durchbrochene Form*, 1995
Amadeo Gabino, *Hommage à
F. Schiller*, 1992
Vera Röhm, *Schattenlabyrinth
(3 Module)*, 2001

Jochen Kitzbihler, Gottfried Honegger, Susanne Specht, Amadeo
Gabino, Gisela von Bruchhausen, Klaus Horstmann-Czech, Herbert
Mehler, Klaus Duschat, Vera Röhm, Christoph Freimann, Claus Bury,
Robert Schad, and others less known, such as Bernadette Hörder,
Gisela Weber, Vera Scholz von Reitzenstein.

Since 1997
Elsa-Brandström-Str. 9
50668 Cologne
Tel. +49 (0)22133668860
Fax +49 (0)22133668869
www.skulpturenparkkoeln.de
info@skulpturenparkkoeln.de

Opening hours:
Apr.–Sept. 10.30am–7pm
Oct.–Mar. 10.30am–5pm

This park was created by the Stoffels, an art-collecting couple, and realised with the help of local institutions that contributed an enclosed garden area of about 3 ha between the Rhine and the zoo, an oasis of peace amid the dense traffic. The works are shown for two years and then moved to another location. They are by well-known artists such as Serra, Chillida, Cragg, Calder, Rückriem, Di Suvero, Graham, Kapoor, Ecker, Core, Forg, and West. Works are not site-specific; many are monumental in scale, and realised in metal or stone. Others exemplify how sculpture can be more than form, material or process – it can express a concept, as seen in the work of Martin Kippenberger, Jenny Holzer or Jorge Pardo.

Tobias Rehberger,
Unmögliche Schönheit (schattig), 1999
Drei ausgesetzte Kinder, 2005

Bernar Venet, *Four Arcs*, 1999

Since 1982
Skulpturenmuseum Glaskasten Marl
Rathaus / Creiler Platz 1   45768 Marl
Tel. +49 (0)2365992257
skulpturenmuseum@marl.de
www.skulpturenmuseum-glaskasten-
marl.de
Dir. Georg Elben

Opening hours:
Museum: Tue.–Fri. 11am–7pm
Sat.–Sun. 11am–6pm
Admission: free
• Access for the disabled
• Pets allowed outside, not inside
• Photographs allowed outdoors
• Guided tours (booking required):
  fee charged
• Audio-guide to 30 outdoor sculptures
• Special audio-guide for blind people
• Exhibition halls with changing shows:
  6–7 per year
• Educational programmes
• Library
• Publications
• Picnic area
• Car park

How to get there:
• By car
• By bus: all buses to Marl-Mitte
Station
• By train: Marl-Mitte Station
• Airports: Dortmund, Dusseldorf

Accommodation & Eating out:
  One-star Golden Tulip Parkhotel Marl
  (50 m)
  Tel. +49 (0)23651020
  info@parkhotel-marl.de
  www.parkhotel-marl.de
  For further information: www.marl.de

The creation of a museum of sculptures in Marl was not an isolated event, as public art had already been installed here previously. In 1953, when the Paracelsus-Klinik Municipal Hospital was built, part of its budget was earmarked for the acquisition of works for its interior and gardens. Since then the city has installed new works in different areas. As part of this program, the exhibition "Stadt und Skulptur" was held at the beginning of the 1970s. After this event, and with the creation of an artificial lake in the middle of the city, the acquisition of works increased. In 1978, Dr. Rüth began to form the Skulpturen-museum Glaskasten, which at first was housed in a small municipal hall, and began to organize small temporary exhibits. Later the exhibition space was enlarged to 1,200 m². In 1982, the museum was made into an institution by the city, with the main objective of creating a collection of sculpture spanning from the beginning of the 20th c. to contemporary works. This collection has grown over time, and

by 2016 consists of more than 300 works, placed at various locations in the city: the museum, the municipal hospital and its garden which since 1990 has formed part of the museum, the surroundings of the artificial lake, and other settings. The permanent collection offers open-air works by Bogomir Ecker, Max Ernst, Emilio Greco, Ilya und Emilia Kabakov, Jan Scharrelmann, Richard Serra, Ulrich Rückriem, Wolf Vostell, Richier, and Ossip Zadkine, among others. Its interior galleries have top-ranking international names, from Gauguin, Rodin, and Giacometti to present-day artists.

Moving beyond sculpture, the Glaskasten-Museum and the Infracor Degussa Factory offer, under the concept of *Landschaftskunstwerk*, the transformation of an industrial ruin; the former installations of the water service have been converted into a "work of landscape art," the *Wasserstände* (Water Levels) by Herman Prigann, located some 5 km from the city centre.

Opposite page:
Jean Arp, *Feuille se reposant,* 1959

This page, from top to bottom:
Herman Prigann, *Wasserstände,*
2000–01
Ian Hamilton Finlay,
A View to the Temple, 1987
Ludger Gerdes, *Neon-Stück,* 1989
Wilfried Hagebölling,
Raumpflug, 1983–84

neuenkirchen **springhornhof**

Since 1967
Stiftung & Kunstverein Springhornhof
Tiefe Straße 4   29643 Neuenkirchen
Tel. +49 (0)5195933963
info@springhornhof.de
vermittlung@springhornhof.de
www.springhornhof.de
Dir. Bettina von Dziembowski

Opening hours:
Outdoor: permanently
Exhibitions: Tue.–Sun. 2pm–6pm
Admission:
Outdoor: free
Special exhibitions: fee charged
* Free guided bicycle tour which we
  offer from May to October on every
  first Sunday in the month
* Pets allowed
* Photographs allowed
* Guided tours (booking required):
  fee charged
* Exhibition halls with changing shows
* Events
* Library
* Publications: leaflet, books
* Bookshop
* Car park

How to get there:
  Neuenkirchen is 70 km from Bremen,
  74 km from Hamburg and 78 km
  from Hanover.
* By car: take the A7 exit Soltau and
  then follow B71 direction to
  Rotenburg
* Airport: Hanover

Accommodation:
  Neuenkirchener Hof (200 m)

The name Springhornhof encompasses a foundation and a cultural association that have worked on creating one of the most singular projects dedicated to open-air art in Europe. According to the organisation, they "promote the notion of artistic engagement with nature, the countryside and village life through a wide-ranging programme of exhibitions, projects and events." Gallery owner Ruth Falazik founded Springhornhof in 1967 as a centre dedicated to the production and promotion of contemporary art. Following her death in 1997, the Falazik family and several friends and collaborators, the federal state of Lower Saxony and the savings bank Kreissparkasse joined forces and created the foundation in 1999.

Since the very beginning, the project has commissioned international artists to create pieces in the countryside around Neuenkirchen. To date, more than 37 outdoor sculptural pieces have been realised within the framework of the Kunst-Landschaft (Art-Landscape) pro-

ject, which brings thousands of visitors to the area every year. The artwork is accessible throughout the year, located in fields, in forests, alongside paths, on lake shores and in nearby scrubland. Whereas the work realised during the 1970s was characterised by the use of materials obtained from natural sources at the site, the scope of the artwork in the early 21st c. has become wider, including architectural sculptures that can be walked on, electronically controlled sound installations, video art, and photographic projects. What unites the work of these acclaimed artists, including Micha Ullman, is their direct commitment to the place of production. The work is conceived as a perceptual tool through which the interested observer can experience new perspectives of the landscape and nature. The newest works by Jeppe Hein, Mark Dion in particular, by artists like Dan Peterman, Tony Cragg, and Michael Asher make explicit references to a wide range of ecological and social questions. The integration of art into an open, cultural landscape, the gradual transformation of the individual pieces within and alongside their surroundings and the con-

Jean Clareboudt, *Windberg,* 1981
Valerij Bugrov, *Himmel und Erde,* 1991

tinuous growth of the sculptural collection are some of the characteristics that make Kunst-Landschaft such a unique project.

The old farmstead of Springhornhof, in the centre of Neuenkirchen,
was converted into an art gallery in the 1960s and "offers an interesting combination of historical structural fabric and modern architecture." It is the point of departure for any and all explorations of the
outdoor sculptural works in the landscape. Furthermore, up to six
exhibitions of contemporary art are organised every year at the old
stables, ranging from traditional media like painting and sculpture to
more experimental and interdisciplinary projects by younger artists.
The programme also includes guided tours, artist lectures, performances, film projections, and conferences. Particular emphasis is placed
on exploring the changing perception of nature and the countryside
through and in art.

The fact that this centre was created in a peripheral location, outside
of the main art circuits of metropolitan cities, is yet another notable
achievement.

Since 1989
Viersen, North Rhine-Westphalia,
about 8 km NW to Mönchengladbach,
about 15 km SW to Krefeld
Outdoor public space
Verein für Heimatpflege e.V.
www.viersen.de/de/inhalt/skulpturen-
sammlung
www.heimatverein-viersen.de/sammlung

The Viersen Sculpture Collection was created by a private initiative as a result of a donation from the American William Pohl, who was once a citizen of the city, and also with the involvement of local institutions. The works are in urban streets and those relevant to this guide in the public park area. New Star, a work by Mark di Suvero, was created in 1992. It was initially the subject of protests by citizens, who finally ended up accepting contemporary abstract art. There are site-specific works by the British artist Tony Cragg: the Bronze Articulated Column (1996), "Chaosmos" by the Chilean Roberto Matta, works by the German Erwin Heerich and the Chinese Wang Du (see photos below), as well as by Wolfgang Nestler.

Erwin Heerich, *Monument*, 1989
Roberto Matta, *Chaosmos*, 2002
Wang Du, *China Daily*, 2010

Since 2008
Skulpturenpark Waldfrieden
Hirschstraße 12
42285 Wuppertal
Tel. +49 (0) 20247898120
www.skulpturenpark-waldfrieden.de

• Villa Waldfrieden, available for
  organisers of events and meetings.
• Closed space for temporary
  exhibitions

Von Haus Waldfrieden zum Skulpurenpark (from the Waldfrieden House to the Sculpture Park, 2011) is a meaningful title. Villa Waldfrieden (1894) was destroyed by bombers during World War II. After that, the paint manufacturer Kurt Herberts commissioned the architect Franz Krause (1897–1979 Wuppertal) to reconstruct it, giving him complete artistic freedom. In 2006 Tony Cragg bought the property, including the empty building, reinterpreting it as a living part of the forest. Today it houses the Archive, the Cragg Foundation, its offices and the artist's study.

Around it are 12 ha of woods with venerable trees such as chestnuts, limes, maples, oaks, and larches, where the autumn gold is fol-

• Guided tours
• Gastronomy
• Concerts

lowed by winter snow, and the reddish leaves of the beeches contrast with the cherries in bloom. Set skilfully among these trees, the sculptures generate a feeling that "the perception of art is bound up with, and inseparable from, an experience of nature". More than three dozen works by Anthony Cragg, Richard Deacon, Thomas Schütte, Wilhelm Mundt, Norbert Kricke and others show a significant range of contemporary sculpture. A closed, minimalist glass room houses temporary exhibitions, offering a radical contrast between the functionalist Modern Movement and the curved and sculptured forms of the Villa.

Everything here is of high aesthetic quality, even its website.

Above:
Tony Cragg, *Points of View,* 2007

Right:
Villa Waldfrieden, 2008,
Temporary exhibitions room

españa

Due to its geographical location, the Iberian peninsula in south-western Europe – between the old world Mediterranean and the new world Atlantic, with Europe to the north and Africa only 13 km further south – has always served as a nexus of global history and culture. 800,000 years ago it witnessed a crucial link in human evolution: the Homo sapiens' forebear, the first Europeans (Atapuerca archaeological site, Burgos). Another milestone, this time in the arts, occurred 40,000 years ago, when Homo sapiens left "negative hands" on the walls of El Castillo cave in Puente Viesgo, Cantabria, along with other figures. The large, mountainous peninsula, of which 85% is Spanish territory, is rich in contrasts and characterised by natural diversity: the expanse of dry land in the south-eastern desert, the green and rainy Atlantic and Cantabrian coasts in the north, enormous riverbeds cultivated over millennia (Ebro, Guadalquivir), endless plains, towering peaks – the Pyrenees of Huesca, 3,300 m, the Picos de Europa, 2,600 m, 20 km from the Cantabrian Sea – snowfall and temperatures below zero, scorching summers reaching 45°C, long springs and lava (Canary Islands), green meadows, Mediterranean woodlands (olive, pine, holm oak, vines), and the most sunshine in all of Europe.

This natural, historical and cultural complexity makes a meaningful summary almost impossible. Highlights include the exceptional cave paintings in the north (Cantabria, Asturias), polychromes of bison from 15,000 BC in the cave of Altamira, Santillana, for which the artist-architect Navarro Baldeweg designed a museum, paradigmatic for its dialogue with the earth and horizon; the megaliths after the Neolithic revolution; the bronze pieces of the El Argar culture, heralding a tradition of precious metalwork that continues today; the founding of Cádiz around 1000 BC, the oldest, existing city in the west, and the gold jewelry of Tartessos (700 BC); the presence of ancient Greek enclaves in the 7th c. BC, which gave Iberia its name; the Roman arrival during the 3rd c. BC and the complete Romanisation under Julius Caesar, giving birth to a Hispania that supplied the empire with philosophers and emperors – two, Trajan and Hadrian, under whom the empire would reach its apogee; the combination of technology and earthly resources in mines such as Río Tinto and Las Médulas, landscapes that now allude to tekne, nature and the beginnings of classical, western art; the political unity of Visigoth Hispania that allowed for continued Roman rule in central Europe; the beginning of Muslim Spain's history and culture in 711, bequeathing, after 8 c. of Islamic and Christian interaction, the possibility of another world, with water and hanging gardens and simple plants, lasting until 1492 when the Catholic Monarchs turned America into the New World and, little by little, the world into one; the 16th–17th-c. Spanish Empire, spread across Europe and three continents; its long decadent decline, briefly interrupted by the Enlightenment in the 18th c. under Charles III – the French gardens of Aranjuez and La Granja; the bloody Civil War of 1936 and the harsh post-war period under the Franco dictatorship. A new era began with the nascent democracy of 1978 and the economic and cultural explosion that followed, bringing with it both shadow – mass tourism, unbridled construction and conse-

Gijón
Kortezubi Hernani
Llanes
Santillana del Mar San Sebastián
Pontevedra
Port-Bou
Vigo Las Médulas
Huesca Girona
Villoslada de Cameros
Zaragoza Cassà de la Selva

Madrid

Cáceres
Malpartida
Baleares

Río Tinto

Jerez de la Frontera
Vejer de la Frontera

Canarias
Santa Cruz de Tenerife
Lanzarote

350 Km

505,988 km², 46.5 million inhabitants,
member of the European Union
since 1986

quent environmental damage, a media empire governed by entertainment, events, banality – and ephemera, for example the creation of centres for contemporary art in many cities.

The past achievements in painting were never reached in sculpture. Classicism continued well into the 20th c., while the young Spanish avant-garde was in Paris. Manolo Hugué created a solid body of work with figures akin to those of Maillol, followed by a radical break initiated by artists who would become some of the most relevant worldwide. Picasso is Picasso in everything. Julio Gonzalez turned iron into a sculptural material and space into an essential, sculptural element in his highly original work, described by David Smith as "the father of all iron sculpture in this century." Gargallo pioneered the use of concave and convex metal surfaces. In Madrid, Alberta created post-cubist work, then left to Moscow and endured Stalinism, whereas Ferrant experimented with mobiles and found objects. Miró and his free surrealism was another global milestone, highly influential in the US after World War II, a time in which Oteiza and Chillida initiated and accomplished their dynamic, spatial explorations. The 21st c. began with the death of Juan Muñoz, invoker and evoker of "placeless places," and different tendencies, from the architectural resonance of Miquel Navarro, Susana Solano and Cristina Iglesias' work to the varied, expressive universe of Jaume Plensa and Perejaume's blurring of artistic boundaries to the ironic and socially critical installations of Pilar Albarracín or MP&MP Rosado.

Madrid is the capital (pop. 3.2 million, 6 million in the area) of the kingdom and the arts, in a decentralised country unlike its European neighbours, conducive to the creation of parks in remote places.

Left:
Gustavo Torner, *Laberinto: Homenaje a Borges*, 1973
Parque García Sanabria, Santa Cruz de Tenerife

Right:
Mark Macken, *Solidaridad*, 1973
Parque García Sanabria, Santa

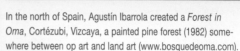

In the north of Spain, Agustín Ibarrola created a *Forest in Oma*, Cortézubi, Vizcaya, a painted pine forest (1982) somewhere between op art and land art (www.bosquedeoma.com).

In nearby Asturias, Llanes, a mediaeval town, with a fishing port where whalers used to set out to the Northern Atlantic, Ibarrola created a work in literal and material dialogue with the sea: *Memory Cubes* (2001) transformed the typical grey cement breakwater blocks into a colourful, ancestral mural that is now very popular. Gijón, which used to be a grey industrial city, now boasts services and open-air sculptures such as those of Miquel Navarro – *Andarín* on the Arbeyal beach and *Homage to Galileo Galilei* by Amadeo Gabino on Cape San Lorenzo. On the Santa Catalina hill, by the beach of San Lorenzo, Chillida installed his *Tribute to the Horizon* (1990) in reinforced concrete, 10-m-high, with its style of harmonic contrast between mass, emptiness, telluric force, etc. Back in the Basque Country, in San Sebastián, Guipúzcoa, on the Paseo Nuevo, in competition with Chillida's *Wind Comb* (see p. 87) is the geometric *Empty Construction* (2002) by the resiliant theoretician and sculptor Jorge Oteiza. Moving to the centre of Castile, in Avila, the Valley of Ambés, Ibarrola painted *115 large granite rocks*, creating a new illuminated nature.

From above to below:
Bosque de Oma, Ibarrola
Cubos de la Memoria, Ibarrola
Rocas pintadas, Ibarrola
Elogio del Horizonte, Chillida
Construcción vacía, Oteiza

cassà de la selva parc art

Since 2003
Parc Art, Parque de las Artes
Contemporáneas de Cassà
Veïnat de Matamala s/n
17244 Cassà de la Selva, Girona
Tel. +34 972463081
parcart@parcart.net
www.parcart.net
Dir. Jaume Roser

Opening hours:
Summer (Apr.–Sept.): Tue.–Sat.
10am–2pm, 4pm–8pm, Sun. 10am–2pm
Winter (Oct.–Mar.): Tue.–Sat.
10am–2pm, 4pm–6pm, Sun 10am–2pm
Closed: 23 Dec.–16 Jan.
Admission: fee charged
• Access for the disabled
• Photographs allowed
• Guided tours: fee charged
• Exhibition halls
• Picnic area
• Car park

How to get there:
• By car, and by train from Girona's
  Station
• By bus from Girona, and San Feliú
  de Guixols
• Airport: Girona Costa Brava

Accommodation & Eating out:
  www.turismegirona.com

The Contemporary Arts Park of the Cassà de la Selva is located 15 minutes from the city of Girona and the beautiful touristic area of the Costa Brava. Situated in the neighbourhood of Matamala, it stretches across a natural environment of some 20,000 m^2 at the base of the Sierra de Las Gabarras, low mountains (maximum altitude 531 m) covered with Mediterranean forests that form part of the coastal range.

A private property, the park contains an ample collection of about 350 open-air works by Spanish and international sculptors, including Néstor Basterretxea, Xavier Corberó, Jakob Engler, Enric Pladevall, Pablo Serrano, Francesc Torres-Monsó and Robert Vandereycken.

The artists themselves select the locations of their works, an interesting and at times decisive element in establishing an authentic dialogue between art and nature. This free selection by each artist contributes to increasing the sculptures' power of communication, as well as drawing out their formal qualities.

The collection includes different materials and formats, but also different artistic languages, which extend from minimalism, formal expressionism and figuration to pure geometric abstraction.

The idea of the *hortus conclusus*, the garden closed to the exterior and forming an agreeable space for domestic life, dates to classic antiquity, was recovered in the Middle Ages, renovated in the Renaissance and extends even into the 21st c. The Arts Park does not overlook this tradition. Conceived as an old garden where art and nature are fused, it offers paradise as a paradigm for the visitor's enjoyment.

The park also realises or participates in activities related to contemporary art, and sculpture in particular. Thus, for example, together with the Fita Foundation, between February and April 2005 it organised the exhibition "Escultura Embrionaria," which sought to bring the general public closer to the different stages of the creative process of a sculpture, from the first idea and early models until it is placed in its final setting.

Since 2000
Museo Chillida-Leku
B.º Jauregui 66
20120 Hernani, Guipúzcoa
Tel. +34 943335963
prensa@museochillidaleku.com
www.museochillidaleku.com
Dir. Ignacio Chillida, Luis Chillida

Opening hours:
Contact the museum
Admission: fee charged
• Access for the disabled
• Photographs allowed
• Guided tours (booking required):
  fee charged
• Exhibition halls with changing shows
• Educational programmes
• Publications
• Shop: books, jewelry, posters, etc.
• Picnic area
• Car park

How to get there:
• By car: Highway A–8, exit 8 to
  Hernani
• By bus: Garayar G2 from San
  Sebastián
• Airport: Fuenterrabia (26 km)

Accommodation & Eating out:
  San Sebastián offers a wide range of
  facilities, from luxury and five-stars
  hotels to pensions for young students. This is an international top
  level gastronomic area with excellent
  cooking and natural food, from luxury
  restaurants headed by some of the
  best chefs in the world to popular
  tapas bars.

"One day I dreamed of a utopia: to encounter a space where my sculptures could come to rest and people could walk among them as if in a forest." (Eduardo Chillida).

The dream of this key figure in the international art of the second half of the 20th c. became reality in 2000, when their Majesties the King and Queen of Spain inaugurated Chillida-Leku, the "space of" or "place of Chillida" in the Basque language. The project began in 1983, when the sculptor and his wife visited the Zabalaga estate, located 6 km south of San Sebastián, and decided to buy part of it. Later they would gradually acquire the rest, including a typical Basque caserío or farmhouse of 1543, which was later restored.

The sculptural space, a single work of art conceived and executed as such by the artist, contains three areas: 12 ha of pasture, with beech trees, oaks, magnolias, and more than 40 sculptures, many of great size, personally and carefully sited by Chillida himself. The Zabalaga caserío contains smaller works, while the service area includes an auditorium, shop, and rest area. The collection consists of a total of about 400 sculptures and some 300 works on paper and "gravitations," which offer the essence of his work.

The outdoor sculptures are made of steel, stone, and concrete. The pieces in corten steel are shaped despite the strength of the material, and their colouring, between rust and orange, changes according to the light. The works in rough or polished granite are deployed around the voids created in their interiors. The interaction with the spectator and the conjugation of art and nature give all the works an extra dimension. The most suggestive way to experience Chillida-Leku is to walk freely and at random among the pieces, as they follow no pre-established sequence or itinerary. In this way, the emotions and pleasures of this enchanted forest are closer to the artist's ideal vision of his space: an enclave of peace and meditation.

Among the activities at Chillida-Leku, the educational programmes are directed to every level, while guided tours, concerts, dance performances, etc. follow the idea so dear to Chillida – whose work often talks about poetry, music, dance, etc. – of fomenting a dialogue between the arts. The shop, available on-line, offers articles of interest for their aesthetic or design quality, as well as books on the artist and his work. The library and documentation centre, with some 4,000 references, is dedicated to research, teachers and students. A small auditorium and the Zabalaga Villa are available for events.

La Casa del Poeta, Estela VII, 1991
View of the forest and several artworks

Since 1995
CDAN Centro de Arte y Naturaleza.
Fundación Beulas
Avenida Dr. Artero s/n, ctra. de Ayerbe
22004 Huesca
Tel. +34 974239893
cdan@cdan.es
www.cdan.es
Artistic Dir. Teresa Luesma

Opening hours: permanently
Admission: free
• Access for the disabled
• Pets allowed
• Photographs allowed
• Guided tours
• Exhibition halls with changing shows
• Educational programmes
• Documentation Centre
• Car park

How to get there:
• To Huesca by car, train, or bus.
• To visit the works of art located in the
  enclaves scattered throughout the
  province, by car, rental car, or bus.
• Airport: Zaragoza (72 km)

Accommodation & Eating out:
  Huesca, Benasque, Abiego, Alquezar,
  Bielsa, Jaca, etc.
  www.dphuesca.es/oferta-cultural
  www.huescalamagia.es

The principal objective of this initiative is to study the relations between art and nature, a goal reached thanks to the quality of the works created and installed, the artists who made them, the theoretical discourse that supports the project and the other activities of its programme.

In the mid 1990s, Huesca's Provincial Government, with years of experience in an intensive programme of cultural activities, decided to launch a project managed by Teresa Luesma and directed by Javier Maderuelo, university professor of architecture, critic, and essayist on art specialising in the landscape and related subjects.

The idea was to create a collection, organised as an itinerary, of works by artists from around the world, in which each work would be designed specifically for its site in different natural locales throughout the province. Each installation involves a reflection on the integration of the artwork in nature, and the use of the natural environment as a material or support for the artist's creative process.

Since 1995, the organisation has invited artists of the land art move-

ment and related areas with experience in such works or interventions. The limits are imposed only by the medium itself and the available budget. The artists and their projects are: Richard Long, who created one of his pathways through a natural landscape in the Maladeta, *A circle in Huesca*, 1994; Ulrich Rückriem, who was interested in studying ways of transforming stone – a grouping of 20 pink granite stelae in Abiego, 1995, and *Estela XXI* in the CDAN garden Huesca; Siah Armajani, *Mesa picnic para Huesca*, in the Pineta Valley, 2000; Fernando Casás, eight black granite monoliths and two centenary living olive trees, in Piracés, 1998–2003; David Nash, *Three Sun Vessels for Huesca*, Santa Lucía hermitage, Berdún, 2005; Alberta Carneiro, an intervention in the grove of Belsué, 2006; and Per Kirkeby's brick constructions in the municipality of Plan and in the CDAN garden. All the works are permanently accessible in their

Ulrich Rückriem, *Three sun vessels para Huesca*, 2005, Berdún
Fernando Casás, *Árboles como arqueología*, 1998–2003, Piracés, desierto de los Monegros

respective locations, and sufficiently distant from one another to create a kind of museological itinerary.

The project organises temporary exhibitions, and educational activities, research grants and especially courses as: *Art and Nature, The Landscape, The Garden as Art, In the City, Public Art*, and *Art and Thought*, and the series of books and publications on cultural construction of landscape, which bring together theorists, historians, critics, artists, and other experts. The conferences and courses proceedings and the publications in 20 years (1995–2015) form a fundamental theoretical base for understanding the relationship between art and nature Since 2006, el CDAN Fundación Beulas is headquartered in the building designed by Rafael Moneo, Pritzker Prize.

fundación césar manrique

Since 1992
Fundación César Manrique
Taro de Tahíche   35507 Tahíche
Lanzarote, Islas Canarias
Tel. +34 928843138
Fax +34 928843463
fcm@fcmanrique.org
www.fcmanrique.org
Dir. Fernando Gómez Aguilera

Opening hours:
Every day (including holidays)
10am–6pm
Admission: fee charged
• Exhibition halls with changing shows
• Educational programmes
• Library
• Publications
• Bookshop
• Coffee shop
• Car park

Accomodation:
   Lanzarote offers a wide range of
   facilities, from luxury and five-stars
   hotels to rural houses.

Through his outstanding work in preservation, using an approach compatible with the creativity of his own time, César Manrique, artist and landscape architect, exemplified the position of commitment to nature and to the tradition of a place.

The island of Lanzarote, with its spectacular volcanic landscape – the last great eruptions were in 1730 and 1736 – was a decisive presence in his life and work. A land of craters, scarce in water, with the sea always visible or nearby, its most dramatic landscapes being in the Mountains of Fire of the Timanfaya National Park, where most of Manrique's interventions are found: his own house and studio, the Timanfaya Restaurant, the habilitation of the Jameos del Agua (a volcanic grotto with a seawater lagoon), the Batería del Río Lookout, and the adaptation of the San José Castle for a small Museum of Contemporary Art. These projects comprise a model of landscape design and architecture that integrate local materials and tropical vegetation, and a minimal alteration of the local environment, a model that has delayed and resisted three decades of the devastating destruction of intensive tourism by generating an unusual sensibility for the natural environment among the local population. Manrique's greatest legacy is therefore the concept of the island as a work of collective art.

The César Manrique Foundation occupies what was his studio-home. The artist himself converted the residence, the domestic staffs' dependencies and the garages into spaces for exhibits and cultural activities. The 30,000 m² estate extends over a bed of lava. On its semi-buried lower level, the construction takes advantage of a natural formation consisting of five volcanic bubbles, which make up a surprising habitable space, while the exterior of the house and its upper level recall the island's popular architecture.

The artist's work is exhibited inside and out: documents on interventions and the environment, murals, mobile sculptures, ceramics, and an ample selection of his pictorial production, together with his collection of other artists' works. The Foundation offers a workshop-residence for artists, and develops activities along three related lines: the visual arts, the environment and cultural thought. Courses, seminars, workshops, lectures, environmental reports, challenges to urban development plans, awareness campaigns, etc. are guided by a critical and alternative spirit. A line of publications gives additional solidity and permanence to the Foundation's labour.

Standing out within the exhibit programme are the art-nature temporary exhibitions, with figures such as Nils-Udo, Thomas Joshua Cooper, Miguel Ángel Blanco, Axel Hütte, Hamish Fulton.

César Manrique, landscape architect and artist
Left: *Energía de la pirámide, series Juguetes del viento*, 1991
Right: murals inside the Foundation's gardens, 1992

Bottom: *Burbuja roja* (red bubble), Foundation's indoor

lanzarote museo atlántico

Since 2016
Bahía de las Coloradas, Playa Blanca
Yaiza, Lanzarote
Canary Islands
museoatlantico@centrosturisticos.com

Opening hours: daily 10am–6pm

Access for snorkelers and divers:
Museo Atlántico de Lanzarote
Puerto Deportivo Marina Rubicón
Urb. Castillo del Aguila, 2,
35580 Playa Blanca
Tel. +34 928 517388
+34 606416701
reservasma@centrosturisticos.com

Statues have been placed under-water before, mostly without any significant interest. The British artist Jason deCaires Taylor (b. 1974) goes much further. His concepts and underwater sculp-ture parks on Isla Mujeres/Cancún and elsewhere are some of the most advanced in terms of their radical interaction between art and nature, aesthetics and sustain-able environment, tourism and protection of the oceans that are under such great threat.
His project *The Silent Evolution,* begun in 2010, is an "underwater sculpture park" (the name Museo Atlántico is misleading). It is in-

stalled on the continental shelf south of the island of Lanzarote and is sponsored by Centros de Arte, Cultura y Turismo, the government institution in the Canary Islands whose mission is to promote the sustainable development of a UNESCO biosphere reserve that must be preserved. DeCaires Taylor creates art and defends the oceans as interconnecting areas: his art installations in pH-neutral concrete create a natural reef, that increases the marine biomass over time; and in turn, the action of the sea makes the sculptures themselves evolve. At a depth of some 12 m in an area of 2,500 m², the exhibit is made up of parts. The central one is a botanical garden containing the following: 1. *The Rubicon*, 35 human figures moving towards the same destination; 2. *The Raft of Lampedusa*, which alludes as much to Géricault's painting as it does to the crisis of abandoned refugees; 3. *Los Jolateros*, children with little boats made of old oil drums, a metaphor of a precarious future; 4. *Content* and 6. *The Photographers,* with a couple taking a selfie; 5. *Hybrid Sculptures,* that are half human, half cactus, and other pieces that allude critically to new technologies, voyeurism and individualism.

The first underwater sculpture park in the Atlantic and in Europe is a suggestive mix of artefacts / nature, and criticism of commercialism.

Since 1992
160 ha, bordered by the M40 motorway to the south, Dublín Street to the west, and Logroño Avenue to the east

Admission: free
Opening hours:
Jun.–Sept.: Mon.–Sun. 7am–1pm
Oct.–May.: Sat.–Thu. 7am–11pm
Fri.–Sat. 7am–12pm

How to get there:
By metro: Campo de las Naciones
By bus: 104,112,122
www.esmadrid.com/informacion-turistica/parque-juan-carlos-i

Centuries ago there was a large olive grove to the north-east of the capital's historic centre. In the 18th c., during the reign of Philip V, when corruption blurred the boundaries between public and private property, the crown treasurer bought around 400 ha for himself using state funds. This was the origin of Olivar de la Hinojosa. In the 1980s the city expanded toward this area. The park was opened in 1992, with an International Symposium on open-air sculpture held there the same year. That was the origin of the Sculpture Path, a specific route that takes you past 19 works by the artists Alexandru C. Arghira (Romania), Yolanda d'Ausburg (Brazil), Miguel Berrocal (Spain), Jorge Du Bon (Mexico), Andrés Casillas / Margarita García Cornejo (Mexico), Jorge Castillo (Spain), Carlos Cruz-Diez (Venezuela), Amadeo Gabino (Spain), Toshimitsu Imai (Japan), Bukichi Inoue (Japan), Mario Irarrázabal (Chile), Dani Karavan (Israel), Leopoldo Maler (Argentina), Samuel Nahon Bengio (Israel), Victor Ochoa (Spain), José M. Utande (Spain), Michael Warren (Ireland).

Begun in 1988 (architectural project by Eduardo Serrano), opened in 1992, with a reform in 2005. It covers an area of 75,000 m² in one of the most densely populated districts in Europe (around 160,000 ha) to the south-west of the city: between La Paz and Santa Paula, near the Cádiz Highway close to the beach.
www.limposam.es

Admission: free
Opening hours: 8am–:
Summer: 1am
Spring and autumn: 11pm
Winter: 10pm

In the city of Malaga, this park is unusual in a number of ways. It is a multi-functional space, with flora, fauna, a lake, water, sporting facilities, children's play area, underground parking, and more. And it is an urban space, a rectangle framed with buildings on three sides and a busy road on the fourth. It is managed by the municipal company LIMPOSAM, and includes enigmatic sculptures by the German artist Stefan von Reiswitz (b. 1931, Munich). It is a community area open to everyone and reflects Danish landscape artist C. Th. Sørensen's concept of playgrounds, mingling greenery (15,000 trees and plants), fountains and a water geyser. All this surrounds the installation of 45 sculptures by von Reiswitz, which show influences ranging from medieval German sculpture to Goya, surrealism, Baumeister, Burri and Marino Marini. They are mythological and fantastical pieces, including fauns, sirens, Minotaurs, dolphins, unicorns and female figures that allude to classical Greece and Rome, suggesting a world that combines the ancestral spirits of the Germanic and Mediterranean worlds.

Since 1976
Museo Vostell Malpartida
Ctra. de Los Barruecos, s/n
Apdo. Correos 20
10910 Malpartida de Cáceres
Tel. +34 927010812
museovostell@org.gobex.es
museovostell.gobex.es
Dir. José Antonio Agúndez García

Opening hours:
Spring–Summer:
21 Mar.–20 Sept.: 9.30am–1.30pm /
5pm–8pm (Tue.–Sun.). Sun. of Jun.,
Jul., Aug. and Sept.: 9.30am–2.30pm.
Mon.: closed. Open on public holidays
Autumn–Winter:
21 Sept.–20 Mar.: 9.30am–1.30pm /
4pm–6.30pm (Tue.–Sun.). Sun. of Oct.,
Nov., Dec., Jan.: 9.30am–2.30pm.
Mon.: closed
Closed on 24, 25, 31 December, 1, 6
January, 9 February
Admission: free on Wednesdays
• Access for the disabled
• Guided tours (booking required)
• Exhibition halls with changing shows
• Library for research purposes
• Publications
• Bookshop
• Café-Restaurant
• Picnic area
• Car park

How to get there:
• By car: take N 521 road to Valencia
  de Alcántara and Portugal
• By bus: from Cáceres to Malpartida
  every hour, from 10am–9pm
• By train: to Cáceres, then by car or
  bus
• Airport: Talavera la Real (107 km)

Accommodation & Eating out:
  Malpartida and Cáceres

Its natural surroundings, location, collection and origin combine to make this a truly unique space. It was created by the artist Wolf Vostell, "citizen of Germany and Malpartida de Cáceres," who introduced happenings to Europe and was linked to the Fluxus movement since its inception in 1962. He also introduced décollage as a tool for intervening in reality, developed through a variety of artistic languages: embeddings, happenings, environments, etc. This museum is not a typical garden with sculptures, but rather a place where, beyond the physical and material presence of open-air works, everything is marked by the desire to bring about a re-encounter between man and nature.

It is located 3 km from Malpartida (pop. 4,400) and 14 km from Cáceres, within the Los Barruecos Natural Monument, a landscape of great geological interest, featuring enormous granite boulders: "Nature's works of art" as Wolf Vostell declared in 1974. In 1976 he installed the first open-air sculpture: *V.O.A.EX (Viaje de [H]Ormigón por la Alta Extremadura*, or "Concrete Trip through Upper Extremadura"), which inaugurated the museum. In 1978, *El muerto que tiene sed* was Vostell's second and final sculpture in Los Barruecos. The museum occupies the former 18th c. Lavadero de Lanas (Wool Laundry) building (14,000 m²), refurbished in 1993–98, and an outdoor area where two other works by the German artist are installed.

The Wolf and Mercedes Vostell Collection galleries house a number of installations that are very typical of his production, showing the conflict of contemporary man and incorporating a political and social critique of the hyper-industrialised world, using cars, TVs and other fetish-objects of the 20th c. The collection is completed with various object-paintings and medium and large paintings.

The Conceptual Art Collection brings together the work of Spanish, Polish and Portuguese artists such as Carneiro, Jerez, Canogar, Partum, Muntadas and Sarmento. Vostell's idea was to create both an exhibition area and place for encounter between artists and the public as a space of reflection and mutual learning. This included the launch of an intensive cultural programme, particularly in the 1970s and 1980s, with "art weeks and days," conferences, lectures, publications, etc., while participating artists donated their own works to the museum. The Fluxus-Gino Di Maggio Donation was added to the museum in 1998 with more than 200 pieces by European, North American and Asian artists, including Kaprow, Maciunas, Paik and Spoerri.

Opposite page:
Wolf Vostell, *V.O.A.EX.*, Los Barruecos,
1976

This page:
Wolf Vostell, *¿Por qué el proceso entre
Pilatos y Jesús duró sólo dos minutos?*,
1996–97
Los toros de hormigón, 1989–90

Since 1999
Illa das Esculturas
Xunqueira do Lérez
36005 Pontevedra
Tel. +34 610530052
xacastro@nvigo.es
www.turismo.gal
Dir. X. Antón Castro

Opening hours: permanently
Admission: free
• Access for the disabled
• Pets allowed
• Photographs allowed
• Guided tours (booking required)
• Fluvial trips
• Publications: guide, leaflet
• Picnic area
• Car park

How to get there:
• By car
• Airport: Vigo (35 km)

Accommodation & Eating out:
  A wide range of hotels and restaurants are available in the city

The reader finds a peculiar project before him, as neither its charac-teristics, its conception, nor even its original idea resemble a "sculp-ture park, a garden, or an open-air museum. It is an island, a contem-porary landscape," as it is described in its catalogue, a territory at once urban and undeveloped. This is how the island of Xunqueira must be understood. Located within the city of Pontevedra, it is a space of recreation and relaxation for local residents, but the birth of this unique idea was provoked by a need to express, to provoke sen-sations beyond those of an ordinary visit. It occupies an area of some 70,000 m² which are shared by the sculptures that populate the land-scape and the native flora and fauna. The location of the project is an important factor to take into account, given that in few sculpture parks the interaction between the space and the artistic works takes on such importance.

The twelve works that occupy the island were installed in the same year as the park's creation. They were all realised by artists of differ-ent nationalities and of the highest international renown in the field, among them two Spaniards and two Portuguese of no less prestige. Some of the artists are close to the language of land art, others to the conception of the work in open spaces, to public art, etc. They have used very different forms of expression for their works, responding to

Clockwise:
Robert Morris,
Laberinto de Pontevedra, 1999
José Pedro Croft, *Untitled,* 1999
Ian Hamilton Finlay, *Petrarca,* 1999

different conceptions of space, but in all of them, in one way or another, a common element is present, Galician granite, a well appreciated material among good architects. Allusions to the past, the present, mythology, love, the passing of time, or solitude are also found: Giovanni Anselmo's *Cielo Acortado*; Fernando Casas' *Los 36 justos*, 36 blocks of black granite over 4,000 m²; José Pedro Croft's *Untitled*, pearl gray granite; Dan Graham's *Pyramid*, 1988–99, pink granite; Ian Hamilton Finlay's *Petrarca*, green slate; Jenny Holzer's *Untitled*, 8 benches of gray granite, engraved; Francisco Leiro's *Saavedra, zona de descanso*; Richard Long's *Línea de Pontevedra*, 37 m long; Robert Morris' *Laberinto de Pontevedra*; Anne and Patrick Poirier's *Une folie o pequeño paraíso para Pontevedra*; an untitled stele by Ulrich Rückriem; and Enrique Velasco's *Xaminorio xunquemenes abay*.

The initiative was sponsored by the provincial government, the Town Council, and the Pontevedra Savings Bank. Ironically, due to its dependence on public administrations, its posterior conservation and maintenance have suffered ups and downs, varying with the changing political tide, which has lamentably resulted in the deterioration of many of the works. For this reason, in 2000 the Illa das Esculturas de Pontevedra Association was formed in order to represent, promote and defend the artistic, social and cultural interests of the project.

Since 2000
Parque de Esculturas Tierras Altas
Lomas de Oro
Ermita de Lomos de Orios
26125 Villoslada de Cameros, La Rioja
Tel. +34 941360667
ceip@riojarural.com
Dir. Roberto Pajares

Opening hours: permanently
Admission: free
• Pets allowed
• Photographs allowed
• Guided tours (booking required)
• Exhibition halls with changing shows
• Educational programmes
• Musical sessions and performances
• Publications: guide, leaflets
• Picnic area
• Car park

How to get there:
• From Villoslada to the sculptures: on
  foot
• To Villoslada: by car and bus
• Airport: Agoncillo (Logroño), and
  Bilbao

Accommodation:
  Villoslada de Cameros (3 km):
  Casa Rural El Quemao:
  tel.+34 941468154
  Posada Hoyos de Iregua:
  tel.+34 941468256
  Camping Los Cameros:
  tel.+34 941747021
  Lumbreras (8 km):
  Casa Rural Arca: tel.+34 941228074
  Albergue El Asilo: tel.+34 941468262
Eating out:
  In Villoslada de Cameros (3 km)
  and Lumbreras (8 km)

This sculpture park was created due to the efforts and vision of the sculptor Roberto Pajares, and the economic support of the Leader II Funds of the E.U. It is located in the Sierra de Cebollera, at an altitude of between 1,100 and 1,415 m, an area under environmental protection since 1995, and covered with oaks, gall oaks, pine groves, and pastures. The works are sited near the Our Lady of Lomos de Orios Hermitage, along the Camino de la Virgen trail, between 20 and 50 minutes by foot from the village of Villoslada and covering a complete circuit of about 15 km. The first work by local sculptor Alberto Vidarte in 1988 was followed, once the park was established, by the works of eight others, among them British artist Lesley Yendell (a colossal glass, plate and spoon among the trees), the Spaniards Luis G. Vidal (an enormous white skull), Carmelo Argaiz, Pamen Pereira, Sotte, and Tomás García de la Santa, and the Cuban Gertrudis Rivalta and Chilean Lucho Hermosilla, who share a common use of natural materials (moss, stones, branches, leaves, and wood), and, at times, a single external resource, painting. Information on exhibits, guided tours and educational activities at the Centro de Interpretación Parque de Cebollera.

Lucho Hermosilla, *Intrusos*, 2001
Lucía Loren, *Madre sal*, 2008

Plaza del Tenis
Paseo del Peine del Viento
20008 San Sebastián

Tel. +34 943481166
cat@donostia.org
www.sansebastianturismo.com

Public space permanently open

Chillida began the *Peine del Viento* series of sculptures in 1952, after his return from Paris. Together with the architect Luis Pena Ganchegui, he promoted it as a public sculpture. San Sebástian was then a small and very conservative city, and the city government at first ignored the proposal. Finally, in 1974 the last Mayor under the Franco Dictatorship proved receptive to the idea. In 1975, on a wild rocky site at the foot of Mount Igueldo that closes the beautiful Bay of La Concha on the west, a place with intimations of the sacred, frequently whipped by the wind and battered by the sea, where others had wanted to build a parking lot, Chillida and Pena were able to realise this true worldwide landmark, a full fusion of architecture, urbanism, landscaping, and sculpture in a design specific to the place and the nature of the sea, the mountain, the air and the light. Pena "interpreted the power of the place in terms of the beginning and end of the city, as an encounter with nature, respecting it and drawing all the richness of the design from it. [...] Thus, he laid out a series of stepped platforms, along the lines of the *crepidomas* of a Greek temple," a plaza that renounces protagonism, subtle to an extreme, and preamble to the sculptor's work, "like a temenos, the sacred precinct before the Greek temple [...] which permits a view to the sea," and with seven orifices, "from which surging water erupts from the subsoil under the plaza on stormy days," a perfect technical solution, and full of aesthetic symbolism (Rispa, ed. 1997). The visitor advances, discovering the three sculptures in corten steel (10 t, 215 × 177 × 185 cm each): first the one on the right, then the one that marks the horizon, and finally the three together – formed by four thick bars of a square section emerging from a trunk anchored into solid rock. But, as the artist says, "… sea, wind, cliffs, horizon, and light. The steel forms mix with the forces of nature, enter into dialogue with them, they are questions and affirmations." A demonstration that the cultural artifact and the natural world are nothing other than a single nature.

vejer de la frontera fundación nmac

Since 2001
Fundación NMAC
Dehesa Montenmedio
Ctra. A–48 (N–340), km 42.5
11150 Vejer de la Frontera, Cádiz
Tel. +34 956455134
info@fundacionnmac.com
www.fundacionnmac.com
Dir. Jimena Blázquez Abascal

Opening hours:
Summer: 10am–2pm. 5pm–8.30pm
Winter: 10am–2.30pm, 4pm–6pm
Admission: fee charged
• Pets allowed
• Photographs allowed
• Guided tours (booking required):
  fee charged
• Indoor galleries
• Educational services
• Library
• Publications
• Restaurants: three inside the Dehesa
de Montenmedio area
• Picnic area
• Car park

How to get there:
• By car: from Cádiz, Jerez, and la
  Costa del Sol, take highway A–48
  (N–340)
• By bus to Vejer: take Transportes
  Comes (www.tgcomes.es) and then a
  taxi
• By train: option 1) take the AVE
  Madrid-Seville, and then the regional
  train to Cádiz, once there, you can
  either drive or take the bus to Vejer;
  option 2) take the Talgo train Madrid-
  Cádiz, and then drive or take the bus
  to Vejer
• Airport: Jerez de la Frontera

Accommodation:
  A wide range of facilities, from luxury
  and five-stars hotels to one-star pensions are available in Vejer, Zahara de
  los Atunes, Conil, Barbate.

The Fundación Montenmedio Arte Contemporánea (NMAC) opened to the public in June 2001. Located in a natural environment 5 km from Vejer de la Frontera (pop. 12,800), it is dedicated to working with contemporary international artists of the vanguard.

It is found in a territory with a double condition: on the one hand, it is 55 km from Cádiz – the oldest city of the West, founded around 1100 BC in an area with archeological remains of up to 2,700 years old, testimony to a cultural heritage that includes sculpture and architecture; and on the other hand, its natural spaces have been humanised following the Mediterranean tradition of creating a balance between man and his environment, which has its particular model here in the Dehesa, the cleared forest where trees and animals live together in a sustainable exploitation.

The NMAC Foundation occupies some 30 ha of the more than 500 ha that make up the Montenmedio Dehesa. Not far from the Atlantic Ocean, it is a land of low hills covered with a Mediterranean-type forest, which occasionally opens to distant views of the hilltop Vejer de la Frontera with its white houses, one of the most beautiful villages in Spain.

The main objective of the Foundation is to create a collection of site-specific installations and sculptures, above all in outdoor settings, and to convert the province of Cádiz into a point of reference in international contemporary art. In addition to these sculptures and installations, there are works of video and photography, located in the open spaces and covered facilities of the Foundation. The works are found along a route which leads through a Mediterranean forest of pines,

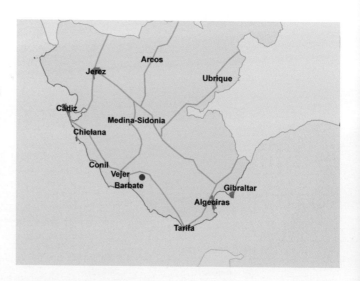

wild olives, mastics, and cork trees. The works of art co-exist with nature, and each appropriates the aromas, colours, and sounds of the diversity of plants and animals that surround it.

All the works were designed specifically for their locations, creating a dialogue between art and nature. But in addition, they have been realised in-situ with the aide of technicians and craftspeople from the area, establishing another dialogue between art and the social environment.

Since its creation, many artists from around the world have visited the NMAC Foundation. They are selected by an advisory committee whose criteria are based on the premise of supporting young creators and offering them the possibility of exhibiting together with better-known figures. Thus, on various occasions the NMAC has been the entry door for foreign creators who had never worked in Spain before. About 20 projects in different formats and by different authors, from Abramovic to Shen Yuan, are permanently placed in the park in 2016.

The dependencies of the Foundation consist of postwar military Quonset huts, which are curved from side to side, their interior walls discontinuous from the ceilings, and uninterrupted by right angles. They contain a reception area, two project rooms, two rooms for photographs, models and drawings of some of the works in the collection, a library, and an installation titled *Hammam* by the Chinese artist Huang Yong Ping. By 2006–07 the plan was a new building designed by architect Alberto Campo Baeza, the building extending longitudinally, closely related to the topography, like an artistic installation. But then came the Great Recession, the financial crisis, and budget cuts.

In addition to producing pieces, the Foundation's second priority is to disseminate information about contemporary art through the artists who have worked here. The works composing the collection are used to illustrate the principal concepts of the art of our time that

Olafur Eliasson, *Quasi Brick Wall*, 2003

NMAC Foundation facilities

Richard Nonas, *River run,
snake in the sun,* 2001
Sol Lewitt, *Cinderblock,* 2001

Opposite page:
MP&MP Rosado, *Secuencia Ridícula,*
2002
Marina Abramovic, *Human Nests,* 2001

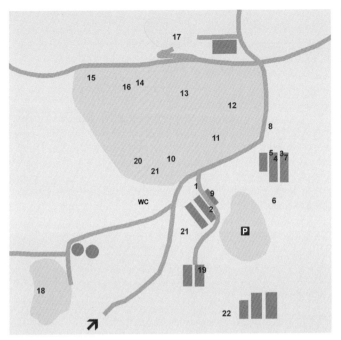

1 MP&MP Rosado, *Secuencia Ridícula,* 2002

2 Michael Lin, *Garden Passage,* 2003

3 Berni Searle, *Waiting 1,* 2003

4 Pilar Albarracín, *La noche 1002 / Lunares,* 2001

5 Marina Abramovic, *The Hero,* 2001

6 Ester Partegàs, *Yo Recuerdo,* 2003

7 Santiago Sierra, *3.000 huecos de*

180 x 70 x 70 cm cada uno, 2002

8 Maurizio Cattelan, untitled, 2001

9 Berni Searle, *Home and Away,* 2003

10 G. Bandolin, *Sky's Impression,* 2001

12 Olafur Eliasson, *Quasi Brick Wall,* 2003

13 Sol LeWitt, *Cinderblock,* 2001

14 Richard Nonas, *River run, snake in the sun,* 2001

15 Susana Solano, *Incienso y mirra,* 2001

16 Shen Yuan, *Puente,* 2004

18 Marina Abramovic, *Human Nests,* 2001

19 Huang Yong Ping, *Hamman,* 2003

20 James Turrell, 2006

21 Aleksandra Mir, 2006

22 Olafur Eliasson, 2006

are offered to the public.

The Foundation promotes a conception of art as a medium of establishing a relation with the world through the works, their forms, gestures, and objecthood. Artistic tendencies, materials, ways of approaching reality and other questions closely related to current issues are the themes that form part of the educational and cultural programme.

The programme of activities offers different levels and focuses so as to reach different sectors of an ample public. The Foundation organises guided visits, and workshops for school groups, adapted to the educational level of each group. Other programmes are directed to the entire family, with particular attention to children, especially during the summer (which in Montenmedio consists of long, hot days – in July and August daylight lasts until nearly 10pm and temperatures

Gunilla Bandolin, *Sky's Impression*, 2001

average highs of 30°C and lows of 17°C, while during the worst days of winter highs are around 16°C and lows around 11°C).

The cultural programme includes lectures, poetry readings, and outdoor concerts, always with the objective of helping to create a more cordial and respectful dialogue between art and the environment. The publication programme follows this general goal and the educational and cultural programme – see bibliography.

To the north of the city of Valencia, Camino de Vera, between the V21 exit of the A7 motorway to Catalonia (V21) and the beach neighbourhood of Malvarrosa UPV

In the wake of the great sculptor Mariano Benlliure (1862–1947), Valencia is a community with notable contemporary sculptors, such as Eusebio Sempere, Andreu Alfaro, Carmen Calvo, Amadeo Gabino, and Miquel Navarro, to cite only a few. The UPV Universidad Politécnica de Valencia has a Sculpture Department on its Vera campus and works

Universidad Politécnica de Valencia, Vicerectorado de Extensión Universitaria, Dirección de Arte
http://wis.fuuh.upv.es/campuescultoric/
Guided tours: Tel. +34 96 3879098 mornings, farteupv@upv.es, vaeu@upv.es
How to get there:
• By bus: www.upv.es/otros/como-llegar-upv/campus-vera/bus-urbano-es.html

From top to bottom, left to right: Adolfo Schlosser, *Velero* 1995; Gerardo Rueda, *Otoño*, 1992; Juan Bordes, *Tres verticales*, 1992; Jorge Oteiza, *Homenaje a Manolo Gil*, 1989; Eusebio Sempere, *Móvil*, 1971; Lorenzo Frechilla, *Obelisco*, 1990

actively on scientific and technical research, development and innovation. Its Sculpture Campus is a little-known but very significant collection of 70 works by the Spanish artists Oteiza, Berrocal, Gabino, Mariscal, Martín Chirino, Miquel Navarro, Basterrechea, Frechilla, Manolo Valdés, Alberto Sánchez, Sempere, Joan Cardells, Rueda, Pablo Serrano, Angeles Marco, and Schlosser; and those of other countries, including Susanne Bayer and the Irish Michael Warren.

finland / suomi

303,899 km², 5.4 million inhabitants, member of the European Union since 1995, capital: Helsinki (pop. 612,000)

Finland lies at the extreme north among the sculpture parks of Europe, with nature playing a very important role in its outlook. Linked to Sweden for more than 700 years, annexed by the Russian Empire in 1809 and independent since 1917, it has a well-known tradition in literature and music, and excellence in the architecture of Eliel Saarinen and his son Eero Saarinen, very sculptural in the latter's TWA terminal in New York as well as in the Gateway Arch of St. Louis, Missouri, USA.

Alvar Aalto is here in Finland, with his masterpiece of global architecture, the Vilpuri Library, its auditorium a roof of waves. His unmistakable designs of furniture and glassware refer closely to sculpture, which has had the figurative artist Wäinö Aaltonen (1894–1966) as its best-known artist.

That is the backdrop to the POAM Penttilä Open Air Museum of the Dutch sculptor Lucien den Arend, a resident of Penttä, who is very act-

POAM Penttilä Open Air Museum
Lucien den Arend
Seppäläntie 860
51200 Kangasniemi
Suomi Finland
www.poam.ws
Tel. +3580442641212
lucien@denarend.com

How to get there:
• By car: 180 km north-east of Helsinki by the E18 motorway

ive in environmental art, land art, and site-specific sculptures. In the park, an old farm closed in the 1950s, set in a forest, his own work forms the collection along with that of international colleagues such as Donald Judd, Oskar Kokoschka, Henry Moore, Richard Serra and Marc di Suvero, and the Finnish artists Theo Niermeijer, Gjalt Blaauw, Gerard Höweler, and Kari Huhtamo.

Parikkala Sculpture Park, or the Veijo Rönkkönen sculptures
Municipality of Parikkala (pop. 5,300), in Southern Karelia, 325 km north-east of Helsinki

How to get there:
• By car: along road 6, a journey of around 4 hours

Parikkala Sculpture Park: very different, because of their initial "strangeness" and suggestiveness are the sculptures of Veijo Rönkkönen in the south-east of Finland, barely 1 km from the Russian border. Rönkkönen (1944–2010) was a Finnish artist and sculptor who lived and worked a solitary and isolated life for half a century, barely setting foot outside his parents' house where he lived. This is the garden or park where the sculptures are located, in strict attention to their nature and function, inexorably part of the land, trees, vegetation, spaces and path. There are over 450 human figures or humanoids, in general forming sculp-

tural and theatrical groups that are not static or hieratic, with a vital dynamism that is frozen like the frame in a film. Some are provocative and even aggressive, others ironic; some appear outside the viewer's life, others look directly into your eyes. Many evoke a feeling of spirituality or harmony. It is a creativity that goes against the trend, outsider art – outside the ruling art system – where life and work are completely fused.

france

Tulleries Gardens, Paris, with interventions from Le Nôtre's (17th c.) to Jacques Wirtz's, 1998

Below:
Bernard Lassus, highway A85 Angers – Tours

The French territory known as the "Hexagon" is characterised by several plains with low plateaus and hills, the high mountains of the Alps and the Pyrenees, the basins of Paris and Aquitaine and the Rhone corridor between the Alps and the Massif Central. Most of the country has a maritime climate with abundant rainfall, moderate temperatures, and oak, beech and apple tree woodlands. The sunnier Mediterranean area, with a landscape of pine, holm oak, olive trees, and grapevines, enjoys mild winters and hot summers. The eastern part, largely covered in thick conifer forests, suffers through long, harsh winters and has only short, mild summers.

The Cro-Magnon man lived here – caves of Dordogne – more than 20,000 years ago and created the cave paintings of Lascaux near Les Eyzies-de-Tayac (pop. 900) in Aquitaine; they are a milestone in art history, most notable for how man used the wall as more than a canvas, integrating the relief into paintings of bulls and horses. Northwestern Brittany has been as deeply influenced by the strong sea along its dramatic coastline as its art has been by granite, from megaliths to cathedrals. The gulf of Morbihan is a popular tourist destination as are the thousands of menhirs in Carnac – 32 km west of Vannes – which date back to 3000 BC. With the arrival of the Celts around 700 BC, the adornment of torques, fibulas, and gold jewelry with natural motifs and geometric forms reached new heights. After Julius Caesar conquered Gaul (52 BC), Roman rule ushered in an exceptionally rich historical period that still resonates today, marked by milestone events such as the area's Christianisation during the late 1st c. and the 3rd and 4th c. This coincided with the arrival of the Franks and their hegemony; the reign and the artwork of the Merovingian dynasty (481–751); the defeat of the Moors at Poitiers by Charles Martel (732); Charlemagne's (768–814) coronation as emperor of the Holy Roman Empire and its cultural rebirth, including Carolingian art, territories from Germany to Italy and a time in which France began to take shape; the Capetian Kings (987–1328) and gothic art, beginning in Saint-Denis (Paris 1147) with the revolutionary Abbot Suger and a shift from opaque walls to wide openings and natural light filtered through stained glass, embodying an integration of art and nature unmatched even today. The Valois (1328–1589) and the Hundred Years' War was followed by the Bourbons and the Renaissance, which led to French neoclassicism in the 17th c. and its emphasis on order, luxury, and grandiosity. France's European hegemony reached its apex during the absolutist monarchy of Louis XIV, the Sun King (1643–1715), as did the overseas expansion and the French garden – exemplified by Le Nôtre's design in Versailles (1662) with parterres, geometric forms, axes, statues, and fountains; an orderly, controlled nature, governed by reason. The Revolution (1789–99) changed the world, but pressure from England and Austria steered it towards Napoleon and his empire (1804–15). Prussia defeated France in 1870, resulting in the 3rd Republic and its creative use of iron, exemplified by the Eiffel Tower. Victorious in World War I, then occupied by the Nazis in 1940,

675,417 km², 66.9 million inhabitants, member of the European Union since 1957

Jardin de la Fondation Cartier
Paris
by Lothar Baumgarten
261, boulevard Raspail   75014 París
http://jardin.fondationcartier.com/fr

The UNESCO by Noguchi
Paris
7, place de Fontenoy, 75352 París
http://www.unesco.org/visit/jardin/

Le Cyclop de Tinguely
Millly-la Forêt
Bois des Pauvres   www.lecyclop.com

European Parliament garden
Strasbourg
by Desvigne + Dalnoky
Parc de Pourtalès, works by Sarkis, Gaetano Pesce, Barry Flanagan, Jimmie Durham, Giulio Paolini, Balkenhol, etc.

The route of European art in Alsace
More than 20 site-specific artworks, by Venet, Gloria Friedman, etc.

France was liberated in 1944 by the Allied landing in Normandy. The 5th Republic – coinciding with the creation of the EEC in 1958 under General de Gaulle created the current presidential system, which was rocked by the Parisian revolts of May 1968 and returned to cultural splendour under the socialist Mitterrand (1981).

Central Paris was once the ancient Roman *Lutetia* and became the world capital of art at the turn of the 20th c.; Rodin freed sculpture from its academic rigour, Bourdelle followed in his wake, and Maillol advanced schematisation. It was the Cubists – Picasso, Braque – who introduced abstraction and Duchamp, Jean Arp, and the Dadaists who paved the way for new artistic forms: the "found object," hybridised counter reliefs using painting/sculpture and performances, thus returning to art's prehistoric origins, its religious rites of chants and dances invoking Mother Earth, fertility, and spring celebrations – the splendour of nature. Then came Laurens, Brancusi, Lipchitz, Zadkine Archipenko and the surrealism of Breton and Eluard. After World War II, kinetic art flourished – Soto, Le Pare – and in 1958 the work/exhibition by Yves Klein "Le Vide" (the void) took installation art into a radical new direction and introduced the New Realists – Klein, Cesar – and their theoretician, Pierre Restany. In the wake of Richier and Bourgeois and the generation of Buren, Pagès, Poirier, and Venet, came a myriad of artists, working with a wide variety of tendencies, styles, materials, and forms that have come to characterise contemporary art and blurring the boundaries between disciplines. This is best exemplified by the development and confluence of gardening, architecture, urban development, landscape design, environmental art: Alphand (Bois de Boulogne, 1852) working with Baron Haussman on the transformation of Paris, Forestier and his parks (Bois de Vincennes, 1887, and others), Guevrekian and his art deco gardens (Paris Exhibition, 1925) all the way to the theory and practice of Bernard Lassus, in which obsolete categories like these disappear. Paris is still France's artistic centre, but the periphery is establishing its independence in areas like art in nature, characterised by a search for compatibility with preservation of historical-artistic legacy.

bignan domaine de kerguéhennec

Since 1986
Domaine de Kerguéhennec
Centre d'art contemporaine
56500 Bignan
Tel. +33 (0)297603184
kerguehennec@morbihan.fr
www.kerguehennec.fr
Dir. Olivier Delavallade

Opening hours:
Open every day of the year, 8am–9pm
Admission: free
Two courses are offered, north and
south of the castle, for a walk to the
discovery of 31 sculptures of the park.
To the North Course (15 sculptures):
around 1.15 hours
To the South Course (16 sculptures):
around 2 hours
Park map with the route
You can borrow seat-sticks for the
park.
An entertainment programme is offered
throughout the year around the park.
• Guided tours (booking required)
• Exhibition halls with changing shows
• Educational services
• Publications: catalogues
• Café du Parc
• Picnic area
• Car park

How to get there:
• By car: take RN 24 from Rennes to
  Lorient, exit Bignan. From Vannes to
  Pontivy, exit Locminé, Bignan
• By train: TGV from Paris, Rennes, or
  Nantes to Vannes
• Airports: Lorient (50 km), Rennes
  (90 km), Nantes (140 km)

The Domaine de Kerguéhennec, a 175 ha park designed by land-scape gardener Denis Bühler in 1872, lies 25 km to the north of Vannes. It was declared a cultural monument in the 20th c. Although its history dates back to the 16th c., it was the Hoggeur brothers, Swiss bankers residing in Paris, who in 1710 built the castle that now houses temporary contemporary art exhibitions. The estate went through a succession of owners until it was acquired by the Count of Lanjuinais in 1872, a representative and later president of the Morbihan General Council. He undertook an important restoration of the castle and the park, adding personal touches and even new areas, such as the arboretum, to Bühler's overall design.

Although the Morbihan General Council purchased the property in 1972, the Domaine de Kerguéhennec remained abandoned until 1986. That year, the DRAC (Direction of Cultural Affairs of the Ministry of Culture) in conjunction with the FRAC (Brittany Regional Contemporary Art Collection) decided to revitalise the estate by creating a sculptural park. To this end, they commissioned sculptural

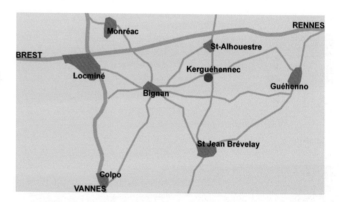

projects from French and international artists – such as Artschwager, for example – to be realised within the property's magnificent forest. The forest at Kerguéhennec is one of the region's most beautiful and home to 100-year-old trees, some of them up to 10 m in height. Many of the species, such as the giant sequoias, are unique to this area. The majority of the trees are clearly identified with plaques stating their name, age, and characteristics, which allows interested visitors to expand their botanical knowledge. The deep forest, the song birds and the indescribably rich landscape can make one forget about the world outside.

Since the park's inauguration, every passing year has seen an increase in the number of sculptures in the forest through pieces created *in situ* by the artists. The placement of the sculptures is characterised by an adaptation to and location within the landscape that is both discreet and in harmony with the surrounding woodland. Some of the selected artists belong to the European land-art tradition, such as Richard Long, Ian Hamilton Finlay, and Ulrich Rückriem, who are all represented in the permanent collection – see map of the park and list of artists and works on p. 100. This collection is complemented by temporary installations; past editions have included the work of Neuhaus, Pat Steir, Calzolari, Franz West, Mullican, and Niele Toroni.

The art's overall integration into the environment is poetic, seamless and without pronounced contrast. The pieces are placed in a subtle, almost imperceptible manner with a considerable distance between them, so that the visitor encounters mostly nature – forest, lakes, and fields – slightly altered, from time to time, by an artwork.

The sculptural park is also home to the Domaine de Kerguéhennec's centre for contemporary art. From the very beginning, it has sought out an international programme and audience.

There are four to five different exhibitions throughout the year, featuring artists of diverse nationalities who are solely dedicated to

Ellisabeth Ballet, *Trait pour trait*, 1993

strictly contemporary creative expression and rigorous investigative work. The exhibitions tend to be individual in nature, retrospectives or related to specific projects, alternating with thematic shows and visiting collections.

The centre also operates an international artists in residence programme, which provides artists with accommodation and studio space for a certain period of time. During their stay, an encounter between the artist and the public is organised to encourage a dialogue with regards to the artistic work.

Some of the artists in residence create pieces that join the permanent collection, such as the *Cristal Cinéma* by Marina Abramovic. The educational programmes are directed at the general public as well as art school and university students.

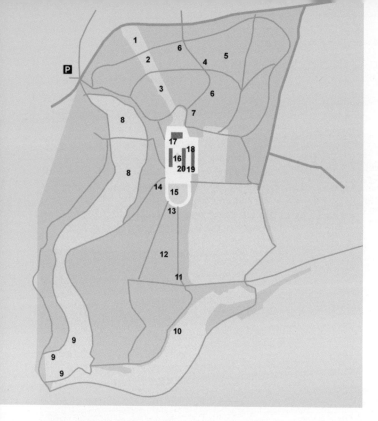

1 Richard Artschwager, *Step to Entropy*, 2003   2 Richard Long, *Un cercle en Bretagne*, 1986   3 Markus Raetz, *Mimi*, 1989   4 Ulrich Rückriem, *Bild Stock*, 1985   5 François Bouillon, *Cène d'exterieur*, 1987   6 Ian Hamilton Finlay, *Noms de plaques, noms d'ar-bres*, 1986   7 Carel Visser, *L'oiseau Phénix*, 1989   8 Marta Pan, *Parcours flottant n.º 1 & 2*, 1986   9 François Morellet, *Le naufrage de Malévitch*, 1990   10 Elisabeth Ballet, *Trait pour trait*, 1993   11 Etienne Hajdu, *Sept colonnes à Mallarmé*, 1971   12 Giuseppe Penone, *Sentier de Charme*, 1986   13 Tony Cragg, *Gastéropodes*, 1988, collection FRAC Champagne-Ardenne   14 Keith Sonnier, *Porte vue*, 1987   15 Toni Grand, *Sans titre*, 1988   16 Malachi Farrell, *Bubbles*, 1993   17 Harald Klingelhöller, *Mit Buchstaben der Worte: Unrecht schreit*, 1995–2003   18 Maria Nordman, *Fragment pour une cité future*, 1987   19 Jean-Pierre Raynaud, *1000 pots bétonnés peints pour une serre ancienne*, 1986   20 Marina Abramovic, *Cristal cinéma*, 1992

Richard Long,
Un cercle en Bretagne, 1986

Opposite page:
François Morellet, *Le naufrage de Malévitch*, 1990
Markus Raetz, *Mimi*, 1989

Digne-les-Bains
Haute-Provence (pop. 16,512, 2013)
Min. 524 m – Max. 1,731 m

Musée Gassendi
64, Boulevard Gassendi
04000 Digne-les-Bains
Tel. +33 (0)492314529
www.musee-gassendi.org
CAIRN Centre d'art informel de
recherche sur la nature
10, montée Bernard Dellacasagrande
Tel. +33 (0)492621173

Refuge d'art
www.refiugedart.fr

Refuge d'Art
Ferme Belon
Access
Important: to visit the Refuge, hikers
must make the request to the Musée
Gassendi. A key will be supplied free of
charge at the museum reception
against an identity card

Nestled in the Alpine foothills of Alpes-de-Haute-Provence, 129 km
north of Marseilles and on a plateau where three valleys meet, Digne
is the focus of projects for combining art and nature that are literally
off the beaten track, both in terms of the established world of art
and in their locations and attributes.

A work commissioned from Andy Goldsworthy in 1996 would
become the start of an unusual adventure in sculpture, with the firm
support of Nadine Gómez, the curator of the unusual Gassendi
Museum of 1889, dedicated to science and the arts, and completely
renewed in 2003. It will end up housing Goldsworthy's well-known
sculpture *River of Earth* and will have a whole room dedicated to his
art. Goldsworthy and artists, including Richard Nonas (photo below,
left) and Herman de Vries, have installed land art, environmental artworks, in the Nature Reserve spanning 269,316 ha, the biggest in
Europe, with steep rocky mountains that characterise the zone, and
with a landscape that draws the viewer in. They invite visitors to discover villages high in the mountains and rural
sites that are abandoned or in ruins, a traditional peasant world that is fast disappearing.
The CAIRN Centre d'art informel de recherche sur la nature was founded in Digne in
2000, jointly by Musée Gassendi and the
Geopark of Haute-Provence. Its main aim is to
create temporary or permanent works of art
set in nature to help sustain this dying rural
environment.
Before that, by 1999, the British artist
Goldsworthy had built the first of three egg-
like *Sentinels* each one a cairn: a human-made
pile (or stack) of stones, used as trail markers
in several parts of the world. Linking up three Sentinels, one located
in a significant point in each of the Asse, Bès and Vançon valleys, the
circuit follows ancient paths among the remnants of an agricultural
way of life.
Pierre Gassendi, a 17th-c. scientist, philosopher, theologian, a
dignois born in the area, answered Descartes' maxim, "I think, therefore I am," with his own: "I walk, therefore I am." Four centuries later,
this is the concept here.
Andy's Refuges d'art:
The artist said: "The sculpture here isn't just
the stone, it's the home, it's the entire trail."
The restoration of ancient footpaths is part
of a unique art project led by Goldsworthy
with the Gissendi museum, the CAIRN
Centre, and the Réserve Géologique.
As reported in The Guardian, "Goldsworthy
wanted to mark the circuit with Refuges in
the form of disused houses belonging to
the non-protected rural heritage, including
chapels, farms and sheepfolds. These have
now been restored, and a specially-designed
sculpture has been incorporated into each

one. They provide shelter for a pause along the route, or indeed, in some cases, the possibility of an overnight stay." Staying overnight in one staying of the ruins that Goldsworthy has rebuilt, these "oeuvres-lieux" is not a very usual thing – for sleeping inside a work of art, see also p. 112.

Refuge d'art is holistic, a single, integral work of art, to be visited over a ten-day hike – or other shorter tours. It is unique in Europe, in-volving an itinerary of 150 km that traverses a number of exceptional landscapes in the nature reserve. It brings together hiking and contemporary art, thereby highlighting both nature and culture. By 2012, six Refuges were renovated and accessible. As of 2016, the

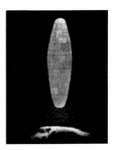

Refuges d'art interactive map
in www.sculpturenature.org

official information lists: Chapelle Sainte-Madeleine, Thoard, 2002; La Forest, St-Geniez, 2008 (photo above); Vieil Esclangon, La Javie, 2005: Col de l'Escuichière, Le Brusquet, 2004–10: Bains thermaux, Digne, 2002; and the three Sentinels: Vallée du Bès | La Robine-sur-Galabre,1999; Vallée du Vançon, Authon, 2000; and Vallée de l'Asse, Tartonne, Plan-de-Chaude, 2000.

The real aesthetic fruition is a "travelling landscape, a place in movement, but on a timescale."

In Goldsworthy's own words: "What has evolved is a project that goes beyond art as an object to be looked at, to something that is part of a landscape to be lived in. That's true. Where things get really interesting is in the subtle interplay between Refuge d'Art, the Sentinels, and the footpaths that link them."

This is, in a way, the dematerialisation of the art object, as John Chandler and Lucy R. Lippard put it (1968), but also materials rooted in 120-million-year-old geological base and the old peasant culture.

Since 1997
Vent des Forêts
Mairie 55260 Fresnes-au-Mont
Tel. +33 (0)329710195
contact@ventdesforests.org
www.ventdesforets.com
Artistic Dir. Pascal Yonet

Opening hours:
1 Mar.–30 Sept.: open daily
Admission: free
• Pets allowed
• Photograps allowed
• Temporary exhibitions
• Guided tour: fee (advanced booking)
• Parking

How to get there:
• By car: from Paris, freeway A4
  to Metz – exit Verdun n.° 30 –
  N35 Voie Sacrée to Bar-le-Duc
  From Metz, freeway A4 to
  París – exit Verdun n.° 31 – D964
  to Saint-Mihiel – turn right to Maizey –
  to arraive to Dompcevrin, one of the
  6 villages of Vent des Forêts
• By train TGV (Meuse TGV station):
  Vent des Forêts is 1 hour from
  Paris, 1h 37' from Strasbourg, 1h from
  Luxembourg
• Airports: Metz, Nancy

Eating out:
  Café de Mme. Simon
  55260 Lahaymeix

Vent des Forêts Association's project arose in 1997 out of the desire of the mayors of six villages around Lahaymeix, to welcome contemporary artists for creative residencies in July each year. 90 works can be seen along 45 km of specially-signposted forest pathways forming seven circular walks, one to four hours long. The artworks produced are exposed to the weather and the passage of time; fleeting or relatively durable, they emphasise a direct link with the environment. They sit waiting to be discovered alongside the pathways through 5,000 ha of forest. The involvement of the artists at the heart of a social, human, geographical and economic environment becomes a part of their creative process: at Vent des Forêts, the artists work in direct contact with the day-to-day realities of a context most original

in its human and technical aspects.
This residency facilitates collaboration with the villagers, the association's volunteers and with local artisans (coppersmith, cabinet-maker, coachbuilder, stone mason, etc.). Thus, the artworks are products of the links which the artists weave with nature and with their chosen partners. Each year, around 25,000 people venture along Vent des Forêts' pathways to discover the artworks. The adventure offers a change from consumption-based leisure activities and attracts a wide social and geographic mix of visitors. Moreover, exploring the pathways demands preparation, careful study of the map and the signposting, and an effort of will, which orientate towards responsible behaviour and sensitise the visitor to the qualities and values of the land. Starting in 2010, Vent des Forêts has launched a programme of projects both innovative and beneficial to the local area, with the the Culture Ministry. One of these projects is the creation of Woodland Houses by the designer Matali Crasset, an industrial designer, who has designed for Vent des Forêts three Woodland Houses, conceived as habitable artworks in the woods, which will allow walkers to absorb the spirit of the place and "snuggle up to it."

Musée de Grenoble
5, place Lavalette
38000 Grenoble
Tel. +33 (0)476634444

The Musée de Grenoble was created in 1798, at the height of the revolutionary wars in France, when many countries were at war. Among its holdings are contributions from Champollion following the Egyptian campaign and pieces from the 13th c. to the most varied trends of the second half of the 20th and early 21st c. The exterior offers an elegant encounter that seems infused with traditions combining art and nature of the Mediterranean parks with sculptures from the 16th c. Access to the Albert-Michallon park is through the Tour d'Isère, a fortified tower dating back to the 14th c. on the banks of the Isère river. Here, in the centre of the city, there are large trees (a Lebanon cedar from 1847) and rare species in a site that reflects grace and distinction.

The sculpture park has evolved gradually since 1988 in a

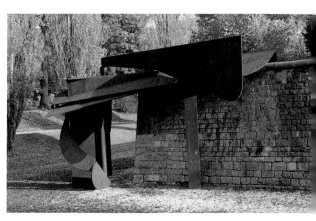

space measuring 16,000 m², including the remains of the city walls that were in place until the 19th c., and which have been used by the British sculptor Anthony Caro as part of his *Le Chant des montagnes* (1993, in the photo above).

The other 14 monumental sculptures are by Léon-Ernest Drivier and Marcel Gimond (1928, bronze), George Rickey (1991, steel mobile), Eugène Dodeigne (1993, Soignies stone), Marta Pan (1991, 3.3 m high, rose granite), Robert Wlérick (1936–42, patina bronze), Morice Lipsi (1978, stone), Gottfried Honegger (1988, painted metal, 5 m high), Ossip Zadkine (1948, bronze), Richard Nonas (1994), Bernar Venet (1992, Corten steel), Eduardo Chillida, Zuhaitz, (1989, Corten steel).

Museum underground parking
Restaurant
www.museedegrenoble.fr

On the François Mitterrand Esplanade, in front of the museum, there are three other large-scale works: a bronze by Marcel Gimond (1934) in front of the 17th c. wall; *Monsieur Loyal* by Alexander Calder (1967), 9 m high in lacquered steel (see photo above left); and *Étoile polaire* by Mark di Suvero (1972), 23 m high and 18 m wide, in painted steel.

le muy **domaine du muy**

Since 2015
Domaine du Muy
83490 Le Muy (Var), France
Tel +33 677047592
www.domainedumuy.com
office@domainedumuy.com

Private park open by appointment
July to October

The park is connected to one of the most prominent French political and cultural families of the 20th and 21st c.: one President of the Republic; one Minister of Culture and Jean-Gabriel Mitterrand, the gallery owner of Galerie Mitterrand, Paris. The Côte d'Azur or French Riviera began as a holiday destination in the 18th–19th c. for the British upper classes and aristocrats: millionaires, billionaires, celebrities, beautiful people.

Only 40 minutes from the coast, from Cannes or Saint-Tropez, about an hour from Nice or Monaco, Domaine de Muy lies in the protec-

Founding President
Jean-Gabriel Mitterrand

Artistic Dir.
Edward Mitterrand

ted valley of Bonne Eau, covered with virgin Mediterranean forests of cork oak, pine and low scrub, a mild and sunny climate 300 days of the year on rugged terrain; an area of more than a hundred ha, in stark contrast to the traditional French rationalist garden of rigid linear geometry constructed by the architect/landscape gardener.

The business model here was created by Parisian gallery owners. It is unique in Europe (see p. 230), and consists of an open-air art gallery with works for sale, specialising in large-scale open-air sculptures and installations, in line with the environment of the upper classes, superyachts, celebrities, museums and art centres, sculpture parks (see p. 108) and important cultural events.

The offer is organised through parcours, with routes that take about 45 minutes, which at the inauguration in the summer of 2015 showed some 40 works.

Opposite page:
Atelier Van Lieshout, *Dynamo*, 2010

This page:
From top to below:
Carlos Cruz-Diez, *Chromosaturation pour une allée publique*, 1965–2012
Claudia Comte, *128 squares and their demonstration*, 2015
Vidya Gastaldon, *Mini Brothers (Oak)*, 2015
Keith Haring, *Sans titre*, 1985
Yayoi Kusuma, *Narcissus Garden*, 1966–2011
David Saltiel, *4 centres délimitant un carré*, 2008
Tomás Saraceno, *Air-Port-City 4 Modules Metal*, 2010–11

In the natural setting, some pieces blend easily, never decoratively, into the forest, while others search for contrast by almost brutal opposition and imposition; some are brought and placed where they can be displayed to their best advantage and others are commissioned from the artist for a specific location or setting. It is a concept that is not common in sculpture parks, the brainchild the curator Simon Lamunière, a Swiss artist and exhibition organiser resident in Geneva. The works are by both internationally established artists and emerging talents. The visit is exclusive: an appointment is required. What the visitor finds in the exhibition will depend on what has been sold or disassembled at each annual parcours; some will remain from one year to the next and others will be added as new installations, as in an urban art gallery.

saint-paul de vence **fondation maeght**

Since 1964
Fondation Marguerite et Aimé Maeght
06570 Saint-Paul
Tel. +33 (0)493328163
contact@fondation-maeght.com
www.fondation-maeght.com

Opening hours:
Oct.–Jun.: 10am–6pm
Jul.–Sept.: 10am–7pm
Closed from 4pm on Dec. 24 and 31
Admission: fee charged
• Pets not allowed
• Temporary exhibitions
• Library
• Publications: guide, exhibition
  catalogues
• Bookshop
• Coffee shop
• Restaurant
• Car park

How to get there:
• By car: highway exit 48 from Nice or
  47 from Cannes
• By bus: line 400 from Nice or Cagnes
  sur Mer
• By train: Cagnes sur Mer Station
• Airport: Nice

Accommodation:
  In Saint Paul de Vence: Colombe d'Or
  Mas d'Artigny, Vergers de Saint-Paul
Eating out:
  In Saint Paul de Vence: Colombe
  d'Or, Café de la Place

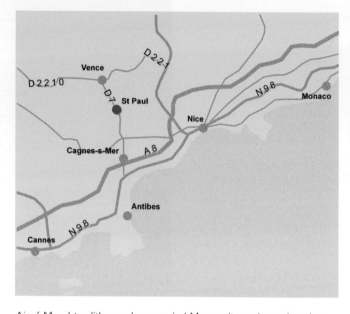

Aimé Maeght, a lithographer, married Marguerite and together they opened a printer's in Cannes in 1930, and six years later an art gallery. In 1946 they inaugurated their Paris gallery, which exhibited the work of Bonnard, Matisse, Braque, Léger, Kandinsky, Miró, Calder, Giacometti, Bacon and younger artists such as Ellsworth Kelly, Tàpies, and Chillida. The Maeghts and their son Adrien were also art publishers, especially of *livres d'artiste*, collectors and patrons, as they decided to create a foundation following the death of their second son. Braque suggested the idea, resulting in the first ever private art foundation in France. A 9,285 m² area on a hill in Saint-Paul de Vence, a beautiful village in the Provence, 12 km from Nice, 16 km from Antibes and 26 km from Cannes was chosen. The elevated, rocky land is dotted with pines and overlooks a Mediterranean landscape. This is where, in 1956, the rationalist, Spanish architect Josep Lluis Sert designed an outstanding and famous piece of modern architecture, an innovative structure to house part of the Maeght's personal collection in both interior and outdoor spaces, serve as a place for temporary exhibitions, store an important 40,000 volume library and accommodate a bookshop, archives, offices, etc.

The building and the natural surroundings are interrelated: a hybridisation of avant-garde architecture and the age-old tradition of spatial arrangements particular to Mediterranean culture. The structure mimics the undulating irregular topography, and the different levels further break the visual monotony. Interior and exterior spaces are accentuated with patios and gardens, and the design uses the stunning natural light of the area, allowing it to enter in a zenithal pattern and flood the exhibition rooms. Sert mostly used brick, stone, and cement and followed local traditions without renouncing expressive forms that were entirely his own, shapes that never lacked functionality, such as the curved coverings resembling enormous tiles. The foundation was inaugurated in 1964 by the legendary French Minister of Culture, Andre Malraux, who declared: "Something has been attempted here that has never been attempted before: to create a world in which modern art can find its place, as well as that other world that used to be called the supernatural."

In the gardens at the main entrance, to the left after entering, is a mosaic by Pierre Tal-Coat, to the right the *Pepin Géant* by Jean Arp, in front and a few metres down a "Stabile" by Calder — *Les Renforts*; to the right of that a mosaic by Marc Chagall — *Les Amoureux*; a few steps towards the entrance a *San Bernardo* by Eugene Dodeigne, next to it *The Fountain* by Pol Bury. In the interior patio of the cloister is a painted bronze by Joan Miró and, nearby, *Les Poissons*, a mosaic fountain by Braque. The Cour Giacometti contains several of the artist's walking men. Between Giacometti and the library lies Miró's *Labyrinth*: terraced environments with pine trees and splendid views, inhabited by the oneiric ceramic work of the Majorcan genius: *four fountains*, the *Wall of the Foundation*, a ceramic mural, the iron and bronze sculpture *La Fourche* — pictured below — several marble pieces — *Oiseau Solaire* and *Oiseau Lunaire* —, etc.

The Maeght Foundation exhibits art not simply as objects but as a lifetime's passion.

Joan Miró, *La Fourche*, 1963
Cerámique ronde, 1973

Since 1983
Centre National d'Art et du Paysage de
l'Île de Vassivière
87120 Beaumont-du-Lac
Tel. +33 (0)555692727
directrice@ciapiledevassiviere.com
www.ciapiledevassiviere.com
Dir. Marianne Lanavère

Opening hours:
Tue.–Sun.: 2pm–6pm
and by appointment
Jul.–Aug.: everyday 11am–7pm
Open all holidays except 25 Dec.
and 1 Jan.
Admission:
• Sculpture park: free
• Access for the disabled
• Pets allowed
• Photographs allowed
• Guided tours (booking required):
  fee charged
• Exhibition halls with changing shows
• Educational programmes
• Library
• Bookshop
• Coffee shop, bar, and restaurant
  Apr.–Sept.: 10pm–7pm, closed on
  Mondays
• Artist residences

How to get there:
• By car: from Paris highway A20 to
  Limoges
  From Toulouse, highway A20, in the
  north of Uzerke exit 42 to Lac de
  Vassivière. In Eymoutiers to
  Beaumont-du-Lac, Lac de Vassivière
• By train: from Limoges to Eymoutiers
  direction Ussel / Clermont-Ferrand
  From Eymotiers by taxi
• Airport: Limoges

Accommodation:
  Limoges: (60 km), about 40 hotels
  Eymoutiers: (16 km), half a dozen
  Auberges, Home Holidays, etc.

The Vassivière Estate owes its name to an 11th-c. term describing an
area to flay sheep. The mansion itself dates back to the 17th c., but
renovations and expansions took place regularly until 1930. The
house is surrounded by extensive grounds, which contain forested
areas and agricultural land for grain cultivation. The construction of a
hydro-electric dam across the river Mauld in 1949 created a 1,000-
ha lake with 45 km of shoreline, effectively turning Vassivière into a
70-ha island at the lake's centre.
Located halfway between Paris and Toulouse and 60 km from
Limoges, the island is essentially an antropic terrain, the result of history and engineering; a protected, largely pedestrian area where the
man-made landscape and contemporary art complement one another perfectly. The area has been a leisure and tourist destination
since the 1970s. In 1983, a dozen artists attending a symposium on
granite sculpture left behind a similar number of pieces, giving birth
to the sculptural park. Two years later more pieces were added by
other sculptors, some of whom went on to gain international
renown.
Among the thirty or so pieces from this period, the majority were

Opposite page:
Andy Golsworthy, *Untitled*, 1992
Fabien Lerat, *Untitled*, 1993
Children playing on a *Dubuffet*

This page:
Aldo Rossi / Xavier Fabre, Centre d'art
contemporaine

created by French artists. David Nash left one piece, whereas, Michelangelo Pistoletto, and Ilya and Emilia Kabakov left one each. David Jones created a piece full of allusions to snakes and ants, and Andy Goldsworthy also realised a site-specific work – see photograph – of which he said: "I explored the border between lake and wood with a wall which itself formed a border. The wall evokes the nostalgic memory of eight villages sunk beneath the lake; its presence provides a key to understanding the true nature of Vassivière." Water, forest, meadow, sand, architecture, art centre, and three marked paths, one about art and nature. In 1986–87, Aldo Rossi and Xavier Fabre built the Center for Contemporary Art, which has become the island's distinguishing mark. Here, removed from the urban context, Rossi has worked out some of his theoretical concepts (adaptation to the spirit of a site, neo-rationalism, building morphology), aesthetic roots (references to De Chirico), and practical architecture: the use of local materials (granite, brick, wood), water-themed symbolism, etc. The space houses temporary exhibitions, an artists' workshop, and services and facilities for cultural and educational programmes.

villars-santenoge **le carré rouge**

Route de Santenoge
52160 Villars-Santenoge

Fondation de France
40, avenue Hoche   75008 Paris
Tel. +33 (03)25842210
fondation@fdf.org

For reservations at the Carré Rouge:
Tel. +33 (03)25842210

Fondation de France is a private entity that aides projects of cultural, scientific, or social patronage. This work is the fruit of one programme and the initiative of Hubert Génin, a resident of Villars-Santenoge, which he presents in the following words: "Instead of having to leave the village for an encounter with modernity, let's have modernity come to us." The project consists of a rural shelter; not in the traditional sense; it's a "painting-refuge," a habitable sculpture, a sculptural work of architecture, an artistic installation where one can sleep. Gloria Friedman's red square, evocative of Malevich's homonymous painting, creates a tension in the relation between art and nature without nostalgia of fusion, offering an experience of the minimal.

Gloria Friedmann, *Le Carré Rouge-Tableau refuge*, 1997

ireland

70,282 km², 4.6 million inhabitants, member of the European Union since 1973

The Lough Mc Nean Sculpture Trail

45 km from Sligo
A sculpture trail for peace between two communities, once divided by enmity and many, long years of violence. A dozen site-specific pieces along a 23-km-stretch unite the villages on the lakeshore and both sides of a border that was once closed to vehicles and pedestrians.
Stonelea Belcoo, County Fermanagh, BT93 5EX
Tel. +353 (0)2866386247

Louise Walsh, *Imagine*, 1999

Ireland is part of the British archipelago, located in NW Europe. The island's linear east coast faces the Irish Sea, which separates it from Great Britain. A ring of coastal mountains – Wicklow, Mayo – with peaks between 926 m and 700 m, frame the wide, central plains. An oceanic climate (median annual of 9°C) and ample rainfall nurture the green Irish countryside, once home to beech and conifer forests. Due to heavy deforestation during the 18th c., only 5% of the surface area is now covered in woodland.

The Megalithic culture flourished during the Bronze Age – stone monuments adorned with spirals and circles. The Celts arrived during the 6th c. BC, introducing their gods, language, ironwork, and a decorative art abstract form. One millennium later, Saint Patrick Christianised the Celtic tribes, and created a strong church, famous for its monasteries, the erudition of its monks, its evangelisation in other parts of Europe and a staunch Catholicism that endures today. Elements of Mediterranean, Coptic, and Syrian culture blended with that of the Celts, resulting in the great Irish art of the 6th and 9th c., including sculptural works such as the stone crosses with the characteristic circle joining the arms, extraordinary manuscript illumination – *Book of Kells* – and abstract art using spirals and intertwined patterns that are unique within western Christianity. In the 12th c., Ireland came under English rule. After a long march towards independence, the majority of the island became a sovereign nation in 1948, the Republic of Ireland, Éire, with Dublin as its capital. The rest of the island, known as Northern Ireland, remained part of the United Kingdom.

Compared with its exceptional 19th- and 20th-c. literature, Ireland's development of a modern, visual art language lagged behind, long out of touch with contemporary movements. It wasn't until after World War II that Ireland produced its most notable abstract sculptor, Oisín Kelly. At the turn of the century, Michael Bulfin, Kathy Prendergast, and Michael Warren are among Ireland's most recognised artists, and James Coleman blurs the lines traditionally separating artistic forms with his installations of projected photographs. Dublin, home to the active IMMA Irish Museum of Modern Art and the splendid 18th-c. gardens and statues in Powerscourt (14 km south), is the epicentre of a flourishing cultural life – film, music, dance – following the economic boom of the late 20th c. Groundbreaking industries like information technology have awoken an innovative spirit that has encouraged new artistic initiatives throughout the country. Some are permanent – Woodland in Wicklow County (the "garden of Ireland," pop. 115,000) south of Dublin (see p. 104); and others are one-time or temporary events – the different sculptural symposia held by the SSI Sculptor's Society of Ireland since 1980, sometimes commissioning permanent objects – the sculptural symposia and artists' residence in Lough Boora (pieces by Jørn Ronnau and others); or the dozen site-specific installations by Peter Hynes, Bulfin etc. (1993) along the Atlantic coast route from Ballina to Blacksod, the Tfr Saile or The North Mayo Sculpture Trail in North Mayo County.

sculpture in woodland

Since 1994
Coillte
Newtownmountkennedy, Co Wicklow
Tel. +353 (1)2011111
info@coillte.ie

Opening hours: daily 9am–7pm
Admission: free
• Pets allowed
• Photographs allowed
• Guided tours (booking required):
  fee charged
• Educational programmes
• Publications: guide, leaflet
• Picnic area
• Car park

How to get there:
• By car: at the roundabout in Ashford
  village, turn left coming from Wicklow
  or take the right exit if approaching
  on the N11 from Dublin. Follow the
  signs for the Devil's Glen Equestrian
  and Holiday village, continue on past
  it and turn right at the next Y-junction
  following the road to Tiglin. The
  Devil's Glen is approximately 800 m
  up on the right-hand side, about
  4 km from Ashford, Co Wicklow.
• By bike
• Airport: Dublin

Accommodation:
  An Oige – Youth Hostel, Devil's Glen
  (2 km)
  Chester Beatty Inn, Ashford (5 km)
  Devil's Glen Holiday & Equestrian
  Centre, Ashford (3 km)
Eating out:
  Chester Beatty Inn, Ashford (5 km)

The Devil's Glen forest is the setting for Sculpture Woodland. Its 218 ha, property of the state forestry company Coillte, were selected due to their rich natural, historic, and cultural patrimony. This patrimony includes a narrow valley (a glen) carved in the glacial era, with a river, a waterfall, beeches, fir trees, Spanish chestnuts, Norwegian spruces, and oaks, a low mountain with moss, laurel, rhododendron, lichen, and ivy, and an animal population including foxes, nutrias, badgers, and squirrels. The forest contains both native and transplanted species. According to a statement by its managers, the sculpture project was established "to help create a greater awareness of wood as an artistic and functional medium. It does this through commissioning artists to create and exhibit contemporary works of artistic excellence." The organisation helps artists create site-specific pieces, and offers the public open access to contemporary works of art free of charge. Seamus Heaney, the Nobel Prize-winning poet who is closely associated with this land, describes this collaboration as "an act of faith in the work of art itself, an act of commitment to the positive values of form and order and solitary contemplation."

The selection of artists is carried out by invitation and competition. Since 1999, each year three commissions are awarded: to an invited Irish artist, to an invited foreign artist, and to an artist selected in a public competition. The installed works of art and the natural settings in which they are found can be contemplated and enjoyed following two marked forest trails. Both walks begin in the parking area, and require footwear adequate for the mountain. Each follows a different route, and Sculpture Woodland asks of all its visitors: "Leave only footprints and take only memories."

The first and shortest walk is 2.6 km long, and it takes about 40 minutes to complete. The second follows a longer trail of 6 km and between one and one and a half hours duration, depending on whether or not the waterfall is included – on both trails, the safety of visitors is their own responsibility.

Sculpture Woodland has an educational programme that, as an additional goal, seeks to involve the local community, with workshops and other activities with local schools that introduce children to the values of art and nature. Thus for example, the children create small works of art with materials they themselves collect in the forest.

Jae-Hyo Lee, *0121-1110=10210*, 2002

Irish artists   Maurice MacDonagh, Michael Warren, Michael Bulfin, Eileen McDonagh, Janet Mullarney, Greenmantle, Michael Kane, Cathy Carman, Deirdre Donoghue, Michael Quane
International artists   Jorge de Bon (Mx), Naomi Seki (J), Kat O'Brien (C), Derek Whitticase (UK) Jacques Bosser (F), Alberto Carneiro (P), Max Eastley (UK), Kristaps Gulbis (LV), Nicos Nicolaou (UK) Lee Jae-Hyo (K)

italia

301,318 km², 60.7 million inhabitants, member of the European Union since 1957

"... rapid heartbeat, dizziness, confusion and even hallucinations" can be experienced "when the individual is exposed to an overdose of beautiful art." This is the Stendhal Syndrome, a psychosomatic condition unique to Italy. This emotional impact, described by Stendhal during a trip to Italy in 1817, is evidence that the reader has arrived at the very heart of western art and culture. The Italian Peninsula lies in the Mediterranean, extending south from the Alps (Mont Blanc, 4,807 m), where the south slopes meet the wide plain of the Po River Valley – Torino, Milan, Venice, Modena, Bologna – and the climate is rainy and continental. The Apennines are the peninsula's backbone, the coastal climate is Mediterranean, the landscape of green hills, cypresses, olive trees and vineyards becomes sunnier and dryer as Tuscany gives way to the Roman countryside – Lazio and the farmland of Mezzogiorno, the Campania (Naples) and, further south, Sicily in a magnificent variety of cultivated and cultured landscapes. The Etruscans settled the Po Valley, Tuscany, and Campania around the 8th c. BC, while the Greeks inhabited the south and Sicily. The founding of Rome in 753 BC began a process of integration that brought the two peoples together. After the Republic (509–27 BC), the empire reached its apex of splendour and territorial expansion during the 2nd c., ranging from the Euphrates to England, from the Sahara to the Danube and leaving behind a legacy that included engineering, law and the art and architecture of Paestum, Rome, Pompeii, Segesta, Agrigento, Syracuse, and Taormina. In the 5th c., the Western Empire came to its end. The next thousand years were ones of darkness and splendour, ruled by a successive political hegemony of Lombards, Franks, Spaniards, and Austrians. The medieval cities that developed, with their international banking and commerce, allowed the Renaissance to flourish. In the 19th c. nationalistic sentiments led to the Risorgimento, the battles of Cavour, Garibaldi, and Victor Emmanuel II in Piemonte and, finally, to a unified kingdom and parliament (1865). Defeated in World War I, the poverty-stricken nation saw the birth of radical socialism and the Communist Party (1921), the subsequent rise of Mussolini's fascism (1922), defeat in World War II and a weak Republic, undermined by a corrupt old party system and a monopolist mass media empire.

In the 1st c. BC, Lucullus introduced the Persian garden, and the Roman hills were soon covered in villas with parks and sculptures. Two centuries later, Pliny the Younger created his own, but the pinnacle of sophistication was reached with the Villa Adriana, an exquisite integration of architecture, lake, water, garden, colonnades, and sculptures that can still be seen from the neighbouring Tivoli. The Renaissance began with the Villa Medici on the Fiesole hills near Florence, designed in 1458 by Michelozzo, disciple of the brilliant Brunelleschi, at the same time as Donatello revealed a new sculptural form. In the 1500s, Michelangelo's genius left its mark on art and architecture, and the Italian garden was defined by the exuberant Villa d'Este with its many sculptures, fountains by Ligorio and Bernini, hydraulic organs (Tivoli 1550) and the Mannerism of architect and theoretician Vignola

Verzegnis

Varenne
Tremezzo Bellagio   Venezia
Varese ●   Cernobbio
Milano
        Pistoia
Santomato
Montecatini Terme   Ponte di Ronca
    Carrara   Firenze   San Gimignano
La Spezia ● ●   Prato
Montemarcello   Pievasciata
    Lucca Pisa   Serre di Rapolano
        Siena   Tuoro di Trasimeno
    Montalcino   Seggiano
Grosseto ●
    Capalbio
        Viterbo   Tivoli
            Roma
                Ravello
                Paestum

            Palermo   Castel di Tusa
        Segesta   ●   Taormina
    Gibellina
                Agrigento   Siracusa

200 Km

Historical gardens in existence today:
Campania: Villa Rofulo and Villa Cimbrone, Ravello, 13th c.
Lazio: terraced gardens at Villa Aldobrandini, by G. della Porta, Frascati, 1598–1603; Villa Giulia, by Vignola, Rome, 1550; the strongly allegorical Villa Lante Bagnala, by Vignola, Viterbo
Lake of Como, Lombardy: Villa Serbelloni and Villa Melzi, Bellagio; Villa Carlotta, 18th c, Tremezzo; Villa Monastero, Varenna, 16th c.
Tuscany: the Boboli gardens, by sculptor Tribolo, 1549, Florence; the Medicis villas in the countryside outside Florence: 3 km north, Villa della Petraia; 5 km north, Villa de Castello, in this town;garden at Villa Reale de Marlia, 8 km north of Lucca, 16th c, modified by Elisa Bonaparte in the 19th c; baroque garden at Villa Garzoni, Montecatini Terme, 17th c.

and his follower G. della Porta. Another exceptional example is the Villa of Prince Orsini in Bomarzo, 20 km from Viterbo, with its sacred forest, dense vegetation and a surreal, sculptural narrative featuring human figures, monsters, animals, and inscriptions by Dante and Petrarca. The 19th c. began with the neo-classical sculptural work of Canova and ended with the creation of the Venice Bienniale (1895), the most important event in contemporary art worldwide (Jun.–Nov.). Medardo Rosso broke new sculptural ground and influenced the Futurists, who would contribute to the development of abstract art in the early 20th c. In their wake came Martini's archaism, Marini's volumetric sense and Manzu's ambiguous "Cardinals," representing the "majesty of form." After World War II, abstract art was spearheaded by Fontana (neon environments), Consagra (enormous works in metal), and Alberta Burri, one of the first to use waste materials and thus an influence on Arte Povera, Germano Celant's term (1967) for the work of Mario Merz, Zorio, and Kounellis. The generation of Luciano Fabro and the experimental Pistoletto worked in conceptual and minimalist art, followed by the transavanguardia (a term by Achille Bonito Oliva) with Sandro Chia, Enzo Cucchi, and Mimmo Paladino. Tuscany continues to attract artists from around the world, who are creating their own gardens or working in the field of environmental art.

Ca' la Ghironda, Ponte Ronca di Zola Predosa, Bologna Emilia Romagna

This 10-ha park in the hills 9 km from Bologna has a botanical garden with 150 plant species and a collection of more than 200 pieces of modern and contemporary sculpture by artists like Pietro Cascella, Manzu, Luciano Minguzzi, Mitoraj, Pomodoro, Zorio.
www.ghironda.it

Gibellina, Sicilia

Gibellina lies in the west of this large, Mediterranean island, in the rather peripheral province of Trapani and a few kilometres on the A29 motorway from the Doric temple of Segesta (430 BC), a man-made creation of utmost elegance and purity located on a lonely hilltop. In 1968 this village of about 6,000 inhabitants was destroyed by an earthquake. It was not rehabilitated, but rather rebuilt at a different location. The mayor, Ludovico Corrao, set out to preserve the village's memories. He met Alberto Burri, who approached the idea for *Grande Cretto* much like he did his paintings. Burri worked on the project in the 1970s, collecting blocks of rubble around 1.7 m in height and covering them with a layer of white cement, kaolin, glue, and pigment. The result was an exciting, large-scale piece of land art that would suffice to include Gibellina in any serious tourist guide, but there is even more: the new urban development plan, designed by Ludovico Quaroni and Vittorio Gregotti; the city hall, social centre, library, theatre and the market (1971) by Giuseppe Samona and Gregotti; the new "historic centre," a complex including a promenade, esplanade and galleries designed by Aprile / Collova / La Rocca in 1981, linked to the landscape. Pietro Consagra realised the Porta del Belice and other artworks. Francesco Venezia designed the minimal Municipal Garden (1984–87) and the museum, both truly site-specific architecture. All these sensitive and telluric projects defy simple classification and do not easily fit into one separate discipline.
www.comunedigibellina.it

Alberto Burri, *Grande Cretto*
Francesco Venezia, Giardino di Gibellina

Partial view of Campo del Sole

I Sentieri dell'Arte, Toscana

In addition to the artwork and parks in Tuscany mentioned on this and the following pages, the art routes – to paraphrase the title used by the Tuscan region to describe how they promote contemporary art in the environment and public spaces – led to several installations, located in unusually close proximity to one another. Based on the diversity and renown of their artists, examples include the Virginia Art Theatrum – Museo della Catastrofe with pieces by Vettor Pisani.

Carrara

Located in the foothills of the Apuan Alps, Carrara has been revered for its white marble since ancient times. The bowels of Mother Earth have been synonymous with sculpture for two and a half millennia, an example of the inextricable link between art and nature, in which the latter is more than merely a background. How can one not feel moved when gazing upon the quarries used by Michelangelo himself to choose the material of such beauty? Since 1957, Carrara's Biennale Internazionale di Scultura, celebrated on a variable schedule, has generated several pieces that now stand in the Parco della Padula, on Via Provinciale Gragnana.

This English garden upon a hill is home to pieces by Robert Morris, Karavan, Parmiggiani, LeWitt, Ian Hamilton Finlay, Luigi Mainolfi, Mario Merz – on the adjacent photograph.
www.labiennaledicarrara.it

Istituto Universitario Olandese, Firenze

Garden with sculptures by Kooning, Karel Appel, Volten, Tajiri, on Via Torricelli 5.
Tel. +39 055221612

Campo del Sole, Tuoro di Trasimeno, Umbria

Tuoro (pop. 3,700) is the site of the Lake Trasimeno battle where, on June 24 in the year 217 BC, 16,000 died when Hannibal defeated the Romans. Nowadays, the shores of the lake, an area of notable, natural interest for its marshlands and birds of prey, house a unique architectural complex comprised of 28 sculpture-columns by international, contemporary artists

Serre di Rapolano, Siena, which can be visited by appointment only, tel.: +39 057704105. Dani Karavan, who installed *Two Environments for Peace*, 1978, created Vivaio per la Pace, a garden-art installation-square (1999) in the old town of **Pistoia**. Meanwhile, in **Montecatini Terme** there are two fountains, one by Susumu Shingu (1998) and a sculptural fountain by Pol Bury in the pine forest of the baths (2004). In **Pratolino**, Florence, Anne and Patrick Poirier created *Petite mise en scene au bord de l'eau* the lake of the Villa

Centro per l'Arte Contemporanea Luigi Pecci, Prato

A dozen pieces in the gardens of the museum by artists like Bizhan Bassiri, Enzo Cucchi, LeWitt, Eliseo Mattiacci, Anne and Patrick Poirier, Staccioli, Fausto Melotti – on the photograph. Viale della Repubblica 277, 59100 Prato
Tel. +39 05745317, www.centropecci.it

such as Nagasawa, Staccioli, Azuma, Pietro Cascella – who conceived the project, 1985–89 – all using the characteristic "pietra serena" stone from the local quarries, grey-black in colour and immensely popular during the Renaissance.
Tel. +34 0758259911
www.trasinet.it

Demidoff gardens, designed for Francisco I of Medici by Buontalenti (second half of the 16th c.) and in which water is a central theme, tel.: +39 0554080721. In the hills and castle of **Romitorio**, Montalcino, Sandro Chia works as an artist, viticulturist and wine-producer. He does not differentiate between his tasks, cultivating the vines with his own hands and saying "I have created wine like I create a painting."
mystudio@sandrochia.com
www.castelloromitorio.com

Nasher Sculpture Garden Peggy Guggenheim Collection, Venezia

This secluded garden in the middle of the city, along the edge of the Gran Canal, is dotted with pieces by Arp, Max Ernst, Duchamp-Villon, Giacometti, Moore, di Suvero, Morris as well as temporary sculptures on loan from the Nasher Collection in Dallas, Texas.
www.guggenheim-venice.it

Pescia Fiorentina
Giardino dei Tarocchi
Capalbio, 58100 Grosseto
Tel. +39 0564895122
www.giardinodeitarocchi.it
www.ilgiardinodeitarocchi.it
tarotg@tin.it

Opening hours:
1 May–16 Oct.: 2.30pm–10pm
Admission: fee charged

How to get there:
• By car: from Siena, the S223 to
  Grosseto, then the Via Aurelia (S1 /
  A12) direction to Rome, pass
  Ortebello and exit Pescia Fiorentina,
  go east (left) and take the second
  road to the left

"In 1955 I went to Barcelona. There I saw the beautiful Park Güell of Gaudí. I met both my master and my destiny, I trembled all over. I knew that I was meant one day to build my own Garden of Joy. A little corner of Paradise. A meeting place between man and nature." (Niki de Saint Phalle)

Site preparations and the first models of the figures to be installed began on a friend's property in Tuscany in 1979. With the intention of creating a magic setting, and the collaboration of artists such as Jean Tinguely, her husband, she enlarged her models to a monumental scale, resulting in a park full of forms and color.

All the works are inspired by, or rather are a likeness of, Tarot cards, in which images and symbols such as the Sun, the Dragon, the Tree of Life, the Hanged Man, the Emperor, the Queen, and the Sphinx appear. From the beginning, the objective was to create a dream world, full of light, where imagination would be limitless, and at the same time, the works would set off the flora and visitors could enjoy themselves.

In the first phase, the figures of the Pope, the Sphinx, the Princess, and the Wizard were made, with the collaboration of friends, artists and technicians. The armatures of these figures emerged in the middle of the garden, and were later decorated as mosaics, with pieces of glass and pottery full of colour and luminosity.

During the production process all the innovative techniques of the 20th c. were forgotten, and work was carried out following the Egyptian style, through molding clay directly over the sculpture and later firing it in the kiln.

In the second phase, the figures of the Emperor, the Sun, the Dragon, the Tree of Life, and the Hanged Man were realised, again with the collaboration of friends, who also designed the paths, benches, and fountains located around the figures. Among these friends were various creators who, in addition to helping, offered their own pieces, such as Pierre Marie Lejeune, who designed some of the ceramic benches and seats of the Sphinx figure. Marina Karella made the sculpture located inside the figure of the Princess, Jackie Matisse created the glass containers that are used as litter boxes, and Jean Tinguely produced one of his kinetic creations in the Tower figure, as well as the Wheel of Fortune in the form of a fountain. With the entry gate built by architect Mario Botta, the Giardino dei Tarocchi opened in 1998.

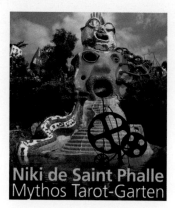

Niki de Saint Phalle: Mythos Tarot-Garten, essay by Jill Johnston and photographs by Giulio Pietromarchi, Benteli Verlag, Bern 2005

castel di tusa **fiumara d'arte**

Since 1986
Parco Scultoreo Fiumara d'Arte
Via Cesare Battisti 4
98079 Castel di Tusa, Mesina, Sicilia
Tel. +39 (0)0921334295
info@ateliersulmare.it
www.ateliersulmare.com
Dir. Antonio Presti

Opening hours: permanently
Admission: free
• Access for the disabled
• Guided tours (booking required)
• Educational programmes
• Library
• Bookshop
• Coffee shop
• Restaurant
• Picnic area
• Car park

• Airport: Palermo

Accommodation:
  Albergo-Museo Atelier sul Mare (see
  above)

Above:
Tano Festa, *Monumento per un poeta
morto*, 1990

Below:
Mauro Staccioli, *Piramide 38° parallelo*,
2010

In Sicilian, Fiumara means "a natural course" or "the bed of a river,
which is dry for most of the year and flows to life again only during
the brief rainy season." The Fiumara de Tusa is located between
Messina and Palermo. Inspired by the place, Antonio Presti, who is a
passionate follower of culture, decided to transform this arroyo into
a "river of art." The first work is an abstract monument. A gigantic
piece in reinforced concrete by Pietro Consagra, which inaugurated
the Fiumara d'Arte Sculpture Park. Half a dozen other installations
have followed, always monumental, site-specific sculptural projects
set in an area covering some 30 km, and donated to the state. The
sculptures are above all by Italians, such as Piero Dorazio, but several
foreigners intervened in the *Ceramic Wall*. Thirty years later, the
works, first subject to demolition orders and then abandoned by
public authorities, are in poor condition. There have been judicial

processes, a regional debate on their administrative situation, attacks
by ecologists who consider them an aggression against the environment, and local, national and international demonstrations of support
by those who love them. It has reached the point that the work of
Tano Festa on the Villa Margi beach was covered with a large sheet
and the sign "Closed," a sarcastic call for attention to a current system that considers art that makes one think to be dangerous.
"Devotion to Beauty, art is not abusive, beauty is not a crime," Presti
proclaims, defending his "counter-museum," a piece of "artistic resistance to cultural genocide."
Over the years Fiumara d'Arte has gone ahead with the hotel-
museum Atelier, which offers an unique experience where the guest
is staying at "author rooms" and becomes him/herself "artwork". On
30 December 2005, the Region of Sicily finally declared Fiumara a
regional park. Later, the *Porta della Belleza* (Gate of Beauty, 2009), in
the neighbourhood of Librino, Catania, is a monumental concrete
wall 500 m long and 10 m high, covered with terracotta pieces made
up by 11 Italian artists and 2,000 students. New works were installed
by Mauro Staccioli – *Piramide*, 2010 – and Giacomo Rizzo (2015).

gallio sentiero del silenzio

Since 2008
Rifugio Campomuletto
via Roma 2 – 36032 Gallio (Vicenza)
Tel. +39 0424445594
    +39 3483162529
www.rifugiocampomuletto.it
www.sentierodelsilenzio.it

Work done by the Comune di Gallio
Projected by architect Diego Morlin
Custodians: Alpini di Gallio

Opening hours: permanently
Admission: free

How to get there:
- By car: From Venezia to Vicenza,
  Sandrigo, Breganze, Luisiana, Asiago,
  Gallio, or: Venezia, Padua, Bassano,
  Asiago, Gallio
- By bus: From Vicenza or Bassano del
  Grappa to Asiago and Gallio
- Airport: Marco Polo of Venice,
  Il Catullo of Verona.
  No train connection

Sentiero del Silenzio (The Path of Silence) is located in a sacred area that was the site of bloody battles during World War I. It is a path for walkers about 3 km long that is suitable for everyone. A meditative and reflective route has been created where visitors can reassess the horrors of war through a new language, that of art.

Visitors come into contact with the atrocities that human beings can unleash when they want to harm others, through an exploration of memory that looks at the past but knows how to offer hope, faith and reconciliation for future generations.

Created by the architect Diego Morlin in 2008 as an innovative concept designed to be different from the more usual sculpture parks, it has become an obligatory stop for people who visit sites dedicated to World War I.

The area consists of 10 large art installations of varied materials with eloquent titles: *Peace Re-Encountered, Piety, Hope, Letters, Witnesses, Armies, Live Flowers, Black Labyrinth, The Immortals, Glorious Fruit.*

Each art installation is accompanied by a text or poem. The project is as non-invasive as possible: any earth-moving that could destroy the blanket of grass have been reduced to a minimum, no tree has been cut, and even the stones have been respected and re-used for new projects.

lusiana parco del sojo arte e natura

Since 2000
Parco del Sojo Arte e Natura
Via Covolo 36046, Lusiana, Vicenza
Tel. +39 0424503173
    +39 3393124946
info@parcodelsojo.it
www.parcodelsojo.wix.com/parcodelsojo
Dir. arq. Diego Morlin

Opening hours:
Open sundays and public holidays
Always available by previous appointment
Access: fee charged

How to get there:
- By car: From Venice to Padua, Bassano del Grappa, Maristica, Luisiana
- By bus: From Vicenza to Marostica and Lusiana
- Airport Marco Polo of Venice, Il Catullo of Verona. Bus service to train stations, but it is not advisable for distances and times

Parco del Sojo Arte e Natura is an innovative project to enhance the value of a 10 ha area that holds extraordinary environmental, historical and artistic interest.

The integration of contemporary art sculptures and their relationship with their natural environment combine to create the perception of a new space and a unique relationship with time.

The idea arose in 2000 as the brainchild of the architect Diego Morlin, and has been brought to life in this park, which is continuously growing and evolving, and which slowly but surely draws in nature and at the same time gives it force and vigour. As it does so, the park rescues nature from the abandonment and degradation it has suffered for so long.

The works of art create what is now a perfect chain of dialogue with the environment in which they are integrated. At times it is in harmony and at other times strident almost to a breaking point, giving life to forms of subtle enforced coexistence.

The magic of the place emerges as visitors follow the paths and experience shifting emotions, as each turning surprises them with a scenario that suddenly changes before their eyes.

The sculpture installations are constructed of a variety of materials, including stone, wood, iron, bronze and clay, some made outside the park and others on site with the natural materials found there. As of 2016 the park houses 80 sculptures by artists from Italy and other countries.

Since 1997
La Marrana arteambientale
Via della Marrana 2
19031 Montemarcello,
Ameglia, La Spezia
Tel. +39 0286463673, +39 3356328606
info@lamarrana.it   www.lamarrana.it
Dir. Grazia Bolongaro

Opening hours:
Open from May to September (August
not included)
Booking in advance, groups minimum
10 people
Information:
• Pets not allowed
• Guided tour (previous booking): fee
• Publications: brochure, catalogues
• Car park

How to get there:
• Sarzana exit from A12 or A15 motor
  way – take direction Carrara –
  continue to the roundabout to Marina
  Carrara and take this direction. After
  the motorway bridge, turn right
  towards Bocca di Magra to get to
  the stop sign, turn right, cross the
  bridge over the river and immediately
  turn right onto via Marrana. After
  700 m, reach the Parco di arte
  ambientale
• By train: to the station of La Spezia.
  Then take a taxi to Montemarcello
  (17 km)
• Airport: Pisa (80km), Genova (120 km)

Accomodation:
  Montemarcello, Relais Golfo dei Poeti
  (Tel. 01876012167)
  Bocca di Magra (Ameglia) 3 km,
  Albergo i Sette archi (Tel. 0187609017)
  Fiumaretta (Ameglia) 4 km, River Park
  Hotel (Tel. 0187648154)
Eating out:
  Montemarcello, Relais Golfo dei Poeti
  (Tel. 0187601216)
  Bocca di Magra, 3 km: Da Ciccio La
  Capannina (Tel. 018765568)
  La Lucerna di Ferro (Tel. 0187601206)
  Zanego (Ameglia) 3 km: La Brace (Tel.
  0187966952)

In 1996 Grazia and Gianni Bolongaro set up the La Marrana
Association in Milan, with the aim of "contributing to the dissemination of contemporary art and opening up new spaces for reflection." One year later, 225 km south in the temperate, holiday climate
of the coast, they created an environmental art park. This space of
30,000 m² on the hills overlooking the sea, 17 km from La Spezia in
the region of La Marrana and within the Montemarcello - Magra
Nature Reserve, is neither a commercial art gallery nor a museum. It

is a private house that opens to the public at certain periods and on
certain occasions, exhibiting the result of a programme of sculptures
and artistic installations specially commissioned for the park.
Every year a show is organised, along with events showcasing artists
of international stature. The artists are given the opportunity to
choose a specific location in the park to create a permanent work,
inspired by its flora, topography, and the historical and social context.
They are free to choose any artistic language, from traditional

sculpture to video-art. To date (2016), this land of olives, cypresses and lush vegetation has hosted 35 works of art.

Visitors become involved in sonic works such as those by Ottonella Mocellin and Nicola Pellegrini or Magdalena Campos-Pons; the vedovamazzei duo, with their "battle seat," taking inspiration from the victorious battle of the Consul Marcellus against the Ligurian Apuanians in 155 B.C. There are also conceptual works such as the art installation by Joseph Kosouth *Located World* (La Marrana, 2004),

Ottonella Mocellin and Nicola Pellegrini, *Things aren't what they appear to be,* 2005
Jannis Kounellis, *Untitled,* 2004

which is made up of 193 m of stones on which the names of cities from around the world can be found. It is a unique art installation in Italy and the third in the *Located World* series after that in Singen (Germany) and Sapporo (Japan); the well containing 4.5 tonnes of bronze bells that Jannis Kounellis has created as a new omphalos on a site away from the park; and the 2005 art installation of the multi-faceted Jan Fabre *The Shelter – For the Grave of the Unknown Computer.*

La Marrana, works by Kegiro Azuma (top) and Jan Fabre (below)

Since 2004
Parco Sculture del Chianti
La Fornace, 48/49
53010 Pievasciata, Siena
Tel. +39 0577357151
info@chiantisculpturepark.it
www.chiantisculpturepark.it
Dir. Piero Giadrossi

Opening hours:
Apr.–Oct.: 10am–sunset. Monday closed
Nov.–Mar.: previous booking
Admission: fee charged
• Guided tour with previous booking:
  gratis for groups of 15 people or more
  conducted in 4 languages
• Access for the disabled
• Pets allowed
• Photographs allowed
• Guided tours (booking required):
  fee charged
• Exhibition halls with changing shows
• Publications: guide, leaflet
• Bookstore
• Picnic area
• Car park
• It is recommended to download
Chiantipark App (free) for smartphones

How to get there:
• By car: Milan-Rome highway, Firenze,
  Impruneta. Certosa exit. Superstrada
  to Siena, Siena Nord exit. Left onto
  SS222, towards Castellina and then
  take a right turn after 1.5 km towards
  Vagliagli. Drive for about 8 km and
  then turn right towards Pievasciata.
  You will find the park at the right after
  about 4 km. From Rome, take the
  highway around Siena, then the Siena
  Nord exit and follow the same above
  instructions.
• Airports: Pisa (100 km), Florence (70 km)

Accommodation:
  Gaiole in Chianti (10 km): 4 hotels:
  Aiolina farmhouse, Borgo,
  Escopeto and Fontanelle
Eating out:
  Michelin one-star Antica Osteria
  Botteganova (8 km). Traditional
  Tuscan cuisine is available in four
  houses (4–6 km)

Located in Tuscany, 11 km north of Siena, the Chianti Sculpture Park
is the personal initiative of the contemporary sculpture collector and
voyager Dr. Piero Giadrossi and his wife Rosalba.

The plan has three objectives: to integrate art and nature, to invite
artists from an international background, and to include a variety of
expressive means. With the initial help of an artistic committee, the
basic criterion in the selection of artists, who come from more than
20 countries and five continents, was to give space to creators well

Adriano Visintin, *Xaris*

established in their country of origin but less known in Europe,
promising talents that would otherwise not be exposed to a Western
audience.

The invited artists create an original work for a site that they personally select. Thus, the pieces are site-specific, with a maximum integration in their surroundings, and become a unique presence in the
corner of woods where they have been installed.

The Giadrossis' project has taken form in the brief space of three
years, with no less notable results.

san gimignano & arte all'arte

Associazione Arte Continua
Via del Castello 11
53037 San Gimignano, Siena
Tel. +39 0577943134
info@galleriacontinua.com
www.arteallarte.org
www.galeriacontinua.com
Dir. Mario Cristiani

Opening hours:
Open air installations permanently
Sept.–Dec.
Indoor artworks: ask for timetable
Admission: free

How to get there:
• By car: highway A1 exit Firenze
  Certosa, then take highway Firenze-
  Siena, the exit Poggibonsi and follow
  signs to San Gimignano
• Airport: Firenze

Accomodation:
  Associazione Strutture Extralberghiere,
  Tel. +39 0577940809
  maurizio@temainf.it
  San Gimignano Pro Loco
  www.sangimignano.com

The beautiful, minimalist, medieval towers of San Gimignano, a free municipality for the past 900 years, rise up from amidst the charming Tuscan countryside, dotted with vineyards and olive trees.
Nowadays (pop. 7,000), it is one of the important small towns in Italy widely renowned for their fascinating historical and artistic heritage. This is the birthplace of the Arte Continua cultural association, which started out by providing guided tours of museums and contemporary art fairs. In 1994, the association began working on the project Arte all'Arte as part of their continuing effort to "combine local culture with aspects of cultural development around the world." Since 1996, four to "six internationally renowned artists of different nationalities" have been invited every year "to realise projects specifically conceived for each one of the six municipalities involved in the initiative (San Gimignano, Poggibonsi, Colle di Val d'Elsa, Siena, Buonconvento, Montalcino). Following a stay in the town, the artists develop their artwork, which is then placed in a public space upon completion."
The subheading of the programme, Arte Architettura Paesaggio (Art Architecture Landscape), is a clear indication of its goal "to create a balance between the city and the countryside and produce new links" between the three, aforementioned domains, "once again giving art a central role in the structuring of the city and the landscape."
The ten editions included the participation of about seventy artists, all of whom have reached a notable level of international prestige – see list below. Each artist works in a different medium and uses formats in their work that are as varied as the entire span of contemporary art at the turn of the century, from sculpture and installation art to video and performance.
About 70% of the projects are temporary in nature, their duration corresponding to the length of the exhibition period, which was usually three months and lasts from September to December. By 2016, the towns also contained approximately twenty permanent objects and installations, thus augmenting their rich cultural heritage by expanding into the world of 20th and 21st c. art – see the list of artists below and artworks on p. 130.
Several artists who had created pieces for previous editions, such as Cai Guo-Quiang, Olafur Eliasson, Alberto Garutti, Anish Kapoor, Tobias Rehberger, and Sislej Xhafa, were invited to participate in the 2005–06 exhibition, primarily because they are among the artists who have best understood and most succinctly interpreted the ideas behind Arte all'Arte.

Marina Abramovic Mario Airò Getulio Alviani Giovanni Anselmo Miroslaw Balka, Per Barclay Lothar Baungartem Louise Bourgeois Tania Bruguera Daniel Buren Loris Cecchini Marco Cingolari A Constructed World Martin Creed Tacita Dean Wim Delvoye Jessica Diamond Wang Du Jimmie Durham Olafur Eliasson Eyse Erkman Alberto Garutti Kendell Geers Antony Gormley Cai Guo-Quiang José A. Hernández Díez Ilya Kabakov Anish Kapoor Tadashi Kawamata Joseph Kosuth Jannis Kounellis Surasi Kusolwong Sol LeWitt Atelier van Lieshout Cildo Meireles Marisa Merz Ottonella Mocellin Gianni Motti Lucy Orta Mimmo Paladino Panamarenko Giulio Paolini Michelangelo Pistoletto Marjetica Potrc Emilio Prini Tobias Rehberger Nari Ward Sislej Xhafa Gilberto Zorio

Previous page:
Antony Gormley, *Fai spazio, Prendi Posto – Making Space, Taking Place*, 2004, Poggibonsi

Below:
Cai Guo-Qiang, *UMoCA (Under Museum of Contemporary Art)*, with Kiki Smith, 2010, Colle di Val d' Elsa

Sol LeWitt, *Untitled*, 1997, Colle di Val d'Elsa   Ilya Kabakov, *The weakeing voice*, 1998, Colle di Val d'Elsa   Mimmo Paladino, *I Dormienti*, 1998, Poggibonsi   Alberto Garutti, *Premiata società corale V, Bellini*, 2000, Colle di Val d'Elsa   Loris Cecchini, *La casa della musica – Sonar*, 2001, Loc, Molinuzzo – Gracciano   Nari Ward, *Illuminated Sanctuary of Empty Sins*, 2001, Loc. Fosci – Poggibonsi   Sislej Xhafa, *Gatti*, 2000, Casole d'Elsa   Jannis Kounellis, *Untitled*, 2001, Montalcino   Marisa Merz, *Untitled*, 2002, Colle di Val d'Elsa   Mario Airò, *Progetto per il Teatro de' Leggieri*, 2002, San Gimignano   Cildo Meireles, *Viagem ao centro do ceu e da terra*, 2002, Siena   Jimmie Durham, *Elsa*, 2003, Colle di Val d'Elsa   Sarkis, *La fontana all'acquerello*, 2003, Poggibonsi   Erminia De Luca, *Progetto speciale per Arte all'Arte 8*, Buonconvento   Marjetica Potrc, *Siena: Urban Agricolture*, 2003, Siena   Joseph Kosuth, *La sedia davanti alla porta*, 1999–2004, San Gimignano   Antony Gormley, *Fai spazio, prendi posto – Making Space, Taking Place*, 2004, Poggibonsi   Tadashi Kawamata, *Porta Nuova*, 2004, Colle di Val d'Elsa   Moataz Nasr, *Lacrime / Tears*, 2004, Siena   Luisa Rabbia, *Il riposo del Tempo*, 2004, San Gimignano   Cai Guo-Qiang, *UMoCA (Under Museum of Contemporary Art)*; 2000–05, Cai Guo-Qiang / Jennifer Wen Ma, *Aeolian Garden*, 2005, Colle di Val d'Elsa

Right:
Mimmo Paladino, *I Dormienti*, 1998,
Fonte delle Fate

Below:
Nari Ward, *Illuminated Sanctuary of
Empty Sins*, 2001, Poggibonsi

Since 1982
Fattoria di Celle, Collezione Gori
Via Montalese, 7
51030 Santomato, Pistoia
Tel. +39 0573479907
goricoll@tin.it
www.goricoll.it
Dir. Giuliano Gori

Access by appointment only
Opening hours:
See "visits" at www.goricoll.it
(This is necessary because the Gori
family often changes the rules about
visits)
Admission: free
• Pets not allowed
• Photographs allowed with previous
  written permission
• Guided tours
• Exhibition halls with changing shows
• Educational programmes
• Publications
• Bookstore
• Car park

How to get there:
See at: www.goricoll.it
• By car: highway A11 Firenze-Pisa,
  exit at Pistoia. Stay right after the toll
  booth and continue straight through
  three traffic lights, exit left for
  Montale, follow indications to Montale,
  after Circa (5 km) you will find the
  large red Alberto Burri sculpture on
  your left in front of the entrance to
  Celle
• By bus: Copit line 19 to Montale, ask
  to get off at Villa Celle (bus stop
  across the road from the main gate)
• By train: to Pistoia Station, then by
  taxi or bus
• Airport: Pisa, Florence

Accommodation & Eating out:
Tourist office in Pistoia
Tel. +39 0573374401
www.turismo.pistoia.it

This cultural institution located just 35 km from Florence thankfully eschews all forms of routine banality. According to its own, precise explanation, "the Fattoria di Celle hosts an important collection of site-specific art;" in fact, the collection "that Giuliano Gori and his family began in the early 1980s" is one of the most relevant in all of Europe. On the 35 ha of this "property, which sits on a hill

overlooking the central Tuscan plain, […] selected international artists have been invited to create installations in the remarkable outdoor spaces of the romantic park and farmland as well as inside the historic villa and various farm buildings. […] Today Celle hosts over seventy completed installations while others are still in progress [and] has become a creative workshop that continuously produces and

Beverly Pepper, *Spazio teatro celle*, 1992

experiments with new vocabularies in the different disciplines of contemporary art." The owners explain that "although documents and some remains indicate that a construction already existed on the site in the year 1000, the Villa Celle and the chapel next to it were built, in their present form, in the late 17th c. by Cardinal Carlo Agostino Fabroni from Pistoia, a great patron of the arts." In 1800 a "local architect, Giovanni Gambini," was recruited "to create an English-style park behind the villa; extending over an area of roughly 20 ha, the park is an extraordinary example of the Romantic ideal of nature. It includes a number of 19th-c. *follies* such as the Tea House, the Egyptian Monument, the two lakes with their bridges, crags and a thundering waterfall." The rest of the park is covered in olive groves. The collection itself is described as follows: "For over forty years, Guiliano Gori's collection has developed through his acquaintance and friendship with artists. [...] In March 1970 the collection, in continuous expansion, was moved to the Celle farm, the Gori family's new residence. [This] made it possible to begin a project which had been taking form in Mr. Gori's mind for some time: he wanted to know how contemporary artists would respond to a new kind of commission in which space would become an integral part of the artwork and not just a container for art. [...] The first nine site-specific pieces in the park and six installations on the top floor of the villa were inaugurated on 12 June, 1982. The idea of site-specific is fundamental for all the projects carried out at Celle. First, the invited artist chooses the place where he wants to create his artwork. Then he carefully analyses all the elements that condition the site [...]; moreover, he must take into account the spirit of Romanticism that

Emilio Vedova,
Non dove, 1985–88

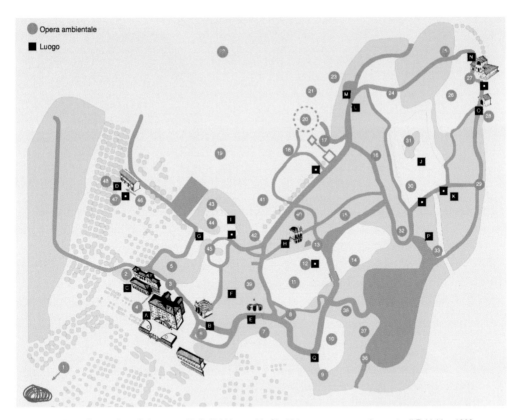

- **Opera ambientale**
- **Luogo**

1 Alberto Burri, *Grande ferro Celle*, 1986

2 Stephen Cox, *Wizard*, 1993

3 Roberto Barni, *Mute Servants*, 1988

4 Fabrizio Comeli, *Sun Dial*, 1997

5 Luigi Mainolfi, *For those who fly*, 2011

6 Robert Morris, *Venus*, 2012

7 Jean-Michel Folon, *The tree of golden fruit*, 2002

8 Ulrich Rückriem, *Untitled*, 1982

9 Robert Morris, *Labyrinth*, 1982

10 Alice Aycock, *The nets of Solomon*, 1982

11 Dennis Oppenheim, *Formula Compound (A Combustion Chamber, And Exorcism)*, 1982

12 Hossein Golba, *The Fountains of Love*, 1993

13 Dani Karavan, *Tea Ceremony*, 1999

14 Beverly Pepper, *Spazio teatro Celle – Omaggio a Pietro Porcinai*, 1992

15 Mauro Staccioli, *Celle Sculpture*, 1982

16 Loris Cecchini, *The Hand, the Creatures, the Singing Garden*, 2012

17 Bukichi Inoue, *My Sky Hole*, 1985–89

18 Ian Hamilton Finlay, *The Virgilian Wood*, 1985

19 Jaume Plensa, *Twins*, 1998

20 Alan Sonfist, *Circles of Time*, 1985

21 Frank Breidenbruch & A. R. Penck, *Spiritual Center*, 1995–97

22 Aiko Miyawaki, *Utsurohi*, 1996

23 Giuseppe Spagnulo, *Daphne*, 1987–88

24 Dani Karavan, *Line I-II-III + IV*, 1982

25 Michel Gerard, *Cellsmic*, 1992

26 Richard Serra, *Open Field Vertical Elevations*, 1982

27 Costas Tsoclis, *Genesis*, 1991

28 Robert Morris, *The Fallen and the Saved*, 2000

29 Hidetoshi Nagasawa, *Iperuranio*, 1996

30 Marta Pan, *Celle Floating Sculpture*, 1990

31 Joseph Kosuth, *Modus Operandi Celle*, 1987

32 Olavi Lanu, *The Three Stones*, 1985

33 Anne and Patrick Poirier, *La morte di Ephialthe*, 1982

34 George Trakas, *The Pathway of Love*, 1982

35 Sol LeWitt, The *Cube Without a Cube*, 1986–88

36 Marco Tirelli, *Excelle*, 2009

37 Susana Solano, *Acotación*, 1990

38 Robert Morris / Claudio Parmiggiani, *Melencolia II*, 2002

39 Richard Long, *Grass Circle*, 1985

40 Fabrizio Corneli, *Grande estruso*, 1987–88,

41 Magdalena Abakanowicz, *Katarsis*, 1985

42 Daniel Buren, *Cabane éclatée aux 4 salles*, 2004–05

43 Luciano Massari, *The Island of Identity*, 2005

44 Fausto Melotti, *Theme and Variations II*, 1981

45 Enrico Castellani, *Enfiteusi II*, 1987

46 Sol Lewitt, *1-2-3-2-1*, 2000

47 Menashe Kadishman, *Morning Light (sheep and sheep)*, 1993–94

48 Alessandro Mendini, *Albero Meccanico*, 2012

connotes the park. […] Thus at the basis of each project, there is a serious investigation of the site and each work becomes tied inextricably to that specific place. Thus the works cannot be moved without losing their meaning. This is what differentiates site-specific art from outdoor sculpture where the pieces are conceived inside an artist's studio and placed in any number of possible settings. At the Gori Collection the artworks originate exclusively for Celle." Given the strict nature of this approach (which includes not accepting donations), it is not surprising that the list of artists represented at Celle see p.135 for their artwork and location – is truly astounding and that more than 200,000 visitors have come to see the collection,

Opposite page:
Daniel Buren, *La cabane èclatèe aux 4 salles*, 2005

This page:
Michel Gerard, *Cellsmic*, 1990
Below:
Joseph Kosuth, *Modus Operandi Celle*, 1987

despite the fact that this private park can only be visited by appointment (information & appointments at www.goricoll.it). Adding to the success of Celle are the temporary exhibitions, the summer performing arts programme at an open air theatre by Beverly Pepper (1992), the video hall for audiovisual events, conferences and concerts and the innovative arts education programme *Arte in Erba* for both children and teachers, nowadays promoted by dall'Associazione Culturale Vivarte (information: "Didattica/scuole" at www.goricoll.it and www.consumoconsapevole.it)

il giardino di daniel spoerri

Since 1997
Il Giardino di Daniel Spoerri
Il Giardino-Seggiano   58038 Grosseto
Tel. +39 0564950457
ilgiardino@ilsilene.it
www.danielspoerri.org
www.ilsilene.it
Artistic Dir. Daniel Spoerri
President: Barbara Räderscheidt

Opening hours:
24 Mar.–6 Nov.: 10.30am–7.30pm
Monday closed
15 Jul.–15 Sept.: open daily
Admission: fee charged
• Access for the disabled
• Pets allowed
• Photographs allowed
• Guided tours (booking required):
  free up to groups of 15
• Exhibition halls with changing shows
• Educational programmes
• Library (by appointment only)
• Publication
• Bookshop
• Coffee shop
• Restaurant
• Car park

How to get there:
• By car: Cassia road (Siena-Rome),
  exit at Bagno Vignoni direction to
  Castiglion d'Orcia-Seggiano (SS 323)
  for 10 km. 500 m after Seggiano villa-
  ge turn left to Pescina-Campo
  Sportivo-il Giardino di Daniel Spoerri.
  Road Siena-Grosseto: exit at
  Paganico, direction to Castel del
  Piano, then to Seggiano.1 km before
  Seggiano, turn right to Pescina-
  Campo Sportivo-Il Giardino di
  Daniel Spoerri
• By train: only to Siena (from Florence)
  and Grosseto (from Rome), then by
  car
• Airports: Pisa, Florence, Rome

Accommodation & Eating out:
  Three apartements with kitchen inside
  the park. See: www.danielspoerri.org

In 1960 the critic and historian Pierre Restany launched the
Nouveaux Realistes (New Realists) in Paris: Yves Klein, Jean Tinguely,
Daniel Spoerri, etc. The latter went on to an adventurous and eclectic
life that includes forays into performance, writing, editing, producing
art multiples – originals by Calder, Duchamp, and others – dance,
choreography, and set design. He even opened a restaurant with a
gallery on the top floor, where he exhibited edible art – Cesar, Beuys,
and others.

He has been labeled a tireless entrepreneur by some and as "one of
the leading showmen in contemporary art" by Chilvers. In 1989 he
acquired Il Giardino, a 16-ha property in the foothills of Monte
Amiata, the highest peak in Tuscany, 80 km from Siena. It is a fierce
landscape with dense, mixed forests; cold and covered in snow in the
winter; dry and hot in the summer; very different from the postcard
image of the Tuscan landscape.

In 1991 and without a specific plan in mind, Spoerri began to place
works donated by artist friends – contemporaries of his, most of

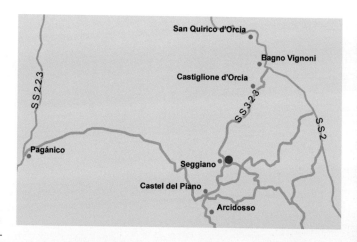

them German or Swiss born around 1930 – in the park. Also
included were a few older artists, such as the surrealist Meret
Oppenheim and the kinetic Jesus Rafael Soto. "In 1993, following the
realisation of the *Unicorn Ring*, the environment began to play a role
in the artwork and the idea for the sculptural and installation park
was defined." The Garden of Daniel Spoerri opened to the public in
1997. A private, non-profit foundation was established, the open-air
collection expanded, young and emerging artists were promoted and
encounters between artistic disciplines and science fostered.

In early 2016, the collection in the park included 110 sculptures and
installations – see map with a list of artists, artwork, and locations on
pp.140–141. About 40% of the work is by Spoerri himself, "easily re-
cognisable, made up of groups of elements and figures, always containing an assemblage of functional, mundane objects, of readymades."
Some are projects specific to the park, others are contributed works.
The immense draw exercised by the founding artist and the Giardino
has resulted in about a dozen friends and artists donating an artwork, or even a few as in the case of Eva Aeppli. Furthermore,

almost two dozen, currently less well-known artists authored another 40 or so pieces.

At the entrance to the park is a sign reading Hic Terminus Haeret – literally "the end sticks here" – a maxim from Virgil's *Aeneid*, said by Dido as she tries to stop Aeneas from leaving. The versatile expression lends itself to a number of modern-day interpretations. It contains polysemy and symbolism, very characteristic of Spoerri, since terminus can also mean area, frontier; transition, and haeret can be translated as to stick, to unite: thus allowing for a number of different poetic intentions by the artist in reference to the creative realm.

Eva Aeppli, *I pianeti, 1975/76–99*

Visitors should note that they are expected to be more than a passive observer of the artwork within this park. The collection effectively "ridicules some of the most difficult subjects of human existence: death, the constant challenges set by the grandiose nature of Monte Amiata, which shows its power at every step." A certain playfulness and "the wild nature of the mountain have had a cathartic effect on Spoerri, noticeable in the traces of a complicated and at times painful personal history that resurfaces among these pieces, in a garden that reflects all kinds of parables about life." This is why visitors encounter "figures against pain and exercises to fight fear" as they wander through this park.

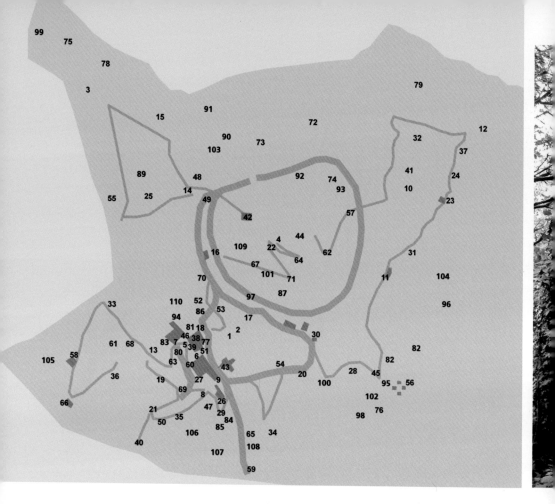

1 Spoerri, *Colonna del Ri-nascimenio*, 1987/91

2 Spoerri, *Tavola di marmo*, 1992

3 Spoerri, *Unicorni, Omphalos, l'ombe lico del mondo*, 1991

4 Spoerri, *Idolo*, 1990

5 Spoerri, *Ingresso vietato senzapanfo-le*, Homage to Joseph Beuys, 1986

6 Spoerri, *Colazione eterna*, Fallenbild: blocked instant,1994

7 Spoerri, *Pranzo eterno*, Fallenbild: blocked instant,1994

8 Spoerri, *Il gocciolatoio dei tritacarne*, 1961/91

9 Spoerri, *La tazza*, 1991

10 Spoerri, *I giocolieri*, 1985

11 Spoerri, *I giurati*, 1985

12 Spoerri, *I manichini*, 1992

13 Spoerri, *Guerrieri della notte*, 1982

14 Eva Aeppli, *Alcune Debolezze umane, I sette vizzi capitali*, 1994

15 Eva Aeppli, *Il Samurai*, 1976/94

16 Spoerri, *Tintin l'elefante*, 1993

17 Spoerri, *L'albero dei crani*, 1993

18 Spoerri, *Mazzo di fiori*, 1994

19 Spoerri, *La bella e la bestia*, 1985/96

20 Spoerri, *Il Diavolo e la Donna Impudica*, 1985/97

21 Pavel Schmidt, *Non aprire prima che il treno sia fermo*, Venus and David among the rejecting, 1996–97

22 Spoerri, *Santo Grappa*, 1970

23 J.R.Soto, *Pénétrable sonore*, pervious sound sculpture 1997

24 Spoerri, *Il Licantropino*, 1997

25 Katharina Duwen, *Discarnica abusiva*, 1997

26 Spoerri, *Cappella dei crani*, Caput Ipse Homo, 1997

27 Spoerri, *La lettrice sarta*, 1997

28 Spoerri, *La tomba del poeta*, 1997

29 Spoerri, *La voliera degli uccelli addormentati*, 1997

30 Spoerri, *La serra dei fiori elettrici*, 1997

31 Spoerri, *Il galletto e la mantide irre-ligiosa*, 1997

32 Esther Seidel – Patrick Steiner, *Il Veggente*, 1996–97

33 Alfonso Hüppi, *La torre degli amanti*, 1997

34 Bernarhd Luginbühl, *Monumento al contadino (Monte Am iata Stengel)*, 1998

35 Spoerri, *Divano d'erba*, 1985/93

36 Spoerri, *Sentiero murato labirintiforme*, 1996/98

37 Spoerri, *Il guardone*, 1996/98

38 Eva Aeppli / Jean Tinguely, *Otello e Desdemona*, 1991

39 Jean Tinguely, *Grande lampadario per D.S.*, 1985

40 Karl Gerstner, *Il bosco di Platone*, 1998

41 Erik Dietmann, *Les nains diabo-liques protègent les oliviers et Dadaníer*, 1997–98

42 Spoerri, *Chambre n. 13 de l'hôtel*

Daniel Spoerri, *Idolo,* 1990; Olivier Estoppey, *Dies irae (il giorno del giudizio),* 2002; Daniel Spoerri, *Guerrieri della notte,* 1982

Carcassonne Paris 1959–65, 1998
43 André Thomkins, *Palindromi,* 1968
44 Paul Talman, *Cattedrale n. 6,* 1987/98
45 Paul Wiedmer, *Drago,* 1998
46 Dieter Roth, *Fax scampanellante,* 1970 ca.–1998
47 Luciano Ghersi, *Le poltrone del Buon Governo II ritrovo dei fachiri,* 1998
48 Eva Aeppli, *Erinni (Furie),* 1977/78–1999
49 Eva Aeppli, *I Pianeti,* 1975/76–1999
50 Johann Wolfgang Goethe, *Agathe Tyche,* 1999
51 Eva Aeppli, *Lo Zodiaco,* 1979/80–1999
52. Meret Oppenheim, *Fontana di Hermes,* 1966–99
   Spoerri, *Bibendum,* 1998
53 Eva Aeppli, *19 aspetti astronomici,* 1977–2000
54 Spoerri, *Forno teste fumanti,* 1995–

2000
55 Luigi Mainolfi, *Terra fertile,* 1999–2000
56 Uwe Schloen, *Villaggio di bunker,* 1994–2000
57 Roberto Barni, *Continuo,* 1995–2000
58 Arman, *Monumento sedentario,* 1999–2000
59 Ursi Luginbühl, *Il guardiano della soglia,* 1997–2000
60 Alfonso Hüppi, *La doccionella pisciona,* 1977–2000
61 Ester Seider, *Un visitatore,* 1998–2000
62 Birgit Neumann, *Coda cavallina,* 1997
63 Juliane Kuhn, *Nanetto schiacciato da giardino,* 2000
64 Kimitake Sato, *La maschera – Zura,* 2000
65 Susanne Runge, *Scala mobile – banco immobile,* 2001

66 Daniel Spoerri, *La fossa comune dei cloni,* 2001
67 Daniel Spoerri, *La piramide della donna sul nodo,* 2001
68 Zoltan Kruse, *Tre troni,* 2001
69 AY-O, *Banzai piece,* 2001
70 Till Augustin, *Nodi gordiani,* 2001
71 Brigit Neumann, *Vaso da notte* per la *Doccionella pisciona,* 2001
72 Eva Aeppli, *L'autre côté,* 2001
73 Daniel Spoerri, *Gli Otto incubi – magri,* 1995–2002
74 Dani Karavan, *Adamo e Eva,* 2002
75 Olivier Estoppey, *Dies irae (il giorno del giudizio),* 2002
76 Jürgen Knubben, *Lenti d'acciaio e cinque geodi,* 1997–2002
77 Herbert Distel, *Pensamento,* 2002
78 Daniel Spoerri, *Il bersagliere,* 2002/03
79 Joseph Pleier, *Pietra solare,* 2003
80 Pavel Schmidt, *Acqua,* 2003

Since 1986
Arte Sella – The Contemporary
Mountain
Corso Ausugum 55–57
38051 Borgo Valsugana (TN)
Tel. +39 0461751251
artesella@yahoo.it
www.artesella.it
Pres. Giacomo Bianchi
Dir. Emanuele Montibeller

Opening hours
Jan., Feb.: 10am–5pm
Mar., Apr., May: 10am–6pm
Jun., Jul., Aug., Sept., Oct.: 10am–7pm
Nov., Dec.: 10am–5pm

Admission: fee charged
• Access for the disabled
• Pets allowed
• Photographs allowed
• Exhibitions rooms/events/concerts
• Publications: catalogues, guides,
  brochures
• Picnic area
• Car park
• Bus-shuttle during summer
• Events and concerts information
  available on the website

How to get there:
The exhibition is in Val di Sella (Sella
Valley) and Borgo Valsugana is the nea-
rest town. The ArteNatura route starts
10 km from the town centre whereas
Malga Costa (Costa Barn) is 13 km from
Borgo Valsugana, 990 m AMSL.
Borgo Valsugana can be reached by
driving along the road SS 47 (Strada
Statale 47) and is about 35 km from
Trento and 100 km from Padua
"Catullo" in Verona and "Marco Polo" in
Venice are the nearest airports. A shut-
tle bus service is available from the air-
port to the nearest train stations
(Verona Porta Nuova or Venezia Santa
Lucia). Borgo Valsugana is on the
Trento-Venezia train line

Arte Sella: the contemporary mountain. This is a unique creative process, which over a period of 30 years (to 2016) has seen the development of a variety of artistic languages, sensitivities and inspirations,
combined in the desire to generate a rich and continuous dialogue
between creativity and the natural world. Founded in 1986, each year
Arte Sella invites artists of international stature to engage in dialogue
with nature and create new works. The works are then handed over
to nature itself, which completes and modifies them over the years,
appropriating them and offering them to us again in a transformed
state that is always new. The visit is a continuous process of discovery,
an emotion that is different every time.
Arte Stella is some 10 km south of Borgo Valsugana, in the province

of Trento, and consists of two routes:

The first, ArteNatura, runs for some 2 km along a forest path off the SP 40 road in the Sella Valley. Access is free. The second, located around the Malga Costa, is a circular route 1 km long. This zone houses a notable number of Arte Sella works, with numerous events held here during the year. "Malga" is the term for the typical barn-type buildings that are common in the Alpine landscape. At one time, the area was home to cows during the summer season and milk and cheese were produced there.

Between May and December Malga Costa becomes a theatre offering performances, seminars, contemporary dance spectacles and classical music concerts in collaboration with the cellist Mario Brunello. As of 2016 the Malga building serves as headquarters for all the activities. There is a charge for access to this second path and the area has pram and wheelchair access.

Giuliano Mauri, *Cattedrale vegetale*, 2001

Above:
Will Beckers, *Attraversare l'animal,* 2015

Below:
Rainer Goss, *Il Quarato,* 2014

Every year the Arte Sella Association selects artists in residence for Malga Costa. They have the chance to enter into harmony with this nature and to get to know the place and its special characteristics.
The residents propose an artistic project that is valued, discussed and finally executed in a completely site-specific way: each work is conceived precisely here and for the place that will house it.
But in addition to artists of international prestige, Arte Sella aims to find an outlet for new art-in-nature talents.
Artists represented in the park included: Giuliano Mauri, Chris Drury, Rainer Gross, Will Beckers, Francois Lelong, Sally Matthews, Jaehyo Lee, Peter Randall-Page, Nils-Udo, Luc Schuiten, Alfio Bonanno, Patrick Dougherty, Aeneas Wilder, and Stuart Ian Frost.

villa di verzegnis **art park**

Since 1989
Art Park
Frazione di Villa di Verzegnis
near the Church Verzegnis, Udine
Tel. +39 0433487779
masicortim@libero.it
www.comunitamontanacarnia.it
www.carniamusei.org
Dir. Egidio Marzona

Opening hours: permanently
Admission: free
• Temporary exhibitions and
  performances

How to get there:
• By car: highway A 23 Udine-Tarvisio,
  exit Carnia towards Tolmezzo, in
  Tolmezzo Carnia go to Verzegnis, then
  to Frazione Villa di Verzegnis
• By bus: from Tolmezzo
• By train: Carnia Station, Vienna line
• Airports: Trieste (80 km), Klagenfurt
  (Austria, 75 km)

Accommodation & Eating out:
  In Villa Santina, Residence Cimenti,
  also an excellent restaurant
  Tel. +39 0433750491
  In Tolmezzo, Hotel Roma,
  Tel. +39 0433468031

The Villa di Verzegnis is a small, isolated hamlet (pop. 943) in the mountains of Carnia, in the Alpine region of Friuli, 42 km from Udine. The German collector, Egidio Marzona, a native of the area, has been inviting international artists, discreetly and away from the media spotlight since the 1980s to come and create large-scale artworks on the rural grounds of his property, recounts the architect Elena Carlini. The result is a "field of contemporary art" that includes land art, minimalist, and conceptual installations by LeWitt, Nauman, Long, Weiner, Dan Graham, Bernd Lohaus and others, but is less well-known than many less noteworthy spaces. The pieces stand in dialogue with a lush landscape of green hills, a river and a lake and, rising up in the background, the triangular silhouette of the village's namesake mountain.

By 2016 the collection consisted of 13 open-air pieces – and other interior ones – characterised by the language of basic geometry, the use of primary materials, and the careful attention given to the artwork's placement within the space. The artists have responded to the environment by creating pieces that take their inspiration from the site and simultaneously relate to it. Richard Long realised a stone circle on the edge of the river Tagliamento, Bruce Nauman a cement pyramid that cuts unexpected vistas into the valley landscape. At first, regulations prohibited the building of "structures" on these fields. The municipal and urban development authorities were, however, conscious of the importance of this long-term project, thus agreeing to declare it an "open air museum zone" – the first ever in Italy – and register it in the new city plan as a special zone dedicated to contemporary art.

Richard Long, *Tagliamento river stone ring*, 1996

latvia & lithuania

Talsi
Riga
Sabile
Vilnius
Druskininkai
150 Km

Latvia
64,589 km², 2.1 million inhabitants, member of the European Union since 2004, capital: Riga (pop. 800,000)

Lithuania
65,303 km², 2.9 million inhabitants, member of the European Union since 2004, capital: Vilnius (pop. 542,000)

The currently bright artistic moment of the Baltic countries, with young artists producing works of great creative intensity in performance, video, and installations, and in an expressionist language of high social content, has attracted the attention of those interested in the most recent art of the early 21st c.

Plains, lakes, and rivers of glacial origin extend along the shores of the Baltic Sea. They are scattered with small hills less than 250 m high, in landscapes little altered over time, where the pastures, alternating with forests of pine and fir, are often covered with snow due to the cold climate. Little populated, these lands were settled in prehistoric times by Ugro-Finnish and Baltic tribes. Dominated and christianised by German knights in the 12th and 13th c., Latvia has lived under Russian and Swedish hegemony since the 16th c. Lithuania swung for centuries between Poland and Russia. Various kings of Poland were Lithuanian, in a Polish-Lithuanian union that lasted until the 18th c., and which was followed by a period of Russian influence.

Both countries were invaded by Germany in the two World Wars. They gained their independence in 1918, only to become federal republics of the USSR in 1940. With the dismemberment of the USSR, they regained independence in 1991, and now look to the West, with parliamentary democracies and market economies.

Amulets from 3000 BC and the unusual *piliakalniai* or citadels of earth, wood, and stone from the Iron Age (1000 BC) of Lithuania did not have a progressive historic continuity. In both countries the importance of handcrafts and the popular arts has been very strong up until the 20th c., and the countries' sculpture has had strong ties to them. In Latvia, stone building only dates from the 13th c., and its greatest native cultural patrimony is the oral tradition: the enormous ethnographic body of folk music, some 60,000 songs inventoried at the beginnings of the 20th c. Many Lithuanian artists emigrated abroad, in waves both before and after World War II, among them George Maciunas, the founder of the neo-Dada group Fluxus.

The plastic arts were stifled here under the social realism imposed by Stalinism – the *Grutas Park*, near Druskininkai, 130 km south-east of Vilnius, now collects abandoned Soviet-era statuary see p. 242. In Latvia, open-air sculpture flourished in the 1960s. The Sculpture Quadrennial of Riga was begun in 1972 (participating artists in 2004 ranged from Abakanowicz to Solveiga Vasiljeva) – and underwent a gradual alignment with Western movements during the generational change of the 1980s – Ojars Feldbergs, creator of the Pedvale Park, and others.

In Lithuania, the assimilation of international trends can be seen in the 1960s, in the work of artists who studied abroad. This trend was accentuated with the turn of the century, as seen in the museum managed under the private initiative of the sculptor Gintaras Karosas, significantly called the "Park of Europe," and the CAC Center of Contemporary Art in Vilnius, which since 1992, under the direction of the Ministry of Culture, presents new international trends. It has been a key to the artistic evolution towards new languages of many local artists, as in the case of Gediminas Urbonas.

Since 1991
Pedvales Brivdabas Makslas Muzejs
Open-Air Art Museum at Pedvale
Pedvale   3294 Sabile
Tel. +371 22401165
pedvale@pedvale.lv
www.pedvale.lv
Dir. Ojars Feldbergs

Opening hours:
May (last Sat.)–Oct.: 9am–6pm
Admission: fee charged
• Access for the disabled: in some
  areas
• Pets allowed
• Photographs allowed
• Guided tours (booking required):
  fee charged
• Exhibition halls
• Educational programmes
• Publications: map, leaflet, etc.
• Coffee shop
• Restaurant: at the museum and in
  Sabile
• Picnic area
• Car park

How to get there:
• By car: from Riga to Ventspils road,
  turn direction Kuldiga to the town of
  Sabile, then follow signs in the town
  showing the direction to Pedvale.
• By bus: from Riga Bus Station to
  Sabile station
• Airport: Riga

Accommodation:
  Guest house Pedvale in a building of
  the museum
  Saule, Talsi, Tel. +371 9177071
  Talsi Hotel, Talsi, Tel. +371 3232020

Located in the region of Kurzeme, 120 km west of Riga and 1.5 km from Sabile, the park is related in its origins to the recovery of the cultural, historic, and natural patrimony of the area. Directed by the sculptor Ojars Feldbergs since it opened to the public, its 100 ha house a collection of works created each season by artists participating in symposiums, workshops, exhibitions, and a resident artists pro-

Hanna Jubran, *The Rim of Fire,* 2004

gramme. All are asked to incorporate their site-specific works to singular natural settings. Pedvale is a project based on the natural landscape, and it encourages artists to use materials friendly to nature, and to experiment, combining new media and technologies.
In 1999 its activities, including festivals and concerts, received the UNESCO's Melina Mercouri Award for its protection of its cultural patrimony.
The collection of some 150 works includes sculpture, land art and site-specific art according to figures of 2005. Works are largely by national artists – several works are by Feldbergs himself as well as artists from the United States, Finland, Netherlands, Israel and Portugal. The museum is set in a natural environment that mixes picturesque ravines with abrupt, narrow paths and the region's characteristically round, flat-topped hills with sloping sides – with places of interest such as the *Idol Lime,* a revered tree, the *Tomb of the Princess,* a memorial to the poet Gertrud von den Brinken, a beaver colony, etc. – as well as a group of historic buildings, among them former houses that now serve as rustic spaces for different activities.

Since 1991
Europos Parkas, Open-Air Museum of
the Centre of Europe
Joneikiskiu k.   LT-15148 Vilnius
Tel. +370 52377077
hq@europosparkas.lt
www.europosparkas.lt
Dir. Gintaras Karosas

Opening hours:
Daily from 10am–sunset
Admission: fee charged
• Access for the disabled
• Photographs (with permission): fee
  charged
• Guided tours (booking required):
  fee charged
• Exhibition halls with changing shows
• Educational programmes
• Conference facilities
• Publications
• Bookshop
• Coffee shop
• Restaurant: indoor and outdoor
• Picnic area
• Car park

How to get there:
• By car: from the centre of Vilnius go
  north along Kalvariju or Gelezinio
  Vilko street to Santariskes rounda
  bout, turn right in the direction of
  Green Lakes / Zalieji Ezerai (the road
  sign indicates "Europos Parkas 11
  km") and follow signs for the park.
• By bus: from Vilnius bus / train sta-
  tion, trolleybus no. 5 until Zalgirio
  stop, then by bus to Skirgiskes
  ("Europos Parkas")
  Check bus schedule at park website.
• By train: to Vilnius, then by bus or taxi
• By taxi: from Vilnius centre
• Airport: Vilnius

Accommodation:
Vilnius (12–19 km): from luxury hotels
to mid-range and low-budget hotels

"Europos Parkas, the Open-Air Museum of Central Europe" was created in 1991 by the Lithuanian sculptor Gintaras Karosas in order to
give artistic significance to the geographical centre of the European
continent (established here according to the calculations announced
two years earlier by France's National Geographic Institute), and to
show the best examples of contemporary Lithuanian and international art.
Located 25 minutes by car from the centre of Vilnius, the exhibit covers an area of 55 ha, and offers more than 90 works by artists from
27 European countries, North America, Ibero-America, Asia, and

Africa. The collection includes large-format works, including some by
famous international artists such as Magdalena Abakanowicz (her
Space of Unknown Growth, whose 22 differently-sized elements of
cement occupy 2,012 m² of space, an impressive landscape), Dennis
Oppenheim (water is the important element in his two enormous
sculptures, *Chair I Pool*, of 1996, and *Drinking Structure with Exposed
Kidney Pool*, of 1998), Sol LeWitt and Karosas himself (his *LNK
Infotree*, composed of televisions, occupies 3,125 m²) and Tei
Kobayashi. The museum has developed through the unity between
nature and works of art. The expressive landscape of the park, with
woods and fields scattered with springs, and with Karosas' own land-

scape architecture, provide a perfect setting for the sculptures. The year the museum was founded coincided with the end of the Soviet era and the opening of new possibilities to produce innovative ideas. Karosas had been clearing the underbrush from the forest, which had been left wild and abandoned for years, before creating his first sculpture, *Symbol of Europos Parkas* (1991), which marks the birth of the park, and which has become the museum's symbol. His landscape project, *Monument of the Centre of Europe* contains references to all the European capitals, indicating their distance and direction from this geographic centre.

Clockwise from above:
Magdalena Abakanowicz, *Space of Unknown Growth*, 1998
Gintaras Karosas, *LNK Infotree*, 2000
Gintaras Karosas, *The Culture*

Since 1993, when the public non-profit institution Europos Parkas was created, international symposiums of sculpture and programmes of artists in residence have been organised. Some 60,000 people visit the centre each year, and it includes buildings and facilities for a variety of services and activities. The park carries out educational activities such as guided tours, close collaborations with schools, workshops, and seminars. A new Education and Information Centre was opened in 2005. Its singular building hosts seminars, meetings, workshops and lectures on art. As the critic Michael Brenson has said, "Europos Parkas is a bridge between different cultures." But it also aspires to be a bridge into art for the general public.

luxembourg

This tiny country is said to be "the pillar of Europe." It is the richest of all European countries in terms of average income per capita. The Grand Duchy of Luxembourg is a founding member of the UN (1945), of the Benelux countries (1947), of the EU, etc. Its capital, Luxembourg (pop. 81,800), is the headquarters of various Europaen institutions.

Born as an earldom (963) with the construction of a castle, it was raised by Charles IV in the 14th c. to the status of a Duchy, and became part of the Spanish Empire, from the reign of Emperor Charles V in the 16th c. until 1714. The exploitation of its iron mines brought a notable economic expansion in the 19th c. In 1867 it was proclaimed an independent state, and its actual constitution and parliamentary democracy dates to 1868. Today its prosperity and elegance have new protagonists – telecommunications, banks, finance – and new symbols – architecture, landscaping, contemporary art, etc.

Bert Thels, *European Pentagon, Safe and Sorry Pavilion*, 2005
Mudam Luxembourg

Located in the watershed of the Moselle River, its high northern country is covered with forests, while its southern sedimentary terrain is broken by crests and cuts. Nature is a very strong presence in the capital city, with a topography marked by serpentine rivers and flat plateaus with sides that drop down to valleys on both sides.

The MUDAM Luxembourg, Musee d'Art Moderne Grand-Duc Jean is located on one of thes plateaus, the Kirchberg Plateau, formerly farm-

Casino Luxembourg –
Forum d'art contemporain
41, rue Notre-Dame
L-2240 Luxembourg
Tel: + 352 225045
info@casino-luxembourg.lu
www.casino-luxembourg.lu
Artist Residencies
Temporary exhibitions and projects

MUDAM Luxembourg
Museé d'Art Moderne
Grand-Duc Jean
Place de l'Europe.
10, avenue Guillaume
L-1650 Luxembourg
Tel. +352 4537851
info@mudam.lu
www.mudam.lu/Museedartmoderne/

2,586 km², 562,958 million inhabitants, member of the European Union since 1957

land and now an area of cultural and office buildings for the EU and new urban development. It stands on the archeological site of Les Trois Glands, on a rocky spur overlooking the river and the Alzette Valley. The project for the museum, begun in 1989, includes a building designed by American architect I.M. Pei that contains a collection of art from 1980 through the 21st c. – from Abramovic and Badiola to Kuitca and Juan Uslé, Chalayan and Margiela, among many others.

Pei has built a museum that raises over the ruins of the Fort Thüngen, its clean very geometrical volumes and indoor spaces offers a good example of art and architecture and landscape links. Nearby, a former wooded garden was transformed into the Dräi Eechelen Park by Michel Desvigne, a landscape architect internationally renowned for his rigorous and contemporary designs – who intervened in Antwerp's Middelheim Museum, see p. 28. He has conceived the park as a work in its

Wim Delvoye, *Trophy*, 1999, Mudam Luxembourg
Max Mertens, *Swings*, 2016, Mudam Luxembourg

own right, but flexible and open to subsequent manipulations, installations, and interventions by artists. By 2016 a dozen artworks are visible in the park.

Also in Kirchberg, and crossing through it, Peter Latz began in 1994 an Arboretum, notably combining geometric and natural forms, while in 2005 Christian de Portzamparc finished the Philarmonie – which was initially to be surrounded by a curtain of elms, and has been realised as an abstract forest of 847 tall columns forming the facade. Until its opening in 1996, the Luxembourg Museum and Casino – an exhibition centre for contemporary art, successor to the 19th-c. Casino Bourgeois, remodeled by the artist-architect Urs Raussmüller in 1994 and again in 2016 by architect Claudine Kaell – has been collaborating on projects involving outdoor works, installations in dialogue with the river. For instance, in 2001 these included works by Daniel Buren, Ian Hamilton Finlay, Wim Delvoye, and Jan Fabre, and in the year 2005 by Ponomarev, Fernando Sanchez Castillo, etc. The MUDAM's Artist Residencies hosts a variety of young artists working in different media.

nederland

No other landscape has been shaped so directly by human intervention, nor borne a name that so literally expresses its essence: the Low Countries. Almost half of the territory – 100 m terraces formed by rivers and glaciers in the east, a delta with hills below sea-level and alluviums along the west coast – would be inundated were it not for complex hydraulic systems. An astounding feat of engineering reclaimed the land from the sea; dikes and artificial polders like the Stormvloed-kering Oosterschelde (1976–87), Haringvilet (1955–71), Afsluitdijk and the Flevoland polders (1950s) are an example of technology creating habitable land. The country lies on the north European plain, the central zone and the Rhine and Meuse River deltas, crisscrossed by tributaries and channels. The humid and maritime climate along the coast becomes increasingly continental inland, with cloudy skies, 200 plus days of rain per year, snowfall, fog, and west winds that move the windmills, as characteristic of this area as the farms that dot these flat landscapes.

Europe's most densely populated country (except for Malta) has a strong democracy, economy, and agricultural sector – Bollenvelde flower fields, south of Haarlem, the Keukenhof National Floral Exhibition. The north-east moors, peat bogs and lucid forests still show traces of the Ice Age, and megaliths, called *hunebed* here, form ancient rows near Emme, where 4,000 years later Smithson turned an industrial quarry into an artwork (see opposite page, below).

Holland's shortage of stone led to sophisticated brick architecture, but prevented sculpture from flourishing until the 20th c.

At the time of the Roman conquest (57 BC), wool-producing tribes lived south of the Rhine, and Celts, displaced in the 3rd c. by Germanic tribes, had settled the north. After the Carolingian Empire was divided, power rested with the ruling houses, which joined the empire of Charles V of Germany and I of Spain (16th c.).

The Reformation, religious conflicts and the Treaty of Munster (1648) led to an independent Republic of the United Provinces, the rule of the bourgeoisie, naval development, foreign colonies, international trade, and economic prosperity. The republic became a kingdom under Napoleon – it is a constitutional monarchy today –, remained neutral in the course of World War I, was occupied by Germany in 1940 during World War II, and joined Benelux in 1947.

The province of the National Park De Hogue Veluwe and the Kröller Müller Museum (see p.158) also includes the four gardens (6.5 ha) of the Het Loo Palace, designed in 1698 by French landscape architect Daniel Marot. The parks and gardens of the 20th c. were influenced by the pioneering architecture and urban design of working-class housing by H. P. Berlage – "new south" of Amsterdam (pop. 780,000) –, the leader of Amsterdam's expressionist school, Michel de Klerk, and J.J.P. Oud. The latter belonged to the De Stijl movement (1915), crucial to the international development of abstract art, along with Mondrian, Van Doesburg, and G. Rietveld – the cubist Schröder House, Utrecht, 1924.

Mari Adriessen might be the most well-known sculptor, but contem-

41,526 km², 17 million
inhabitants, member of Benelux,
member of the European Union

Caldic Collection, Blaak 22,
3011 TA Rotterdam,
Tel. +31 (0)104136420
(booking required)

Emmen

Amsterdam   Zeewolde

Otterloo

Utrecht

Den Haag   ⊙

Arnhem

Rotterdam

Zwijndrecht

Tilburg

75 Km

Opposite page:
NEXT architects, *Elastic Perspective*,
2014, Rotterdam

Below:
Partial view of the garden with Anya
Gallaccio, *Blessed*, 2001
Robert Smithson,
Broken Circle – Spiral Hill, 1971,
Emmen

porary art really began in 1948 with the CoBrA group: Appel's expressionist pieces in wood and later aluminium, Constant Nieuwenhuy's constructivist sculptures and the radical, utopian project *New Babylon*. Meanwhile, Carel Visser made collage-sculptures with metals and *objects trouvés* (found objects) and Jan Schoonhoven (Nul group, 1960) created monochrome reliefs. The 1970s included Van Bakel, who died young, and Jan Dibbets, a conceptual artist who used landscape photography in his "perspective correction" and preceded European land art and landscape art, followed by Henk Visch's figurative work and Irene Fortuyn-O'Brien's objects and installations. The artists of the early 21st c., like the Atelier van Lieshout, have blurred the lines between artistic disciplines, an impulse mirrored by architecture-urban planning-landscape design: Stedelijkmuseum gardens (Amsterdam 1992) and the White Orchard (1994) by Petra Blaisse in the Rotterdam Museumpark, also the site of a "mental space" by French artist Yves Brunier (1993), the VSB gardens (Utrecht 1995) and Interpolis (Tilburg 1998) by Adriaan Geuze I West 8, and alternative concepts like Lars Spuybroek's biomorphic "textile tectonics."

Gemeentemuseum Den Haag
Stadhouderslaan 41
2517 HV Den Haag
Tel. +31 703381111
www.gemeentemuseum.nl

Celestial Vault
Machiel Vrijenhoeklaan 175
Kijkduin
2555 NA Den Haag
Behind the restaurant De Haagsche
Beek

There are 300 sculptures, statues and monuments in the capital dating from the 19th c. to the present. The Beeldenpark Gemeentemuseum Den Haag is a sculpture garden right by the Municipal Museum. It is a small open-air collection with pieces by first-rate contemporary international artists such as *Large Locking Piece* (1965) by Henry Moore, *Untitled Object* (1983) by Donald Judd [1], and *Model voor het reliëf met geometrische figuren* (1988–90) by Sol LeWit. There are also works from between 1949 and 2006 by Dutch artists such as Fransje Carbasius, Piet Esser, Carel Kneulman, Jan Maaskant, Charlotte van Pallandt, and David Bade, the so-called "six sculptures," *Zes skulpturen* (1985) by Carel Visser [2], a sculptor

1
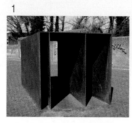

2

who had previously studied architecture, and one by Jürgen Partenheimer, a highly rated unusual German artist from the early 21st c. Kijkduin is a neighbourhood to the east of the city that is best known for its long beach of sand and dunes, less popular than the capital's main beach, Scheveningen (see p. 163), a little further north. At the top of one of these dunes is James Turrell's *Celestial Vault* (2010), an elliptical bowl measuring 40 × 30 m with an earthen wall around it. To get to this crater, you have to climb the wooden steps in the dune and walk through a concrete passage. Inside, the walls of the bowl are grass and the centre is a large stone where two people can lie back and observe the sky like a vault. On a higher dune, there is another stone from which you have a panoramic view of the beach and sea, across an increasingly flat horizon: light and space in an earthwork where the visitors are no longer passive spectators but performers, and where the work is only a work when the observer observes from it – photo below.

flevoland: constructed nature

From sea to land, from Zuiderzee to Flevoland. This is the youngest province in the Netherlands, created in 1986 and the result of a huge project lasting 60 years; the work of human spirit and effort, but also of intelligence, and the engineering of the great Cornelis Lely, 1854–1929, thus the name of its capital, Lelystad – and aesthetics. It could be said that this nature created by humans is a work of art in itself, the holistic fusion between engineering, architecture, urban planning, land art, landscaping, and visual arts. Within this Mondrian landscape, there are some individual artefacts that embody the *Zeitgeist* and *Genius Loci* of Flevoland. They are land art, earthworks, site-specific works, environmental art – the avant-garde of the last third of the 20th c., mini-malist aesthetics facing the huge and wild sea, but no less firm and solid than the resilient effort of the human race when it aims for utopian goals for the future. The pioneer was *Observatorium* (1971) by Robert Morris near Lelystad (see p.16). Marinus Boezem has a green, plant cathedral based on the floor plan of the Nôtre Dame in Paris: *De Groene Kathedraal* (1987–99) is located in Turuluurweg, close to Almere [1, 2]. Also close by is Pampeshout, the *Polderland Garden of Love and Fire* (1997) by the architect Daniel Libeskind [3, 4]. By Richard Serra there is *Sea Level* (1996) in Zeewolde [5]. Like the *Observatorium* by

1

2

3

4

5

Morris, there is another notable creation in Eastern Flevoland, *Exposure* by Antony Gormley, which since 2010 has provided a visual landmark, that transforms greatly in the changing views in these low, flat waters and lands. Gormley himself explains: "My concept of how sculpture works in the landscape is that it is a still point in a moving world." This crouching man is a metallic structure, 25 m high, weighing 60 tonnes, which is a perfect example of the Dutch idea of "Landschapskunst," or landscape, and "Landschapskunstwerk," landscape work of art. Located 1 km from the shore of Lelystad, on the dyke that connects it with Friesland, it is the most complex work by this British artist, a digital design created with the University of Cambridge and other centres, with 547 nodes and 14,000 bolts. But this milestone is not all there is in Flevoland. Among other works of land art is the 50,000 m^2 of *Ardzee* (1982) in Vogelweg, Zeewolde by the Dutch artist Piet Sleger, who has another work in Lelystad, as well as the sculpture park of the Kröller-Müller Museum in Otterlo (see p. 158). Finally, planned for the end of 2016 is *Pier + Horizon* by Paul de Kort.

Since 1938 (museum), 1961 (park)
Kröller-Müller Museum
Houtkampweg 6   6731 AW Otterlo
Tel. +31 (0)318591241
info@krollermuller.nl
www.krollermuller.nl
Dir. Lisette Pelsers

Opening hours:
Tue.–Sun.: 10am–4.30pm
Open on bank holidays
Closed on Monday and 1 Jan.
Admission:
Combined ticket park and museum:
fee charged
• Access for disabled
• Pets not allowed
• Photographs allowed
• Guided tours (booking required)
• Exhibition halls with changing shows
• Educational programmes
• Library
• Publications: leaflets, guide, books
• Bookshop
• Coffee Shop
• Restaurant

How to get there:
• By car: from A1, A50, and A12
  highways follow the signs for Park
  Hoge Veluwe / Kröller-Müller
  Museum
• By bus: from Apeldoorn and
  Ede/Wageningen/Arnhem stations
• Airport: Amsterdam

Accommodation:
  Several hotels are available at
  Otterlo

The Kröller-Müller Museum has one of the biggest sculpture gardens in Europe, covering 24 ha in which modern sculpture has found its natural habitat. The garden is open all year round, and each season gives life to a different environment. In 1888, Helene Müller, the daughter of the owner of a German shipping company, married Anton Kröller, who was working in the company's Dutch headquarters in Rotterdam. When Helene's father died, at the age of 27 Anton became the company's director, and worked in the Netherlands on its expansion until it became a corporate giant with interests worldwide. Thanks to the company's enormous capital, between 1907 and 1937 the couple collected over 11,000 works of art, a great collection of 19th- and 20th-century masters, with Van Gogh (paintings and drawings) at the core, including sculptures and ceramics. In 1909 the couple acquired a 6,000-ha hunting reserve including woods, moors and sandy terrain. In 1935 the property became part of the Stichting het Nationaal Park De Hoge Veluwe foundation. A little later the art collection was donated to the Dutch

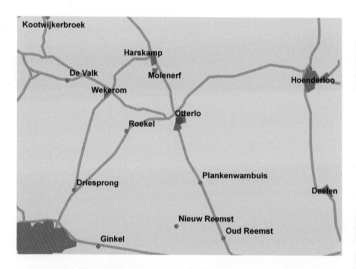

State on the condition that it should be exhibited in an appropriate space in the park. The great Belgian architect Henry van de Velde designed the museum (1938) and added a sculpture room (in the early 1950s) that engages in a clear dialogue with the natural environment. From an early age Helene was greatly interested by the relationship between architecture, art and nature. A number of elements dating back to her lifetime still remain in the park. But it was not until after her death when the plans for a sculpture park really took shape. At the start of the 1950s, the Museum's director Bram Hammacher began to acquire sculptures to amplify the collection. Together with the landscape architect J.T.P. Bijhouwer he prepared a plan to convert the forest surrounding the museum into an area for exhibiting modern sculpture. The large field by the entry to the garden still reflects the environment of the period of its inauguration in 1961. These "exterior rooms" carpeted with grass show the works of artists such as Rodin, Maillol, Lipchitz and Henry Moore. The white sculpture

Drijvende sculptuur (Floating Sculpture) by Marta Pan, together with the lake specifically designed for the work, remain among the biggest attractions in the garden. In 1963 Rudi Oxenaar was new director. His greatest interest were works in which architectural organisation plays a role. He commissioned large-scale works in specifically chosen locations from artists such as Snelson, Volten, Richard Serra, Di Suvero, Dubuffet. The landscape of the garden was no longer a mere decoration; it had become part of the artwork itself. There was also a reconstruction of the famous Sonsbeekpaviljoen (the Sonsbeek pavilion) by the architect Gerrit Rietveld, a member of the De Stijl Neoplasticism movement: it is an excellent place for exhibiting sculptures, and at the same time an impressive spatial construction. In

Joep van Lieshout, *Mobile Home for Kröller-Müller*, 1995

1990 Evert van Straaten took over as director. Together with the landscape architect Adriaan Geuze (West 8) he designed a new plan, with an extension, the new "Sculpture Park". Now the garden is the landscape of imagination, where you can walk and find all kinds of mis-en-scène and elements that inspire or incite reflection. The projects of Van Lieshout, Tom Claassen, Krijn Giezen and Chris Booth always demand a different form of contemplation. Most recently, the Aldo van Eyck pavilion and the Marta Pan amphitheatre were added, once more an encounter between architecture and art. Since 2012 the director Lisette Pelsers, again with West 8, has developed new concepts for the garden with new "exterior rooms". And in 2016 Pierre Huyghe creates his environment called *La Saison des Fêtes*.

Above: Richard Serra, *Spin Out
(for Robert Smithson)*, 1972–73
Jean Dubuffet, *Jardin d'émail*, 1974

Opposite page:
Marta Pan, *Floating sculpture
"Otterlo,"* 1960–61

1   Ulrich Rückriem, *Untitled*, 1988
2   Carel Visser, *Untitled*, 1988
3   Piet Hein Eek, *Portiershuis* (Porter's lodge), 2002
4   Jan van Munster, *+ -*, 1987
5   Lee Ufan, *Relatum*, 1979–80
6   Per Kirkeby, *Baksteensculptuur voor Kröller-Müller / Brick sculpture for Kröller-Müller*, 1988
7   Richard Serra, *One*, 1987–88
8   Sol LeWitt, *Six-sided tower*, 1993
9   Isamu Wakabayashi, *Otterlo Mist*, 2001
10 Tom Claasen, *18 Liggende houten mannen / 18 Men in Wood*, 2000
11 John Rädecker, *Gewei / Antlers*, 1923–28
12 Giuseppe Penone, *Faggio di Otterlo*, 1987–88
13 Luciano Fabro, *La doppia fàccia del cielo*, 1986
14 Joep van Lieshout, *Mobile Home for Kröller-Müller*, 1995
15 Chris Booth, *Untitled*, 2005
16 Hermann Maier Neustadt, *WD-Spiral Part One CINEMA*, 2001
17 Arno van der Mark, *The library*, 1988
18 Evert Strobos, *Palissade / Palissade*, 1973–91
19 Lucio Fontana, *Concetto spaziale natura*, 1959–60
20 Eugène Dodeigne, *Sept.*, 1993
21 Jean Dubuffet, *Jardin d'email*, 1974
22 Ian Hamilton Finlay, *Five Columns for the Kröller-Müller: por a Fifth Column for the Kröller-Müller: or Corot-Saint-Just*, 1980–82
23 Mario Merz, *Igloo di pietra*, 1982
24 Henry Moore, *Two-piece reclining figure II*, 1960
25 Gerrit Rietveld, *Rietveld paviljoen / Rietveld pavilion*, 1955–65
26 Aristide Maillol, *L'air*, 1939
27 Jacques Lipchitz, *Le Chant des voyelles (Song of the vowels)*, 1931–32
28 Christo, *56 vaten / 56 barrels*, 1966/1977
29 Marta Pan, *Sculpture flottante "Otterlo"*, 1960–61
30 Kenneth Snelson, *Needle tower*, 1968
31 Aziatisch Laantje / Asian lane
32 Richard Serra, *Spin out (for Robert Smithson)*, 1972–73
33 R. W. van de Wint, *View*, 2001

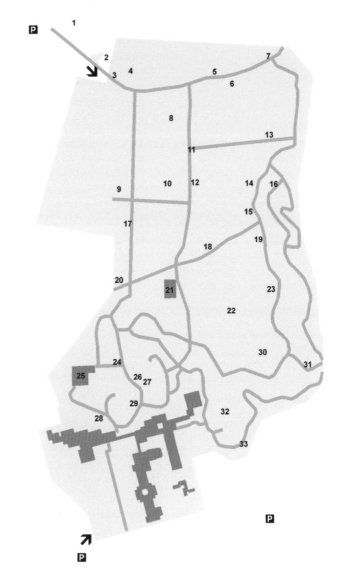

Other artists in the Kröller-Müller Sculpture Park and Sculpture Forest
Hans Äschbacher, Pawel Althamer, Jean Amado, Tony Andreas, Kenneth
Armitage, Joannis Avramidis, Antoine Bourdelle, Stanley Brown, Sjoerd Buisman
Chen Zhen, Wessel Couzijn, Cor Dera, Jacob Epstein, Henri-Etienne Martin,
Chohreh Feyzdjou, Irene Fortuyn-O'Brien, Otto Freundlich, Shamai Haber, Liet
Heringa / Maarten van Kaslbeek, Oscar Jespers, Ödon Koch, Bertrand Lavier,
Arturo Martini, Marcello, Mascherini, Umberto Mastroianni, François Morellet
Pjotr Müller, Eduardo Paolozzi, Alicia Peñalba, Constant Permeke, John
Rädecker, Germaine Richier, Oliffe Richmond, Cornelius Rogge (2 works), Piet
Slegers, Tony Smith, Carel Visser (4 works), André Volten (5 works), Albert van
der Weide, Lawrence Weiner, Oswald Wenckebach, Magdalena Wiecek, Fritz
Wotruba (3 works), Jurjen Zeinstra / Ira Koers / Mikel van Gelderen

R.W. van de Wint, *View*, 2001

Since 1994
Museum Beelden aan Zee
Harteveltstraat 1
2586 Den Haag – Scheveningen
Tel. +31 (0)703585857
info@beeldenaanzee.nl
www.beeldenaanzee.nl
Dir. J.J.Teenwisse

Opening hours:
Tue.–Sun.: 11am–5pm
The museum is closed on Christmas Day,
New Year's Day and Three Kings Day
Admission: fee charged
• Access for the disabled
• Pets not allowed
• Photographs allowed
• Guided tours (booking required):
  fee charged
• Exhibition halls with changing shows
• Educational programmes
• Library
• Publications: leaflet, guide, books
• Bookshop
• Coffee Shop
• Car park

How to get there:
• By bus: bus terminal, lines 8, 14, 22,
  23
• By tramway: lines 1, 9
• By train: The Hague Central Station
• Airports: Rotterdam, Amsterdam

Accommodation:
  A wide range of facilities is available
  at Scheveningen and The Hague
Eating out:
  More than 45 restaurants at less than
  900 m from the museum

In the past, Scheveningen was a picturesque fishing village on a long stretch of sandy beach, immortalised on canvas by Dutch painters since the 17th c. As early as the 19th c., the town served as a tourist destination, famous for its wharf, the sea museum and this particular sculpture museum.

The private collection of the art lovers Lida and Theo Scholten consists of more than 780 pieces from the 19th to the 21st c.

In 1983 the architect Wim Quist – a specialist in museum design, such as the expansion of the Kröller-Müller in 1969 – designed the facilities that would house the sculptural work. The structure integrated a neo-classic pavilion built by King William I in 1826 on top of a dune overlooking the Atlantic Ocean. The four rooms, two wide hallways, three patios, and three terraces were conceived as an extension of the beach, maintaining the same colouring as well as the intensity of the natural light.

The artwork is exhibited in both the interior spaces and the terraces and exterior sections that look out across the beach. This also includes the section added in 2005, known as "the area of the Fairy Figures at the sea."

The predominantly stone, iron, and steel sculptures are by both Dutch and international artists ranging from Alfaro to Zadkine to Balkenhol, Chadwick, Manzu, and Tajiri. Despite the fact that no pellucid dialogue exists between art and nature, the dune landscape and the sea do play a significant role in the placement of the pieces.

Tom Otterness, *The Crying Giant and the Herring Eater*, 2004

wijk aan zee beeldenpark een zee van staal

Since 1999
Wijk aan Zee
Municipality of Beverwijk
www.eenzeevanstaal.nl

"Sea of steel" is the name of this sculpture park; extremely appropriate, as it is the main material that the works have been made from. Wijk aan Zee is a small fishing village in the north of the Netherlands with a 19th-c. holiday beach, on the shores of the Atlantic, known for its expansive sand dunes.

The park was created by the sponsorship of the British-Dutch steelmaker Tata Steel. It lies in the dunes, to the side and under the smoke shadow of the factory here, the Corus Group. It began in 1999, with a number of works, which were added to in the following years, notably in 2009. Of particular note from that time is the sculpture *White Rhythm* (1999) by the British artist Robert Erskine (see photo below). Also from that year is *The Messenger* by Aleš Veselý. The Dutch are represented by Herbert Nouwens: *Beeldengroep Corus: Arie, Piet, Loes, Henk en Ludwig* (2003), Niko de Wit: *Zonder titel* (2003), and the architect and sculptor R. W. van de Wint: *De Poort* (2009), who also has an interesting work in Flavoland (see p. 155). Other sculptures, more than a dozen of them, have been created by a number of international artists: the Italian Luciano Dionisi, the Greek Apostolos Fanakidis, the British Colin Foster, the German Karl-Heinz Langowsky, the French José Rault, the Spanish Mercedes Cano-Redondo and Antonio Sobrino-Sampedro, the Estonian Jaak Soans, and the Dutch Nico Betjes and Paul Schabel.

beeldenpark drechtoevers

Since 1996
Beeldenpark Drechtoevers
Noordpark, Zwijndrecht
Tel. +31 (0)786933070
info@beeldenparkdrechtoevers.nl
www.beeldenparkdrechtoevers.nl

Opening hours: permanently
Admission: free
• Access for the disabled
• Pets not allowed
• Photographs allowed
• Guided tours: fee charged
• Temporary exhibitions
• Educational programmes
• Picnic area
• Car park

How to get there:
• By car, bus, waterbus, or fastferry
• Airport: Rotterdam
Accommodation:
  Hotel Ara, tel. +31 (0)786231780

The city of Dordrecht forms an urban area with Zwijndrecht (pop. 45,000) and is across the river from Papendrecht (pop. 30,000), the two towns included in the Drecht Riverbank Sculpture Park. This is an initiative of the artist members of the Kring van Beeldhouwers – The Circle, an association of Dutch sculptors – and fruit of the labour of the town of Zwijndrecht and the Drecht Riverbank Project Team.

During the first phase, different artists of the association donated their works, and other Dutch sculptors were invited to follow their example. In 1996 the Park was inaugurated by Her Majesty Queen Beatrice. Planned to extend along 35 km of the river; the Park seeks to be an element that will eventually connect the six towns of the area. One of its most singular characteristics is that it is owned and managed by the artists themselves, who are mainly of Dutch nationality.

Although the works are generally not site-specific, all are sited and installed by the sculptors personally, with the river always in the background. The sculptures and their authors – from Lucien den Arend to Margot Zanstra – change regularly. The largest number are sited in the Noordpark of Zwijndrecht, others in Papendrecht, a Dutch dike town founded in the 13th c., where the De Rietgors Museum of Modern Art is located, an institution that has mounted some exhibitions with the park.

norge

Occupying the western portion of the Scandinavian Peninsula and bordering the Atlantic, Norway partially lies beyond the Arctic Circle and is home to Europe's northernmost city. Norway's landscape was shaped during the Ice Age, the hard rock yielding to glaciers that formed the famous *fjords*. The depression of Trondheim with its gently sloped fjord divides the country in two: in the north, granite mountains rise up to 2,000 m in height, then descend to narrow coastal plains, such as the Nordland strip, with dramatic coastlines and countless islands; the Atlantic Coast extends to the south with mountain peaks between 1,400 m and 2,500 m in height, and in the southeast a terraced plateau gradually descends to the Strait of Skagerrak. The country is sparsely populated, 13 inhabitants per 1 km^2, and the majority of the population is concentrated in this latter area, where Oslo, the capital (pop. 510,000, founded in 1048), is located.

Most of the surface area (71%) is uncultivated. Conifer woodlands cover 26% of the land, whereas barely 3% is used for agricultural purposes. 21 national parks and nature reserves protect areas of singular, ecological interest within a country where untouched nature and five active glaciers exist alongside a road network connected by 17,300 bridges. Due to the temperate Gulf Stream, the ports along the Atlantic Coast, unlike those on the Baltic Sea, never freeze – median temperatures in Nordland range from 4°C in January to 13°C in July – which contributed to the development of Norway's long-standing and rich fishing tradition. The sea also yielded other, more recent sources of wealth – oil and natural gas.

Populated after the Ice Age by Lapps in the north and Danes and Swedes in the south, Norway entered the annals of history with the Vikings and their conquest, plundering and settling of Scotland, England, Ireland, Iceland, and Greenland between the 8th and 10th c. The country was unified by Harald I Harfager (ca. 875), christianised during the 11th c. by Danish king Canute the Great, reached its peak during the 13th c. under Haakon IV and became part of Denmark and Sweden in 1397. The country gained its independence in 1905, granted women suffrage in 1913, remained neutral during World War I, prospered economically during the 1930s and was occupied by Germany during World War II.

The cave paintings in Alta, in the north of the country, date back 6,000 years. Located above the Arctic Circle, the county of Nordland measures 38,237 km^2 and is characterised by a rugged landscape, lit up by the midnight sun in the summer and by northern lights in the winter. Close to the city of Bodø (1,215 km from Oslo) is Svartisen, the second largest Norwegian glacier; to the north-west, the austere beauty of the Lofoten Islands, dotted with red fishing cabins built in the vernacular style of the 12th c.; located 30 km from the urban centre is the country's largest maelstrom (whirlpool), Saltstraumen.

Here one also finds interesting cave paintings as well as one of Europe's most unique art projects in the environment – see p. 168.

Norway's culture is young by southern European standards. Stone architecture was not introduced until the 12th c., and the wooden

385,156 km² (except the Svalbard archipelago in the Arctic Ocean), 5.2 million inhabitants, in 1972 rejected to be part of the European Union

Lofoten

Andøy

Skånland

Øksnes
Sortland   Tjeldsund   Evenes

Bø   Navik
        Hadsel   Lødingen
                              Ballangen

Bodø

Vågan
                    Hamarøy
        Vestvågøy
Flakstad
        Moskenes

Trondheim

Røst

                Fauske
        Bodø
                Skjerstad
        Gilsdeskal   Saltdal

Oslo

                Beiarn
        Meløy

                Rana

Leirfjord

Alstahaug
            Velsn

Vega   Vevelstad
                        Hattfjelldal
        Brønnøy
        Sømna

150 Km

stave churches Stavkirker (12th–13th c.) are an example of an original style. The refined architectural work of Sverre Fehn, subtly and thoroughly integrated into the landscape, enjoyed international acclaim during the 1970s. Long after the woodcarvings of the stylised Viking ships, Gustav Vigeland developed his monumental, Scandinavian style, exemplified by 227 sculptures at the Vigelandsparken, designed and laid out by the artist in the middle of the enormous and exceedingly popular Frogner Park in Oslo. In the spotlight at the beginning of the 21st c. are Norwegian artists like Per Barclay, Sissel Tolaas, or the young Danish-Norwegian couple Elmgreen & Dragset.

bodø **skulpturlandskap nordland**

Since 1992
Skulpturlandskap Nordland
Prinsensgt, 100   8048 Bodø
Tel. +47 756000
skulpturlandskap@nfk.no
www.skulpturlandskap.no
Dir. Maaretta Jaukkuri

Opening hours: open air public space
Admission: free
• Pets allowed
• Photographs allowed
• Temporary exhibitions
• Publications
• Bookshops
• Restaurants
• Picnic areas
• Car park

How to get there:
• By air, bus, car, or by train
• Airport: Bodø

At the end of the 20th c., the County of Nordland in cooperation with Art in Norway began several innovative projects in the cultural sphere, with a particular focus on contemporary art. One of these projects is the collection of open-air sculptures known as Artscape Nordland, which was developed between 1992 and 1998 from an original idea by the Norwegian artist Anne Katrine Dolven. A second programme, in execution in 2009–10, is known as Artistic Interruptions, and consists of a series of site-specific works in interior and exterior spaces. It can be considered a continuation of Artscape Nordland

Artscape Nordland: artists, works, and places – see map on p. 167
1 Raffael Rheinsberg, *Island Museum*, Andøy   2 Inghild Karlsen, *After-images*, Øksnes   3 Sigurdur Gudmundsson, *Ocean Eye*, Sortland   4 Sarkis, *Days and Nights*, Hadsel   5 Kjell Erik Killi Olsen, *The Man from the Sea*, Bø   6 Dan Graham, *Untitled*, Vågan   7 Markus Raetz, *Head*, Vestvågøy   8 Toshikatsu Endo, *Epitaph*, Flakstad   9 Cristina Iglesias, *Laurel leaves*, Moskenes   10 Luciano Fabro, *The Nest*, Røst   11 Steinar Christensen, *Stella Maris*, Hamarøy   12 Tony Cragg, *Untitled*, Bodø   13 Jan Håfström, *The forgotten Town*, Gildeskål   14 Per Kirkeby, *Beacon*, Meløy   15 Waltercio Caldas, *Around*, Leirfjord   16 Sissel Tolaas, *House of the Winds*, Alstahaug   17 Oddvar I.N., *Opus for Heaven and Earth*, Vevelstad   18 Kain

and a step further in the concept of pieces commissioned specifically for a given place, in which the best possible locations are sought for the works.

Artscape Nordland is a collection of sculptures unique in various ways, consisting of 33 works by 35 artists from 18 countries, which are sited in 35 municipalities scattered throughout the area, and whose governments are the owners of the pieces. With nature as their frame, they are permanently accessible to the public, without any other limitations than those deriving from the Nordic climate. Artscape Nordland owes its origins to an exhaustive debate on the role of art in society and the theme of "centre and periphery." The large County of Nordland, with 45 municipalities and 240,000 inhabitants, has no museum of art, and people must travel long distances to see modern art in museums and galleries. Thus the idea arose to create a collection of modern art for this county environment, with a work of sculpture in each municipality and using the landscape as a "gallery." The particular Nordic characteristics of the natural environment of the region were used as the basis for the artistic selection. The sculptures are found in natural scenes of great beauty and variety, often untamed landscapes of the Atlantic coastline, in widely ranging locales over an area of 40,000 m². The collection thus constitutes the largest park of open-air sculptures in the world.

The project has been the subject of a permanent debate in important artistic forums, as it is considered one of the most interesting initiatives realised in any part of the world in the last decade of the 20th c. The demand for information on Artscape Nordland and the research projects that focus on it is considerable, both in Norway and in other countries.

Artistic Interruptions, planned to incorporate some 20 new site-specific works by international artists, attempts to defy conservative notions of cultural identity. It gives great importance to a close dialogue between artists and local communities. Communication and friction are the crucial aspects of these encounters. The objectives of the project are to investigate questions related to the local context, communicative potential, and the function of art in contemporary society, as well as to foment a theoretical debate about the concept of site-specificity in the double sense of artistic genre and strategy.

Antony Gormley,
Havmann, 1995, Rana

Tapper, *A new Discussion*, Vega   19 Erik Dietman, *Steinar Breiflabb*, Brønnøy
20 Dorothy Cross, *Shark-Cow-Bathtub*, Sømna   21 Hreinn Fridfinnsson, *Elf's Castle*, Hattfjelldal   22 Hulda Hàkon, *Three Èldar*, Vefsn   23 Antony Gormley, *Havmann*, Rana   24 Kari Cavèn, *Today, Tomorrow, Forever*, Beiarn   25 Gediminas Urbonas, *Four Exposures*, Saltdal   26 Kristjan Gudmundsson, *Protractus*, Skjerstad 27 Per Barclay, *Untitled*, Fauske   28 Bård Breivik, *Untitled*, Narvik   29 Martti Aiha, *Seven Magical Points*, Skånland   30 Bjørn Nørgaard, *The Stone House*, Evenes 31. Olafur Gislason, *Media Thule*, Tjeldsund   32 Inge Mahn, *Heaven on Earth*, Ballangen   33 Anish Kapoor, *Eye in Stone*, Lødingen
Curator: Maaretta Jaujuri.

Above: Anish Kapoor, *Øye i stein* (Eye in Stone), 1998
Below: Markus Raetz, *Hode* (Head), 1992

Artistic Interruptions: artists and
project sites
Goksøyr & Martens, Bolga
Markus Renvall, Hemnesberget
Steven Stapleton & Collin Potter,
Svolvær
Cathrine Evelid & Sophie Brown, Vågan
Baktruppen, Stamsund
Lisa Karlson & Charlotte Thiis-Evensen,
Nyksund
Rikrit Tiravanija – Kamin Lertchaiprasert
– Geir Tore Holm – Sossa Jorgensen,
Sørfinnset
Simon Starling, Øksnes
Carsten Höller, Nesna
Winter & Hörbelt, Brønnøysund
Svein Flygari Johansen, Lurøy
Maria Bustnes, Lødingen
Elmgreen & Dragset, Tranøy
Mobile Homes & MiN ensemble, Bodø
Jeppe Hein, Bodø
Alexandra Mir, Narvik
Project director: Per Gunnar Tverbakk

Above: Per Barclay, *Untitled*, 1993; below, right: Per Kirkeby, *Varde* (Beacon), 1992

Since 1999
Kistefos Museum
Samsmoveien 41
N-3520 Jevnaker, Norway
Tel. +47 61310383
post@kistefos.museum.no
www.kistefos.museum.no

A/S Kistefos Træsliberi (founded in 1889) was a factory for producing wood pulp. In 1955, production halted and in 1999 it re-opened as a monument of Norwegian industrial cultural heritage.

From the beginning the idea was to open a sculpture park as well. The first few years it displayed mainly Norwegian contemporary sculptors: Nico Widerberg, Beate Juell, Kristian Blystad, Lekenede Hest, Bjarne Melgaard, Kjell Nupen, Nils Aas, Edgar Ballo, and then Olafur Eliasson, Anne-Karin Furunes, Siri Bjerke. A more international approach came with works by the Colombian Fernando Botero, the Englishman Tony Cragg, the Italian Fabrizio Plessi (who in 2005 unveiled the first site-specific work here), the Norwegian-Danish artist duo Elmgreen & Dragset, the Japanese artist Shintaro Miyake, the Welsh Petroc Sesti, and the very international Anish Kapoor.

In 2009, another site-specific work was installed, *Tumbling Tacks* by Claes Oldenburg and Coosje van Bruggen, heavily inspired by the site's industrial history. 2011 was Marc Quinns' year: *All of Nature Flows Through Us*, a bronze in the middle of the river. 2013 was *Pulp Press (Kistefos)* by the Irish John Gerrard. In 2014 they unveiled *Slektstrea, Genbanken* by Norwegian Per Inge Bjørlo. The 30th sculpture in the park arrived in 2015: *Free to Frolic* by Phillip King, one of Britain's most significant contemporary sculptors.

Michael Elmgreen and Ingar Dragset,
Forgotten Babies #2, 2005
Olafur Eliasson, *Viewing machine*, 2001

Since 2013
Ekeberg Hill, south-east of the city
Kongsveien 23, 0193 Oslo, Norway
Tel.: +47 242191
http://ekebergparken.com/en

Opening hours: permanently
Admission: free
• Guided tours available
• Art conferences
• Offers for children, youth, education
Eating out:
    www.ekebergrestauranten.com
    Outdoor seating (in summer)

The Ekeberg Hill landscape inspired the backdrop of the famous Edvard Munch's acclaimed painting *Der Schrei der Natur* (The Scream of Nature), four versions, 1893–1910. The area of pines, ashes, black alders, maples, willows, and firs fell into neglect during the second half of the 20th c. In the 21st c. it has regained its former glory with a high-quality, elegant sculpture park. It is the result of efforts by Norwegian billionaire, entrepreneur and art collector Christian Ringnes through a foundation that he set up. More than 35 sculptures by famous masters, modern and contemporary artists are spread out across its 26-ha territory, displaying works from Rodin to Ann-Sofi Sidén.

Four female figures are very significative: *Nue sans draperie* (1921) by Aristide Maillol; *Eva* by Auguste Rodin (1881); Salvador Dalí's *Venus de Milo aux tiroirs* (1936); Louise Bourgeois' (*The Couple* 2003) consisting

of two aluminium figures hanging between two huge pine trees. Other works are the big steel *Open Book* of Diane Maclean, which reflects its readers / viewers and their background in a continually changing array of colours; James Turrell's *Ekeberg Skyspace* provides an interplay between light and colour, and three dozen works by Lynn Chadwick, Tony Cragg, Dan Graham, Jenny Holzer, Richard Hudson, Tony Oursle, Auguste Renoir, the Chapman brothers, Sarah Lucas, Knut Steen, Sarah Sze, Aase Texmon Rygh, Per Ung, Dyre Vaa, Guy Buseyne and others. Ekebergparken has become in a short time a pride and joy of the city: the hill is packed with visitors during weekends.

Aristide Maillol, *Nue sans draperie*, 1921
Auguste Rodin, *Eva*, 1881
Louise Bourgeois, *The Couple*, 2003

polska

Agriculture did not reach these gently rolling plains until around 4200 BC, and they remain agricultural today – cereals, red beets, potatoes. 28% of its area is forest, mainly beeches and pines, with a continental climate influenced by masses of cold Arctic air, producing cold winters with abundant snowfall and hot and rainy summers.

The wood and earth fortresses known as *grody* date to the 5th c. BC. The Slavic tribes that occupied the area in this century were joined together by the 10th c., giving rise to the first national dynasty of the Piasts, and bringing contacts with the West, with the first buildings in stone. Under the Jagellons, the union with Lithuania extended their domains from the 14th c., making Poland the most powerful state of Eastern Europe. Its decadence led to its disappearance as a nation after successive repartitions to Russia, Austria, and Prussia.

Independent again in 1918, in 1939 it suffered the invasion and inhuman repression of the Nazis. In 1945 it became a People's Republic, communist and part of the Soviet Bloc. An era of Socialist Realism in art and an industrialisation based on coal, steel, and shipbuilding began. In 1989 it entered the orbit of parliamentary democracies and free-market economies.

The Baroque flourished here, and in sculpture, the neoclassical influence of Canova and Thorvaldsen extended into the early 20th c. Ksawery Dunikowski's work relates to Rodin, achieving in the monuments of his maturity a mix of art and architecture. His works were donated to the State in 1948 and are housed in the Krolikarnia Palace, whose gardens on the banks of the Vistula River contain the Sculpture Park. Against this figurative line, Poland has had a more active role in the historic avant-garde than is normally thought. From the end of World War I the formistas group included futurists, cubists, and expressionists, and abstraction was developed throughout the 1920s. Soviet Constructivism and Suprematism inspired the Bloc group, and the career of Katarzyna Kobro, the first of the three great figures of the 20th c. Polish sculpture (all of them women) flourished with Malevitch's visit and exhibition in Warsaw (pop. 1,745,000) in 1927. Almost all of Kobro's sculptures, which are found in Lodz's Sztuki Museum, are without volume, quasi-architectural, minimal *avant-la-lettre*. Two key events occurred in 1965, when the Krolikárnia opened. The first in Paris: Alina Szapoczników developed assemblages, "sculp-

Magdalena Abakanowicz, *Unrecognised*, 2001–02, Cytadel Park, Poznan

Opposite page:
Artur Brunsz, *Untitled*, 1965, Biennale Form Przestrzennych 1965, Elblag

312,685 km², 38.5 million
inhabitants, member of the
European Union since 2004

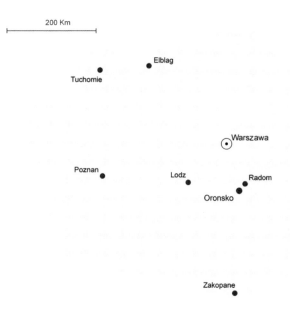

200 Km

Elblag
Tuchomie
Warszawa
Poznan
Lodz
Radom
Oronsko
Zakopane

ture-objects," and "habitable sculptures," close to but beyond new realism; the other in Poland: the Biennials of Spatial Forms began in Elblag. Until the last Biennial (1973) and the reunion of the artists (1986), permanent works were left in parks and streets. One of the participants became Poland's third great sculptor, Magdalena Abakanowicz – of the greatest international relevance, her works are collected from the US to Japan; she is a personal creator who brings together an extraordinary fusion of natural force and artistic expression. In a country where sculpture is not among the most popular arts, the Poznan Biennial has taken place since 1976, and new sculpture parks (the Wladyslaw Hasior in Zakopane, or the one in Tuchomiu) have opened. Younger artists such as Igor Mitoraj, Miroslaw Balka, or Ryszard Wozniak, members of the Gruppa group, assure the creative future in "objects" and installations.

Muzeum Rzeźby im. Xawerego Dunikowskiego
Królikarnia Palace
ul. Pulawska 113a   02–707 Warszawa
Tel. +48 228431586   www.mnv.art.pl
królikarnia@mnv.art.pl

International Sculpture Biennal, Poznan
Centrum Kultury Zamek
ul. Swiety Marcin 80–82

61–809 Poznan   Tel. +48 618536081
www.zamek.poznan.pl

Park Rzeźby im. Hasiora
Muzeum Tatrzanski   Zakopane

Europejskie Laboratorium Sztuki
ul. Pochya 4   77–133 Tuchomie
Tel. +48 598215815
www.piwarski.pmk-essen.de

Since 1981
Centrum Rzeź by Polskiej
ul. Topolowa
26–505 Oronsko
Tel. +48 486184516
Fax +48 486184470
sekretaria@rzezba-oronsko.pl
www.rzezba-oronsko.pl
Artistic Dir. Mariusz Knorowski

Opening hours:
Monday closed
Park exhibition (open air):
permanently, 8:00–dusk
Other facilities: see timetable
Admission: fee charged
• Access for the disabled
• Pets allowed
• Photographs allowed (different fees)
• Guided tours (booking required):
  fee charged
• Temporary exhibitions
• Educational programmes
• Library for professionals, artists,
  academics, students
• Publications: guide, leaflets, books
• Bookstore
• Cafeteria & Restaurants: in the
  Centre, Café Art and a canteen with
  full-board
• Picnic area
• Car park

How to get there:
• By car: domestic road no. 7 between
  Warsaw (120 km) and Cracow
  (180 km)
• By bus: from Warsaw to Radom, from
  Cracow to Radom, then from Radom
  to Oronsko (16 km): line K (shuttle)
• By train: from Warsaw or Cracow
  stations to Radom
• Airport: Warsaw

Accommodation & Eating out:
  Guest-rooms in the old manor gra-
  nary, now The Sculptor's House
  In Oronsko: Motel Billy (3 km),
  Starowiejska Inn, 500 m to the Centre

The Centre of Polish Sculpture in Oronsko (pop. 1,500) is located on an aristocratic 19th c. estate with a complex of buildings and a historic park. Its cultural tradition dates to the middle of that century, when Józef Brandt, a painter of historical scenes connected with the Academy of Munich, created the Free Academy of Oronsko here, which was frequented by artists and disciples from all over Poland. But it was not until 1965 that the first outdoor sculpture exhibition was organised in the park, launching the sculpture programme. A year later the Centre for Sculptors' Creative Work was founded. Since 1981 it has depended on the Ministry of Culture, which restored the manor house and the other historic buildings.

The entire 12 ha of the park is dedicated to the creation, exhibiting, and documentation of sculpture. Every year, about 200 artists, mainly from Poland, are invited to participate in a residency programme, and to direct or attend workshops, academic sessions, seminars, lectures, symposiums, temporary exhibitions, and open-air events. Józef Brandt's mansion contains a museum of 19th-c. furniture and decoration. The former Chapel and Orangerie – which was Brandt's studio – are today spaces for temporary exhibitions, and the former garages (1905) are a permanent sculpture gallery. A new building was opened in 1992, and houses the Museum of Contemporary Sculpture, while the artist and professor Grzegorz Kowalski organises sculpture exhibitions

in the picturesque and romantic garden, of a notable value as landscape and nature preserve, with poplars, chestnuts, ashes, alders, and abundant ivy.

By 2016 the collection consists of 621 artworks, including sculptures, objects, installations, drawings, paintings, and tapestries. Among the artists presented in the museum are great masters such as Abakanowicz, unclassifiable talents such as Hasior, and consolidated figures such as Jerzy Jarnuszkiewicz. The open-air park exhibits half a dozen sculptures of unknown authorship from the 18th and 19th c. which offer a historic counterpoint to the large contemporary collection. With 93 works, this is dominated by European sculpture, especially from Poland and, to a lesser degree, Germany, and with a few pieces from Japan and the United States. The works are by 77 artists, many little known or members of recent generations, such as Teresa Murak and others.

The Centre offers a foundry, pottery kilns, and workshops for carpentry, stone, etc. for resident artists, as well as a variety of educational and outreach activities. Documentation and publication activities include an updated database on Polish artists, and a library with material on current trends in Polish and international art. The Centre publishes its own books and magazines, including *Oronsko*, and the annual Rzeźba ba Polska (Polish Sculpture), a prime reference source.

Opposite page:
Tadashi Hashimoto, *Untitled,* 1998

Below:
Andrzej Bednarczyk, *The Field where Angels Whispers,* 1998

portugal

Situated on the western extreme of the Iberian Peninsula, Portugal's hills and rivers smoothly descend from the Spanish meseta to the Atlantic Ocean, which bathes a low and regular coastline. Of a Mediterranean climate modified by the influence of the Atlantic, the country is dry towards the south and very variable and moist towards the north. The dominant vegetation of the flat landscape in the south consists of maritime pines, olives, and cork trees, while the more accidental topography of the north is green with fields, woods – oaks, birches – and grapevines. The valley of the Duero is "wine country," with its capital in Porto (pop. 303,000), the Roman Portus Cale that gives Portugal its name.

In April 1974, the "Revolution of the Carnations" brought dictatorship to an end and inaugurated a new era. The Second Republic, semi-presidential, and with a social-democratic political outlook, inherited a poor agricultural country with a high level of unemployment and emigration, and large inequalities in all areas, including the contrasts between a backward rural realm and urban areas and cities, where generous cultural and artistic offerings are concentrated (Lisbon, capital of the nation, pop. 547,000, the Roman *Olisipo*).

In a land inhabited since the remotest of times, the human hand has left works of art in its natural environment that date to very early periods: designs on stone in the valley of Côa (18000 BC); megaliths near Lisbon, and numerous dolmen – here called *antas* – such as the Anta Grande of Zambujeiro, near Evora, the largest in Europe; sculptures from the Bronze Age in Beira, Alentejo, and Algarve. By the turn of the 21st c., Portugal had abandoned the periphery of the artistic world. Modern centres of art have been established or strengthened, and great collectors have appeared on the transnational scene, as well as many artists, with Julião Sarmento at their head, as well as Cabrita Reis, Croft, Joana Vasconcelos (the one who perhaps refers most to her own context), Chafes, Tabarra, Vasco Araujo, and other young emerging talents. Critics and art professionals have also joined the international discourse and circuits, many titling their works in English.

Porto and its neighbouring Santo Tirso (30 km) house two sculpture parks (see pp.162–165). In Porto, avant-garde landscape design is found in the Passeio Atlántico (2001–04) by Manuel de Solà-Morales, and the works of João Gomes da Silva: his intervention in the gardens of Serralves (1996–2000) and, 70 km outside Porto, the plaza and garden of the luminous church of Marco de Canavezes by Alvaro Siza. In Lisbon, the Belém Centre offers programming of constant interest, including retrospectives of artists from around the world.

The Gulbenkian Foundation, a private institution – the majority of cultural institutions depend on the government – is renowned worldwide for its Calouste Gulbenkian Museum – tapestries and Oriental objects – and offers a more current selection of works at its Centre of Modern Art, in its programme that invites emerging artists to create specific projects in its home and gardens. Finally, the Tajo Park (1998) features the art and landscape architecture of Georges Hargreaves.

92,391 km², 10.6 million
inhabitants, member of the
European Union since 1986

100 Km

Santo Tirso
Porto

Açores

Lisboa

Madeira

**Fundaçao Calouste
Gulbenkian**
Centro de Arte Moderna
José de Azeredo Perdigão
Rua Dr. Nicolau de Bettencourt
1050–078 Lisboa
Reception +351 217823474

Information / Booking +351 217823474
www.gulbenkian
camjap@gulbenkian.pt
Opening hours:
Tue.–Sun.: 10am–6pm Mon.: closed
Admission: fee charged
Children, students, and seniors: free

Gabriela Albergaria, *Disguise /
performance in the garden*,
Fundaçao Calouste Gulbenkian,
Lisbon

Since 1989
Fundaçao de Serralves
Rua D. João de Castro, 210
4150–417 Porto
Tel. +351 226156500
serralves@serralves.pt
www.serralves.pt
Dir. João Almeida

Opening hours:
Oct.–Mar.: Tue.–Fri. 10am–6pm; Sat.–
Sun. and public holidays 10am–7pm
Apr.–Jun.: Tue.–Fri. 10am–6pm;
Sat.–Sun. and public holidays
10am–8pm
Jul.–Sept.: Mon.–Sun. and public
holidays 10am–7pm
Admission: fee charged
• Access for the disabled
• Photographs allowed
• Guided tours (booking required)
• Exhibition halls with changing shows
• Educational programmes
• Library
• Publications: book, map, and leaflets
• Bookstore: museum bookshop
• Shop
• Cafeteria & Restaurant (3 areas):
  buffet service and open air terrace,
  sandwiches, Tea House, restaurant
  at night (booking in advance)
• Car park: fee charged

How to get there:
• By car and taxi
• By bus: lines 201, 203, 502, 504
• By train
• Airport: Porto

Accommodation:
  From luxury and five-stars hotels to
  low-budget rooms

The mission of the Fundação de Serralves, as an international cultural hub, is "to stimulate interest and knowledge among people from different origins and ages in contemporary art, architecture, landscape and the critical issues for society and its future, doing so in a way that is fully part of its exceptional heritage." The 18 ha of land in the centre of the city was acquired in 1986 by the Portuguese state, which in partnership with half a dozen other entities created the Foundation in 1989 for the purpose described above. The Foundation's complex of heritage sites has been a national museum since 2012. It includes the Serralves Villa, an Art Déco building constructed by Carlos Alberto Cabral, 1895–1958, with decorations by the most relevant figures of the time, such as Lalique, the park, and the Museum of Contemporary Art, the work of Pritzker Prize-winner Álvaro Siza, 1999, as well as some other installations.

The Serralves Villa includes space for the museum's temporary exhibitions. Its collection has the firm aim of creating a dialogue between international and Portuguese art from 1960 to the present day. It includes artists such as Helena Almeida, Leonor Antunes, Baldessari, Alberto Carneiro, Jimmie Durham, Liam Gillick, Dan Graham, Cildo Meireles, Gerhard Richter, Ruscha, Julião Sarmento, Robert Smithson, and Monika Sosnowska.

The Park is a unique part of the landscape heritage of Portugal: a complex unity of various parts, the result of a process that is now in

Opposite page:
Claes Oldenburg, Coosje Van Bruggen,
Plantoir, 2001

Above:
Dan Graham, *Double Exposure*,
1995–2003

its third century: remains of a 19th-c. Romantic garden, the surroundings of the former Quinta do Mata-Sete estate, the garden of the
Serralves Villa and the new gardens of the Contemporary Art
Museum designed by João Gomes da Silva. Its variety of areas and
sections, each with its own characteristics, including a small, romantic
lake, come from a fusion between natural space (dense wild woods)
and designed and constructed nature, all with great contrasts of
colour, shadows, textures and vegetation. Of particular note due to
their variety and quality are the rose garden, fruit trees and dense
wooded areas.

In this environment of interaction between art and nature, significant
works have been installed on a permanent basis: *Plantoir (Almocafre)*,
Claes Oldenburg / Coosje Van Bruggen, 2001; *Double Exposure*, Dan
Graham, 1995–2003, *Walking is Measuring*, Richard Serra, 2000; *Um
Jardim Catóptrico (Teuseus)*, Ângelo de Sousa, 2002; Ser Árvore e
Arte, Alberto Carneiro, 2000–02; Monte Falso, Francisco Tropa,
1997–2001; *For a New City*, Serralves Museum & A Working Farm,
Maria Nordman, 2000–01; *Pour Porto*, Veit Stratmann, 2001; *Pour le
Parc*, Veit Stratmann, 2007; *Sem título*, Fernanda Gomes, 2008–09; *La
Baigneuse Drapée (La Seine)*, Aristide Maillol, 1921.

The Museum's exhibitions include the park, where the works aim to
enhance the relationship between art and nature. They present
established and emerging artists, both Portuguese and international.
The exhibition *Squatters*, 2001, achieved particular notice, with artists
from the whole world working on specific projects in all the corners
of the natural environment of Serralves.

Since 1996
Museu Internacional de Escultura
Contemporânea de Santo Tirso
Câmara Municipal de Santo Tirso
Praça 25 de Abril
4780–373 Santo Tirso
Tel. + 351 252830400
gap@cm-stirso.pt/pages/1862
www.cm-stirso.pt
Dir. Álvaro Moreira

Opening hours: permanently
Admission: free
• Access for the disabled
• Pets allowed
• Photographs allowed
• Guided tours (booking required)
• Educational programmes
• Library: Museu municipal Abade
  Pedrosa
• Bookshop
• Car park

How to get there:
• By car, train, bus, on foot
• Airport: Francisco Sá Carneiro, Porto,
  26 km from Santo Tirso
  Nearest main cities: Porto, Guimarães

Accommodation:
  Hotel Cineday (Santo Tirso)
  Santo Thyrso Hotel, Santo Tirso

The MIEC_ST Museu Internacional de Escultura Contemporânea de Santo Tirso has its origins in a proposal made by the sculptor Alberto Carneiro to the municipality of Santo Tirso in 1990, to hold symposiums on contemporary sculpture, in particular public sculpture. After four symposiums, in 1996 the creation of the MIEC_ST Board was approved to organise sculpture symposiums, guarantee the maintenance and conservation of the collection, promote it and implement a set of other related activities.

The museum was opened in 1997 by the President of the Republic, Jorge Sampaio. In 1999 two artistic organisers were recruited: the sculptor Alberto Carneiro and the art critic Gérard Xuriguera.

Since 1990, the city of Santo Tirso has hosted Simpósio Internacional de Escultura, which brings together artists with a variety of origins.

Some artists of the park:
Alberto Carneiro, Carlos Cruz-Díez,
Angelo de Sousa, 1990; Pedro Cabrita
Reis, 2001; Mauro Straccioli, 1996;
Peter Klassen, 2004; Rafael Canogar,
2015; Miquel Navarro, 2015; Pierre
Marie Lejeune, 2015

MIEC_ST is a space for dialogue and discussion, dissemination and debate on public sculpture. It is a privileged space for reflection and a hub for innovative projects, taking advantage of the singularity of its nature and the privileged relationship between the pieces; a plural place for complete interaction between people and art. Set within the urban boundaries of the city of Santo Tirso, it offers a self-contained and unrestricted visit. The works, located in a variety of public areas, are the result of the symposiums held between 1991 and 2015. In 2016, with 54 sculptures, MIEC_ST is divided into six main centres: Parque D. Maria II y jardines; Praça do Município; Parque dos Carvalhais; Praça Camilo Castelo Branco; Parque Urbano de Rabada; Parque Urbano de Gião. Some of the artists present, both Portuguese and international, are listed at the side.

Opposite page:
Denis Monfleur, *Le Porteur de vid*, 2015

Above:
Pino Castagna, *Canyon*, 2012

Right:
Carlos Nogueira, *Casa comprimida com árvores dentro*, 2012

sverige

449,964 km², 9.8 million inhabitants, member of the European Union since 1995

Although Sweden is the epitome of advanced modernity and formal sophistication, the forces of nature – long winters, snowfall, lakes, forests – pervade the daily life and the culture of its people. Sweden occupies the eastern part of the Scandinavian massif, which descends in large plateaus towards the Baltic Sea, its peaks demarcating the border with Norway. The landscape, with lakes covering 40,000 km², was shaped by weather and glaciers; 50% of its surface is covered in pine, fir, and birch woodlands and only 7% is cultivated land. The mountainous, northern part of the country is marked by an inhospitable, polar climate. Central Sweden, with a continental climate, large lakes, and urbanised areas like Stockholm (pop. 1.5 million; –3°C in January, 17°C in June; founded in the 13th c.), is the country's core region. In the south, separated from Denmark by the Strait of Oresund, is the Skåne region, rich in agricultural production, with a more temperate climate, and the city of Malmö (pop. 250,000), located directly across from Copenhagen.

Covered in ice during much of the Paleolithic, cave paintings in the N depict humans and animals in a highly naturalist style, figures that appear further south in Tanum (Gothenburg and Bohus) during the Bronze Age. During the Iron Age craftsmen produced remarkable work in gold and silver. Populated by the Svear in the E and the Goths in the W, Sweden was first mentioned by Tacitus in his *Germania* during the 1st c. The Viking's western expansion ushered in a period of Christianisation during the 9th c. Eric IX conquered Finland (1157, under Swedish rule for five c.) and created the bishopric of Uppsala (1164). Sweden, then under Gustav I of Vasa, abandoned the Kalmar Union with Denmark (1523), which was followed by several Nordic wars. The height of Sweden's dominance in the Baltic during the 17th–18th c. and the onset of the "era of freedom" (parliament and two parties, 1720) were followed by an alliance against Napoleon, the addition of Norway to Swedish territory, neutrality, industrialisation, a liberal monarchy, and a shift in power from the nobility to the people, freedom of the press (1812), mandatory, coeducational schooling for both genders (1842, 1849) and religious tolerance (1859). Starting in 1905, after Norway seceded from Sweden, a succession of socially democratic governments introduced a wave of social reform and new freedoms that turned the country into one of the most advanced in terms of universal suffrage (1909–18), retirement pension (1913), the 8-hour workday and women's right to vote (1919). The second half of the 20th c. witnessed landmark events like the support for developing nations, the Earth Summit in Stockholm (1972) – which heightened ecological awareness around the world; the assassination of prime minister Olof Palme (1986) and the consequent loss of hope for a different world – based on the "Scandinavian Model": moderate socialism and real freedoms – as an alternative to rampant capitalism and communist dictatorship.

A national identity in Swedish sculpture did not emerge until the 19th c. and produced its leading figure in the early 20th c., Carl

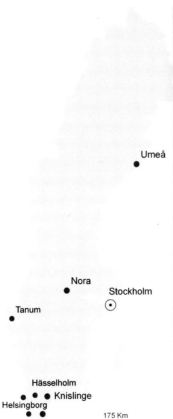

Umeå

Nora
Stockholm
Tanum
⊙

Hässelholm
● ● ● Knislinge
Helsingborg
● ●
Lund   Skåne   ├─────┤ 175 Km

Milles, once assistant to Rodin. His monumental pieces are exhibited in their own open-air museum, the Millesgarden – Italian-style terraces with fountains and columns, located on the outskirts of Stockholm, about 5 km from Norrtull. Abstraction did not achieve a level of importance until 1947 with Arne Jones and his work in metal. Since then, the integration of Swedish artists into international movements has accelerated, environmental, minimal, Olle Baertling. A significant number of contemporary artists are drawn to the interrelationship of art/nature, man/environment. Håkansson, Bandolin, Sidén, Svensson, Gyllenhammar, etc. explore these ideas through sculpture, installation, video-art, photography, and even sound installations. Swedish architecture, from the first known buildings – 11th-c. wooden stave churches – to the refined austere work of Erik Gunnar Asplund has always worked in dialogue with nature. The Chapel (1918) and Crematorium at the Woodlands Cemetery (Skogskyrkogården) in Stockholm (1935–40) exhibit a subtleness and affinity to the spirit of the site that is rarely seen in later sculptures and art installations and are far removed from the banal placement-of-pieces-in-green-spaces or the oft abused creation of self-proclaimed site-specific artwork. The contribution of landscape architecture is equally important, from the Sundbyberg Park near Stockholm (1937) by the socially conscious architect Sven Hermelin and the parks of Erick Glemme (Norr Malstrand, Tegner Grove, the transformation of the Vasa Park, 1941–47) in the capital to Sven-Ingvar Andersson's designs for parks in Stockholm, Malmö – Gustav Adolf Square, 1997 – and Lund – around the train station, 1997 – in which he unites garden art, ecological questions, and the latest trends in visual art. Finally, other immensely popular parks include those in Malmö, especially Pildammsparken, designed for the Nordic Exhibition in 1914, and the five thematic gardens Trädgård and Norr in Umeå (pop. 105,000).

Above:
Roxy Paine, *Impostor*, 1999, Wanås
Foundation, Knislinge

Since 1987
The Wanås Foundation
Wanås, S–28990 Knislinge
Tel. +46 (0)4466071
e-post@wanas.se
www.wanas.se
Dir. Mattias Givell and Elisabeth Millqvist

Opening hours:
Park: 8am–7pm daily
Indoor exhibitions: May–Nov.:
Mon.–Sun. 10am–5pm
Admission: fee charged
• Access for the disabled
• Pets allowed
• Photographs allowed
• Guided tours (booking required)
• Exhibition halls with changing shows
• Educational programmes
• Publications: catalogues, books
• Bookstore, shop and deli
• Coffee shop
• Restaurant
• Picnic area
• Car park

How to get there:
• By car: from Malmö, road E22 to
  Kristianstad / Kalmar, then road 19 /
  23 to Osby, in Knislinge turn right to
  Hässleholm / Wanåsutställningar, in the
  next crossing turn left to Hässelholm /
  Wanås. From Hässleholm / Göteborg /
  Helsingborg /Stockholm: from
  Hässleholm go N on road 23 to Växjö,
  turn right to Broby (before Ballingslöv),
  in Norra Sandby turn right to Knislinge /
  Wanås (approx. 25 min.).
• By train: Hässleholm Central, then taxi,
  or to Kristianstad and bus 545 to
  Knislinge
• Airport: Copenhagen, then by train to
  Hässleholm, Malmö

Accommodation:
  Kristianstad (25 km) and Hässleholm
  (25 km)
Eating out:
  In Knislinge (2 km), Broby (10 km),
  and Kristianstad (25 km)

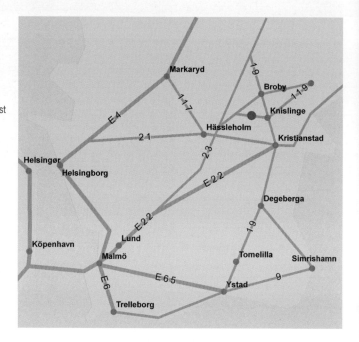

The non-profit Wanås Foundation is located 150 km from Malmö on an extensive property in the north of Skåne, the country's southern-most province. The grounds comprise a castle, a farm, large expanses of forest and a sculptural park.

The first fortress on the property was built in the 15th c. and, given its location on the northern border between Skåne and Småland, it played an important role in the wars Sweden and Denmark fought between the 16th and 18th c. The original fortress was destroyed by the Swedes during the Seven Years War (16th c.). In 1566 the current castle was built on the foundations of its predecessor and little has changed in its overall appearance since then. Following the Snapphane War (1675–79), Lena Sofia von Putbus undertook a com-plete restoration of the castle and, between 1767 and 1817, another renovation took place that amplified the lake, added two large grana-ries – which now serve as exhibition spaces for contemporary art – and laid out the tree-lined avenues. In 1901 half of the moat encir-cling the castle was covered and the lower part of the western sec-tion was constructed. Since then it has served as the private resi-dence of the Wachtmeister family, who manage both thefoundation and the farm. Since 1987, the park has housed an ever increasing col-lection of artworks by contemporary, international artists, charac-terised by the development of projects specifically related to art in nature.

In a succession of yearly exhibitions, more than 250 artists of differ-ent nationalities have worked here and exhibited their art – sculp-tures and installations – in the castle gardens and forest. "The exhibi-tion in 1996 included the participation of eight North-American artists." At this stage, the sculptors used materials and natural resources from the region in the creation of their projects. Between 1996 and 2001, the programme consisted of group shows, each fea-

Yoko Ono, *Wish trees for Wanås*,
1996–2011

turing the work of more than ten artists, most of them from
Scandinavian countries and North America. At the beginning of this
century, the approach shifted to inviting a smaller number of artists,
who have worked on increasingly challenging and ambitious projects.
This has entailed the participation of artists like Jenny Holzer,
Charlotte Gyllenhammar, Dan Graham, and Ann Hamilton. In 2002,
three large-scale installations were thus completed, whereas in 2004
only one invitation was extended to an artist – Maya Lin, who executed her first, large-scale installation measuring 500 m in length
(see photograph on the following page) in Europe. Wanås, however,
also likes to work with young or emerging artists. In 2006, invitations
went out to eight US artists, who have been asked to create site-
specific installations. Among others, Jeppe Hein in 2013, Carl F.
Reuterswärd in 2014, Nathalie Djurberg & Hans Berg in 2016.
In addition to the exhibitions in the old granaries and stable, the
foundation develops an educational programme to promote the
understanding, knowledge and study of the sculptural projects as well
as the latest tendencies in contemporary art. The programme offers
guided visits and provides workshops about the pieces in the sculptural park, designed to foster a dialogue between the public, the
experts and the artists.
The Wanås Educational Centre regularly collaborates with universities in the region and other Swedish cultural institutions. The programme Youth Projects gives high school students the opportunity to
realise temporary sculptures. Wånas reaches its apex of public activity between the months of May and August, when the plants are in
bloom and the forest attracts many visitors who spend their day
enjoying a picnic in nature. The harsh winters give way to a white
wonderland in which the sculptures take on a magical presence and
a walk among the enormous trees turns into a singular experience.

Right:
Dan Graham, *Two anamorphic surfaces*, 2000

Below:
Maya Lin, *11 Minute Line*, 2004

1 Igshaan Adams, *I Am You*, 2015
6 Marina Abramovic, *The Hunt Chair for Animal Spirits*, 1998
7 Miroslaw Balka, *Play-pit*, 2000
8 Gunilla Bandolin, *Pyramiden*, 1990
9 Janet Cardiff, *Wanås Walk*, 1998
10 Kari Cavén, *Cow Chapel*, 1993
11 Jacob Dahlgren, *Primary Structure*, 2011
12 Gloria Friedmann, *Stigma*, 1991
13 Marianne Lindberg De Geer, *I Am Thinking About Myself – Wanås*, 2003
14 Antony Gormley, *Together and Apart*, 2001
15 Dan Graham, *Two Different Anamorphic Surfaces*, 2000
16 Tue Greenfort, *Milk Heat*, 2009
17 Charlotte Gyllenhammar, *Vertigo*, 2002
A Ann Hamilton, *lignum*, 2002
18 Molly Haslund, *Swings – Coordination Model 2*, 2014
19 Molly Haslund, *Three double wall bars – Coordination Model 6*, 2014
20 Jeppe Hein, *Modified Social Bench#11*, 2012
21 Jene Highstein, *Grey Clam*, 1990+2001
22 Jene Highstein, *Horisontal*, 1990
23 Malin Holmberg, *I will stop loving you*, 2010
24 Jenny Holzer, *Wanås Wall*, 2002

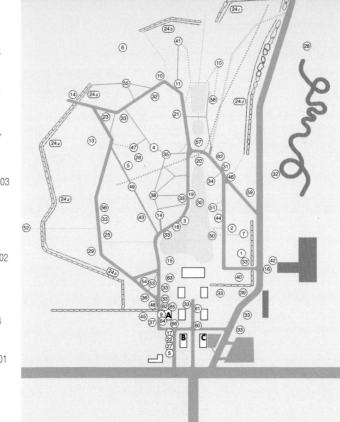

B Juan-Pedro Fabra Guemberena, Carl Michael von Hausswolff & Jan Håfström, *Graf Spee*, 2007–14
25 Henrik Håkansson, *The Reserve (001)*, 2009
26 Michael Joo, *Mediator*, 1998
27 Tadashi Kawamata, *Tree Hut Wanås*, 2014
28 Tadashi Kawamata, *View Tower Wanås*, 2014
29 Per Kirkeby, *Wanås*, 1994
30 Bernard Kirschenbaum, *Cable Arc*, 1987
31 Lone Larsen, *Altar I*, 1996
32 Maya Lin, *Eleven Minute Line*, 2004
B Mikael Lindahl, *Foundation of a Building*, 2010
33 Allan McCollum, *Parables*, 1998
34 Melissa Martin, *Dining Room*, 2006
35 Thom Merrick, *Whitney Outhouse of American Art*, 1996
36 Richard Nonas, *La Colonne Terminée III*, 1990–97
37 Yoko Ono, *Wish Trees for Wanås*, 1996–2011
38 Roxy Paine, *Impostor*, 1999
39 Roxy Paine, *Façade/Billboard*, 2010
40 Srinivasa Prasad, *In and Out*, 2012
41 Martin Puryear, *Meditation in a Beech Wood*, 1996
42 Andrea Ray, *Recall*, 2006
43 Carl Fredrik Reuterswärd, *Interlettre*, 1984–85

44 Raffael Rheinsberg, *Svart Linje*, 1988
45 Jason Rhoades, *Frigidaire (cold wind)*, 1996
46 Jorge Satorre, *The Erratic. Measuring Compensation*, 2009–10
47 Kathleen Schimert, *Untitled*, 1996
48 Sarah Schwartz, *Mother*, 1989
49 Sarah Schwartz, *Reflexion*, 1989
C Esther Shalev-Gerz, *Les inséparables*, 2000–08
50 Ann-Sofi Sidén, *Fideicommissum*, 2000
51 Pål Svensson, *Sprungen Ur*, 1996
52 Jan Svenungsson, *The Eighth Chimney*, 2007
53 Anne Thulin, *Double Dribble*, 2010
54 Hanne Tierney, *Love in the Afternoon*, 1996
55 Sissel Tolaas, *Terra Maximus*, 1989
56 Marianna Uutinen, *The hearts*, 1994
57 Stefan Wewerka, *The Little Bridge*, 1988
58 Robert Wilson, *A House for Edwin Denby*, 2000
59 Dan Wolgers, *Allt är förlåtet*, 1992–2010
60 Johan Celsing, *Monk*, 1998
61 Lars-Erik Falk, *Modul skulptur*, 1990
62 Carl Magnus, *Bon Voyage*, 1993
63 Richard Nonas, *Some Comfort*, 1998
64 Pål Svensson, *Enhet*, 1998
65 Sara Szyber, *Spring*, 1998
66 Karin Tyrefors, *Taurus*, 1998

Per Kirkeby, *Wanås,* 1994
Ann Hamilton, *Lignum,* 2002
Jenny Holzer, *Wanås Wall,* 2002

Antony Gormley, *Together and Apart*, 2001 (1998)
Miroslaw Balka, *Play-pit*, 2000

Since 1980
Ladonia: Nimis, Arx, Omfalos
Kullaberg Nature Reserve
Skåne
Tel. +46 42345354
lars.vilks@swipnet.se
www.ladonia.org
Dir. Lars Vilks

Opening hours: permanently
Admission: free
• Pets allowed
• Photographs allowed
• Guided tours (booking required)
• Publications: guidebook
• Library
• Bookstore
• Picnic area
• Car park

How to get there:
• By car: 35 km north of Helsingborg,
  on the north side of Kullaberg
  Reserve. Look for Himmelstorp, from
  there, 20 minutes walking (1.2 km)
• By bus: from Helsinborg
• Airport: Copenhagen

Ladonia is best described as a happening or performance that has lasted more than a quarter of a century, carried out by judiciary officials, police, bureaucrats, authorities, a cultural foundation dedicated to the destruction of art, and the general public, all incited by a professor and artist in collaboration with other citizens and a few international colleagues, the likes of Joseph Beuys and Christo. Ladonia is many things simultaneously. When asked, its founding father replies: it "is a nation, created in 1996. It is 1 km² in the nature reserve Kullaberg in the south of Sweden. The creator, the Swedish artist Lars Vilks, began in 1980 to work on a huge sculpture and a conceptual project. The pieces to be found are the enormous *Nimis*, made of wood, *Arx*, made of stone and concrete and *Omfalos* [...] is a rather small piece, 1.60 m of concrete and has been removed by the authorities. This sculpture is now in Moderna Museet in Stockholm. There is a memorial on the spot where *Omfalos* was placed, an 8 cm concrete small sculpture. Ladonia is to be found in a remote place, but can rather easily be reached. [...] More than 30,000 visitors every year."

Others, like professor Karnell of the Stockholm University, have also made their voices heard. In a mountainous and largely inaccessible place, full of precipices and caverns, where few people venture, *Nimis* (excess), 150 m long and 15 m tall, was created from driftwood and books nailed into the "walls." The open land belongs to the Gyllenstiernska Krapperup Foundation and has been declared a nature reserve. The county discovered *Nimis* in 1982 and, as it was considered a building, ordered its removal. Several judicial proceedings have followed since then, treated by Vilks much like a performance. In 1991, he erected the sizeable *Arx* (fortress) out of stones and cement. Just like the Viking rune stones, *Arx* is a book: officially published by the publisher Nya Doxa, it has 352 pages that cannot be turned. Readers can sit on the 352nd page and contemplate *Arx* in its entirety. The judge believed that if it was a book, then it was a matter of freedom of expression, which is protected by the constitution. He called a public hearing with both parties present, which Vilks announced to the press much like a theatrical event – several people called to reserve tickets. *Omfalos* was created in 1999; a reference to the *omphalos* at the Greek temple in Delphi, which represented the navel of Gea, the

Above: *Omfalos*

Below: *Nimis* and *Arx*

earth. The aforementioned foundation for the arts and culture report-ed Vilks for building the piece without their permission, demanding its removal as well as that of *Nimis* and *Arx*. The judge ruled that *Omfalos* had to be removed, but acquitted *Nimis* and *Arx*. The police declared that it would be impossible to determine the authorship of *Omfalos*, but the judge decided it had to be Vilks, thus dictating what was art and who its author was (he denied it) and changing the age-old pre-rogative of the art world itself. Appeal upon appeal followed, eventually reaching the Supreme Court. Meanwhile, the artwork was bought by the acclaimed Swedish artist Ernst Billgren. Despite prior warnings, the officials seriously damaged the piece during the removal process. Vilks asked the county council for permission to erect a memorial, and a monument not exceeding 8 cm in height was authorised. It was in-augurated in 2002 and established Sweden's legal height limit for public sculptures not requiring a permit. Vilks, now that a judge had declared him the author of the piece, sued the government for the damages. And Billgren, its owner, donated it to the country's most prestigious art institution, the Moderna Museet, which, contrary to the other state authorities, accepted it. One question remained: would *Omfalos* be exhibited or archived? For now, according to Cecilia Widenheim, the museum's curator, *Omfalos* "is being institutionalised [...], measured and weighed, photographed and classified, and put into a warehouse."

An example of what defines art, architecture, and landscape design; the boundaries between individual authorship and collective work; freedom of expression and property rights; aesthetics, ethics, and legal norms. An example of authorities as artistic material – the title of a book by Vilks; an expression of the post-modern approach to art and nature; a contribution to the debate about art as entertainment; the book as the safeguard of free art and culture; a critique of a sys-tem that defines the ownership of land and art; a triumph of imagina-tion over bureaucracy; ideas and more ideas. The objects are in them-selves interesting installation pieces, habitable sculptures or land art, as degradable as life, inseparable from the natural environment which inspired and created them. Ladonia is all that and more, questioning the concept of "citizenship" in a world connected by the internet with its ironic "declaration of independence" in 1996, which not only convinced the 4,000 Pakistanis who asked to be naturalised, but also a western graduate in fine arts, who wrote at length and in great detail about this "nation." It is truly a work of meta-art, possibly bril-liant and undoubtedly thought-provoking.

stockholm **moderna museet**

Since 1958
Moderna Museet
Skeppsholme
Exercisplan 4
Stockholm
Tel. +46 852023500
www.modernamuseet.se
Dir: Daniel Birnbum
Co.Dir: Ann-Sofi Norning

Opening hours:
Mon.: closed
Tue.: 10am–8pm
Wen.–Sun.: 10am–6pm

The Museum of Modern Art houses Sweden's national collection of the visual arts which proceed from the royal collection – 1792, the first public museum in Europe outside Italy. It is located on Skeppsholmen Island (Island of the Boats) in the centre of the city. Soon after its founding it had become one of the leading world institutions in its field. For example, with regard to sculpture, the Moderna Museet was the setting in 1966 for an enormous creation by Niki de Saint Phalle *Hon*, considered a pioneering work in environmental and installation art, and in 1968 it sponsored the reconstruction of Vladimir Tatlin's model for the *Monument to the Third International* (1920), a key work in contemporary art and architecture. Since 1994 the museum has a new building designed by the architect Rafael Moneo, who has always been dedicated to creating his work from the spirit of the place, and setting it in profound dialogue with its surroundings.

There are not many outdoor sculptures in and around the garden, but they constitute a small and yet splendid group. Dating to 1961, *The Four Elements* is one of Alexander Calder's monumental iron mobiles. *The Fantastic Paradise*, a sculptural group of 16 pieces, seven in iron and nine in fibreglass, is a joint work by Tinguely and Saint Phalle (1966). *The Lenin Monument* is by Bjorn Lovin, while Dan Graham's *Pavilion Sculpture II* (1984) and Rückriem's *Black Swedish Granite* (1981) are found along the route to the Östasiatika Museet. Per Kirkeby has a piece from 2000 on the dock facing Nybroviken.

The Man on the Temple is by Bjørn Nørgaard (1980), and *Louisa* is by Thomas Woodruff (1987). *The Monument to the Last Cigarette* (1975)

and the *Monumental Figure* (1927), by Swedish artists Erik Dietman and Christian Berg respectively, are situated close to the most admired sculptures of the collection: the *Déjeuner sur l'herbe group* (1962) by the Spaniard Pablo Picasso.

Niki de Saint Phalle, *Le Paradis fantastique*, 1966
Yayoi Kusama, *Ascension of Polka Dots on the Trees*, 2016, installation view
Pablo Picasso, *Déjeuner sur l'herbe*, sculptural group by Carl Nesjar, 1964–66

Since 1994
Umedalen Skulptur
Aktrisgränd 34   90364 Umeå
Tel. +46 90744990
galleri@gsa.se
www.gsa.se
Dirs. Stefan Andersson and Sara
Sandström Nilsson

Opening hours: permanently
Admission: free
• Access for disabled
• Pets allowed
• Photographs allowed
• Guided tours (booking required)
• Exhibition hall with changing shows
• Publications: leaflet, catalogue

Stefan Andersson and Sara Sandström are the owners of a contemporary art gallery, carrying both their surnames, founded in 1980, which has since grown to become one of the most important galleries of its kind in Sweden. They have two gallery spaces, the largest gallery space in Stockholm, and the gallery space in Umeå, which is situated in a former hospital compound, owned by a local real estate developer, Balticgruppen, Umeå. For 20 years, From 1994 to 2014, the gallery has cooperated with Balticgruppen, to build a sculpture park in the compound. Over the years, they have organised sculpture exhibitions in the hospital park, every summer from 1994 to 2000 and every other year from 2002 to 2014. Balticgruppen have through the years purchased 45 sculptures, which form one of the largest sculpture parks in Europe, with works by Louise Bourgeois, Tony Cragg, Antony Gormley, Cristina Iglesias, and many others. The park is open 24/7 all year round, with free admission, and is maintained by Galleri Andersson Sandström and owned by Balticgruppen, Umeå.

• Coffe shop
• Restaurant
• Picnic area
• Car park

How to get there:
• By car, bus and train
• Airport: Umeå

Some of the artists and art works in the permanent collection:
Bård Breivik, *Untitled*, 2001   Miroslaw Balka, *30x60x10, 250x1958x795, 30x60x10, 250x521x174*, 1996   Kari Cavén, *Skoggsunge*, 2002   Tony Cragg, *Stevenson (Early forms)*, 1999; *Not Yet Titled*, 2003   Cristos Gianakos, *Beamwalk*, 1996   Antony Gormley, *Still Running*, 1990–93; *Clearing II*, 2004   Carina Gunnars, *Untitled*, 1994   Claes Hake, *Five stone Bows*, 1995   Anish Kapoor, *Pillar of light*, 1991   Clay Ketter, *Homestead*, 2004   Richard Nonas, *55 meter long double-line of doublebolders*   Roland Persson, *Untitled*, 1998   Anna Renström, *Alliansring*, 2000   Buky Schwartz, *Forest hill*, 1997   Anna Steake, *Larger than life*, 2002

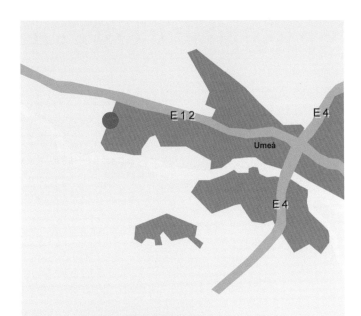

The Art Guys, *Love Song for Umeå: Banner Work #7*, 2002
Louise Bourgeois, *Eye Benches II*, 1996–97

Hans Castorp left Hamburg, his hometown, to keep his cousin company during a 3-week stay at the Berghof Sanitarium, at the foot of the Magic Mountain, Zauberberg. Enthralled, Hans stayed on for seven years. Thomas Mann, like his character and other geniuses, was fascinated by the Alps: Turner painted mountains, snowstorms, and sunshine; Nietzsche made Zarathustra into a Superman, who returns to his human state upon descending; Jung wrote "this is it, my world [...] the secret, where one can be without having to say anything"; Percy Shelley wrote verses and Hesse had the Great Spirit come to humanity here, amidst "this silent and cold grandeur." The two mountain massifs, the north-west Jura and the Alps, which cover 75% of the territory, are divided by a central plateau with many lakes, Mittelland, home to 70% of the population. The Alps are covered with thick mantles of snow and about 2,000 m² of glaciers with crests as high as 4,000 m. Cultivated land and pastures end at 1,500 m, where the thick conifer forests begin – fir, silver fir, larch, cembran pine. The colourful Alpine meadows, dotted with blueberries, martagon lilies, edelweiss, purple gentian, and annunciation lilies, grow at 2,200 m. The only thing surviving at 3,000 m is the mineral kingdom, lichen, and moss. It is a unique and unpredictable Alpine climate, cold up high – -40°C in the Jura – and continental in the valleys below, with abundant rain and snowfall and dramatic temperature changes. The valleys are human terrain, an idyllic landscape of pastures, meadows and wooden country houses surrounded by grandiose, majestic nature.

Germany, France, and Italy have all influenced Switzerland and its languages. During the 2nd c. BC the Helvetians settled here. Augusta Raurica (near Basel, pop. 180,000) was founded after the Roman conquest (58 BC). Nordic Burgundians and Alamanni tribes came between the 2nd–4th c., followed by the Franks in 530. Irish monks on evangelical missions created monasteries like Saint Gall. Germania's rule lasted from 1032 until 1291, when three cantons established the Helvetic Confederation. During the 16th c., the Reformation divided the population into Calvinists and Catholics. Since 1674 Switzerland has been neutral; it became a federal state in 1848. Now comprised of 26 cantons, Switzerland is a financial centre famous for its banking industry, a refuge for exiles, home to several international organisations, a strong economy with a high standard of living, a society with an erudite tradition, an art market – Basel Art Fair, galleries – and collectors, especially in the private sector, and a direct democracy with active citizens and municipalities. In 1992, the country declined to join the EU.

Tradition and innovation live side by side here. The medieval, covered, wooden bridges – like the one in Lucerne, based on an unusually light and resistant design by the brothers Grubenmann (1760–70) – are particularly noteworthy. Sculpture reached a high point during the 19th c., when it played a central role in the new urban design of public spaces. Vincenzo Vela used naturalism in his defense of the oppressed, and Herman Obrist's modernism sought

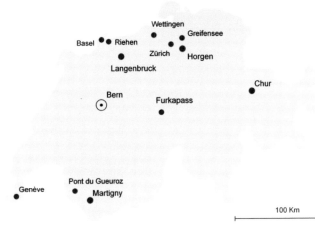

41,290 km², 8.3 million inhabitants

Wettingen

Greifensee

Basel • • Riehen

Zürich

Horgen

Langenbruck

Chur

Bern
⊙

Furkapass

Genève

Pont du Gueuroz
• Martigny

100 Km

Opposite page:
Salginatobel Bridge, 1932, Robert Maillart

Below:
Kienast Vogt, Swiss Re (Bank Vontobel), Zurich, 1995

to unite art and nature in his studies of the spiral. In 1916 Hugo Ball opened the Café Voltaire, which would serve as a stage for the Zurich Dadaists: Tristan Tzara, Jean Arp, Huelsenbeck, Janco, Hans Richter, Sophie Taeuber-Arp. The Arps later moved abroad, as did Paul Klee, Le Corbusier, Johannes Itten (Bauhaus), Giacometti – one of the most significant sculptors of the mid-20th c. – and Meret Oppenheim, an active and popular member of the Parisian surrealists in the 1920s. Max Bill worked here, an architect and sculptor who focused on mathematically-based minimalist forms that later inspired the concrete art of Lohse. During the 1950s–60s, the cosmopolitan Jean Tinguely combined kinetic art with performance and waste or junk art at museums in Freiburg and Basel. The protagonists of the 1960s–70s: Bernhard Luginbuhl and the Fluxus members, Andre Thomkins and Karl Gestner; in the 1980s, Markus Raetz and John Armleder; and in the 1990s, Thomas Hirschhorn.

A nature with such imposing spaces required an equally daring human spirit in return, leading to the design and construction of dams – Grand Dixence and Mauvoisin, in the Valais; roads – Sustenstrasse, 1938; railway viaducts – Wiessen, near Davos; and, yet again, bridges: Robert Maillart revolutionised the use of reinforced concrete, endowing it with a new aesthetic and form – the elegant bridge of Salginatobel, Schiers 1929. In addition to the traditional parks in Geneva or the Civic Park in Lugano, close attention has been paid to the study and preservation of structures and the design of new landscapes. Descombes created public parks in Laney, Geneva (1986), and Freiburg (1999) and the 35 km circuit *La Voie Suisse* around the Uri Lake (1990). Dieter Kienast expressed his ideas through site-specific designs and rigorous, minimal geometric compositions that unite nature and culture – *Et in Arcadia ego*, Uetliberg 1989; two projects in Chur; *Mimesis*, Greifensee 1995; others in Appenzell, Basel, Riehen, Zurich; in Germany (Frankfurt, Erfurt, Karlsruhe, Berlin, Magdeburg) and France. His disciple Udo Weilacher has selected more than 450 Swiss gardens and landscapes from the 12th to the 21st c. – see bibliography. All of this explains why the country has so few sculptural parks. There are some exceptions to this rule, such as the Furka art project; the Bex outdoor sculpture triennial established in 1981; the Village Plaza of the CS Crédit Suisse in Horgen by Karavan (1994); the Atelier Amden project established in 1999 and the International Land Art Festival in Grindelwald, where temporary pieces are created from natural materials.

Since 2000
Stiftung Sculpture at Schoenthal
Schoenthalstrase 158
CH–4438 Langenbruck
Tel. +41 (0)617067676
mail@schoenthal.ch
www.schoenthal.ch

Opening hours:
Fri.: 2pm–5pm
Sat., Sun. and holidays: 11am–6pm
Admission: fee charged
• Exhibition halls with changing shows
• Publications
• Car park, limited space available

How to get there:
• By car: half an hour from Basel
• By bus: from Langenbruck

Accommodation:
  Bed and Breakfast in Schoenthal's
  Guest House or in hotels in
  Langenbruck

Sculpture at Schoenthal coexists in dialogue with the tranquil Alpine landscape of the Jura region and the Romanesque art of a former monastery. A little over 800 years ago, the church of the Benedictine monastery, with its now-famous facade, was consecrated. Closed by the Reformation in the 16th c. and sold by Basel to a private owner in the 19th c., it has been a protected historic building since 1967. The Sculpture at Schoenthal project was set up in 2000, with a private initiative after the restoration of the complex.
Access to the 30 works on permanent display is by footpaths, and among the international artists featured are Richard Long, David Nash, Tony Cragg Nicola Hicks, Ian Hamilton Finlay, Ulrich Rückriem, Ilan Averbuch, Nigel Hall, William Pye, Hamish Black, Not Vital and Swiss artists such as Roman Signer or Peter Kamm. Temporary exhibitions share the space with classes, lectures or residences.

Opposite page:
Nicola Hicks, *Minotauro*, 2003

Above:
Nigel Hall, *Soglio*, 1994

Below:
Ulrich Rückriem, *Tempel*, 1987

Fondation Pierre Gianadda
rue du Forum 59   1920 Martigny
Tel. +41 (0)277223978
info@gianadda.ch
www.gianadda.ch

Opening hours: permanently
Admission: fee charged
• Access for disabled
• Guided tours
• Exhibition halls with changing shows
• Educational programmes
• Bookstore and boutique
• Coffee shop
• Restaurant
• Picnic area
• Car park

How to get there:
• By car: highway A9 from Montreux or
  from Sion, road 21 from Grand Saint
  Bernard tunnel
• By bus: CFF station (bus stop at
  Fondation Pierre Gianadda)
• By train: Martigny-Orsières (Martigny-
  Bourg Station). Panoramic train
  Chamonix-Mont Blanc-Châtelard-
  Martigny (1 h 45). From Paris (Lyon
  Station): Lausanne (TGV)–Martigny (5h)

Accommodation:
  Hotel du Rhône, Tel. +41 (0)27722224
  (closed from 15 Nov.–15 Dec.)

Tucked in between natural forests and terraced hillsides with vine-yards is the Alpine town of Martigny, 75 km from Aosta in Italy, via the Grand-St-Bernard Pass, and 40 km from Chamonix in France. Set against a scenic backdrop of pristinely white snow in the winter and bright greens and flowering plants in the spring, is the Pierre Gianadda Foundation. Its public spaces feature modern sculptures, such as *Tige Martigny* by Bernhard Luginbuhl (1957–99), as well as a cultural complex that includes a sculpture park, temporary sculpture and other visual arts exhibitions, the Gallo-Roman Museum, the Automobile Museum, concerts, etc.

Although its landmark is the round, medieval tower of La Batiaz, the city also holds memories of the Roman era – such as a 74 × 61.7 m

amphitheater for 5,000 spectators – one of the smallest built under Roman rule, some well-preserved thermal baths and drainage sys-tems, and a Mithraeum – and of the flourishing bourgeoisie of the 17th c., as can be seen in the peaceful and picturesque Rue du Bourg. The modern city is built on the shores of the Dranse River, just before it flows into the Rhône, and the outskirts still show the influ-ence of last century's rationalist movement. Towards the north, en route to Salvan, the bridge of Gueuroz (1932), a delicate design in reinforced concrete by Alexandre Sarrasin, crosses the narrow pass of Trient at an altitude of 187 m, demonstrating the confluence of art and engineering and expressing a subtle but effective dialogue between the object and nature that is both mathematical and beautiful.

In the spring of 1976, the industrialist Leonard Giannada discovered the remains of an ancient Gallo-Roman temple, the oldest of its kind in Switzerland. Shortly thereafter, his youngest brother, Pierre, with whom he was very close, died in an aviation accident. He decided to establish a cultural centre under a foundation bearing his brother's name, dedicated to archaeology, the arts, modern and contemporary music, and culture. The centre, built upon the vestiges of an ancient temple dedicated to Mercury, was inaugurated in 1978.

The umbrous gardens are home to the archaeological remains of thermal baths and the wall of a temenos set amidst trees and pools of water. In this idyllic setting are several permanent artworks by illustrious modern artists, making these gardens a veritable tour through

Opposite page:
Foundation terrace and archeological remains

Above:
Alexander Calder, *untitled mobile*, 1965

the history of 20th c. sculpture — see list on p. 205. The pieces are by artists of international renown, from Maillol to Vernet and Chillida. Another unique spot is the "Chagall Court," home to a monumental mosaic commissioned by Ira Kostelitz in 1954, and moved here, into its own pavilion, in 2003.

In addition to the works featured on these pages, the collection also includes pieces such as a *Reclining Figure* (1982) in bronze by Henry Moore and another bronze, *Le Sein* (1965), by César. Then there is *Roue Orifamme*, a 1962 steel sculpture by Jean Arp, Dubuffet's *Element of Contortionist Architecture V*, Segal's *Woman with Sunglasses on Park Bench* and Rodin's *Meditation with Arms*. One of the interior halls is home to a permanent exhibition of the Collection Louis et Evelyn Franck, which includes the work of Cezanne, Van Gogh, James

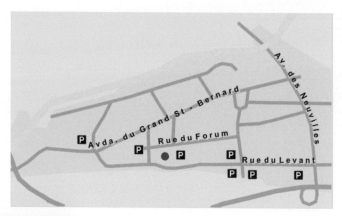

Constantin Brâncuși, *Le grand coq,*
1949
Alicia Peñalba, *Le grand double,* 1979

Ensor, Picasso, and Van Dongen. The temporary exhibitions of modern and contemporary art have long been a mainstay of the institution, adding up to about 100 editions since 1980. They take place three to four times a year and have featured celebrated artists such as Goya, Picasso, Klee, Gauguin, Schiele, Manet, Degas, Braque, Kandinsky, Dufy, Modigliani, Renoir, Matisse, Giacometti, and Cartier-Bresson. The exhibitions also cover other subject matter: The classical music concerts have brought an equally impressive roster of international talent to the auditorium, including Menuhin, Isaac Stern, Rostropovitch, Ashkenazy, Zukerman, Raimondi, Cecilia Bartoli, Barenboim.

Above:
View of the sculpture park: the Foundation building in the centre, and the *Reclining figure* by Henry Moore, 1982

Right:
Joan Miró, *Tête*, 1974–85

Artists at the permanent sculpture park:
Arman (Armand Fernández) Jean Arp Max Bill Émil-Antoine Bourdelle
Constantin Brâncuși Pol Bu Alexander Calder César (César Baldaccini)
Marc Chagall Eduardo Chillida Roland Cognet Niki de Saint Phalle Dubach
Jean Dubuffet Elisheva Engel Hans Erni Max Ernst Robert Indiana
Jean Epoustéguy Willem de Kooning Lalanne Aristide Maillol Marino Marini
Etienne Martin Joan Miró Henry Moore Alicia Peñalba Antoine Poncet Jean
Pierre Raynavel Henry Laurens Germaine Richier Auguste Rodin Rouiller
George Segal Stahly Szafran Tapies Tommasini Bernar Venet

united kingdom

A few thousand years ago, the Thames was a tributary of the Rhine and modern-day Britain the W part of the N European plain. Towards the end of the last Ice Age, rising sea levels created the British Isles.

The N and W highlands – Scotland and Wales – consist of plains and low mountains, whereas the E and SE lowlands – England – are marked by gentle, rolling hills. Ulster, a portion of neighbouring Ireland, and several other islands complete the British territory. The western winds off the Atlantic and the Gulf Stream contribute to the humid climate, cloudy skies, fogs, mists, little sunshine, changeable weather, abundant rainfall – strong in the mountains, more moderate in the SE – and consistent, mildly cool temperatures. The landscape is full of contrasts: a highly urban population (large conurbations with millions of inhabitants) and sparsely populated rural areas.

Only 5% of the population lives in the countryside, which is unsuitable for cultivation and largely unproductive (18%). Pastures and meadows predominate (46%), agriculture covers 27% and forests, decimated over centuries, now only account for 10% of the land.

The megaliths at Avebury (4000 BC) and the extraordinary Stonehenge (2900–1500 BC) were the original nexus between man and cosmos. Celtic tribes settled here around 700 BC. Claudius conquered the island (44 BC). The Roman Empire's influence reached its apex with Hadrian's Wall (122). Starting in 407, invading Angles, Saxons, Vikings, and Danes ushered in five centuries of small warring kingdoms and Christianisation. The Norman Conquest led by William I in 1066 instilled a sense of national unity for the first time, expressed by the *Great Domesday Book* (1086). Gothic art and royal hunting forests flourished under the many royal dynasties succeeding William I. During the 16th c., colonial expansion began under Elizabeth I. Cromwell's political revolution (1649) and Newton's scientific revolution lasted throughout parliamentary rule, fueling an interest in natural science and technology that would drive the Industrial Revolution (1760), its progress, coal mines, exploitation of the earth, factories, working-class masses, iron architecture, and engineering and maritime expansion. Romanticism emerged as a response, exalting the individual and, with Burke, establishing new aesthetic categories for what constitutes the beautiful and the sublime in nature, exemplified by the Lake District, home and beloved landscape of poets – Wordsworth, Coleridge, Southey –, theorists and critics – John Ruskin, 19th c. – and writers and artists – Beatrix Potter, Schwitters, 20th c. – or by Constable's paintings of rural Suffolk and Turner's renditions of natural, urban, and industrial landscapes.

The English garden developed in the early 18th c. Whereas the French garden used strict symmetry and straight lines, the English variety attempted to recreate a wild, "natural" nature through informality and an emphasis on trees and plants rather than structures, thus creating vistas akin to landscape painting. Gardeners, landscape designers, architects, and theorists gave birth to a myriad of such gardens and books about this style, which garnered immediate, international acclaim. Initiated by Switzer and Capability Brown, it turned pictur-

243,305 km², 65.1 million inhabitants, member of the European Union since 1973. In 2016, 52% voted to leave

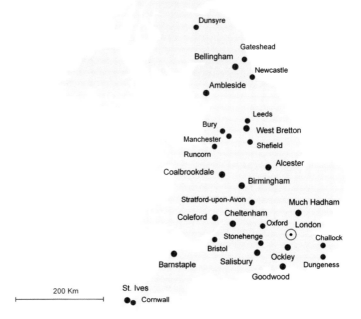

Dunsyre

Gateshead

Bellingham

Newcastle

Ambleside

Leeds

Bury

West Bretton

Manchester

Shefield

Runcorn

Alcester

Coalbrookdale

Birmingham

Stratford-upon-Avon

Much Hadham

Coleford

Cheltenham

Oxford   London

Stonehenge

Challock

Bristol

Salisbury

Ockley

Barnstaple

Dungeness

Goodwood

St. Ives

200 Km

Cornwall

Pitmedden Garden, 23 km north of Aberdeen, A. Seton, 17th–18th c.
Stowe Gardens, Chiltern Hills, Buckinghamshire, Bridgeman since 1714; William Kent; Capability Brown, Head Gardener since 1741
Blenheim, Oxfordshire, Bridgeman since 1709, Capability Brown (altered)
Kensington Gardens, London, with interventions by Bridgeman, 18th c.
Stourhead, Wiltshire, near Salisbury and Stonhenge, 1743, H. Hoar, the first to avoid symmetry and geometrical forms
Hampton Court Gardens, London: since 1660, Maze (1690); Great Vine by Capability Brown (1768)
Cornwall Corniche, Truro, near St Ives: Trewithen, 18th c.
Trelissick Garden, 1750–1825
Chatsworth, Derbyshire, since 1696, Capability Brown 18th c., Paxton is Head since 1826
Victoria Park, Hackney, London, 1842, by Pennethorne, the first public park
Kew Gardens, London: Royal Botanic Garden, Orangerie, pagoda, templetes,1756–61, by Chambers; Palm House by Burton, 1848

esque under Price and Knight, evolved into the Victorian Garden with Repton and the publisher Loudon and culminated with Paxton: Chatsworth and Crystal Palace (1850) marked an entire international era. During the Victorian Age (1837–1901), the dramatic rise of capitalism was accompanied by middle-class rule, new proletarian urban centres, Marx and *Das Kapital*, the first public parks, social legislation (1871), Howard's garden-cities (1898) and Gertude Jekyll's gardens in the early 20th c.

The empire was then the world's foremost power, covering a quarter of the earth. Victory in World War I was followed by the empire's steady decline. Epstein's bronze work was the only notable contribution to sculpture at the time. In 1933, *Unit One* stepped onto the scene with abstract art pioneers like Ben Nicholson and his *white reliefs*, Barbara Hepworth, Henry Moore and his organic forms – first in stone, later in bronze – inspired by Sumerian and Mexican primitivism and surrealism. Again victorious in World War II, Britain continued the process of decolonialisation. As the empire came to an end, New Towns were created at home, and Geoffrey Jellicoe spearheaded landscape design. The anthropomorphic sculpture of Butler and Armitage and Lynn Chadwick's schematic work defined the 1950s. The 1960s began with large-scale iron pieces and walking spaces by Anthony Caro, followed by the singular work of Finlay and concluding with the new and radically different land art of Richard Long and others, including Andy Goldsworthy and Hamish Fulton. In 1981, the ICA in London showcased the New British Sculpture of Woodrow, Julian Opie, Tony Cragg, Richard Deacon, Anish Kapoor (three Turner Prize winners, along with Antony Gormley and his installations), all cosmopolitan artists of the 21st c.

Singing, Ringing Tree

2007, Tonkin Liu Near Burnley, Lancashire, 21 miles (34 km) north of Manchester. Located on a hill overlooking Burnley, it is a "musical sculpture." As the wind passes through the different lengths of pipe, it plays different chords. Each time the visitors sit under the tree, looking out through the wind, they will hear a different song. The work was "named as one of the 21 landmarks of 21st c. Britain, voted by the readers of The Independent News and BA's High Life magazine" and won a RIBA National Award.

The studio Tonkin Liu practices art, architecture, landscape, etc. and as of 2016 has won seven RIBA Awards.

Ian Hamilton Finlay

Scottish poet, sculptor, gardener and editor, whose concrete poetry – in which the typography and lay-out of the page contribute to the overall meaning – led him to work with other media, such as stone, wood, ceramics, and even neon tubes. In 1967 he moved to Stony Path with his wife Sue, a farm in "Strathclyde, the infernal region," as he calls it, far removed from all tourist activity. They created their own, private garden where, surrounded by diverse flora, 275 artworks have been arranged within the space: poetry objects, inscriptions of phrases that range from enigmatic, ironic, and clearly political, neo-classical architectural elements, Corinthian capitals, obelisks, pyramids, little bridges, sun dials, columns, small fountains, etc. Little Sparta is an entity comprised of many parts, a total work of art, in which the whole is so much more than its individual parts. Its influences can be traced back to the Renaissance Bomarzo of Prince Orsini (see p. 116);

it is a poetic garden full of metaphors, global in character, moral and philosophical in its assessment of the French Revolution and the pre-Socratic visions of nature. Finlay uses the garden to explore the complex relationship between wild nature and societal change, between the world and the capacity of the written word to express it. In short, he moves beyond the generally "respectful" placement of sculptures in natural surroundings. It is a complete discourse born from words, sculpture and an altered and molded natural environment. He has created more than 50 similar installations in the United States, continental Europe and Great Britain, Perth, Glasgow, Borough of Luton, Dudley, Durham, London. Little Sparta, Stony Path, Dunsyre nr. Lanark, ML11 8NG, Scotland, 32 km SW of Edinburgh on the A702, Jun.–Sept., Wed., Fri. & Sun.: 2.30am–5pm Tel. +44 (0)1556640244 info@littlesparta.co.uk www.littlesparta.co.uk

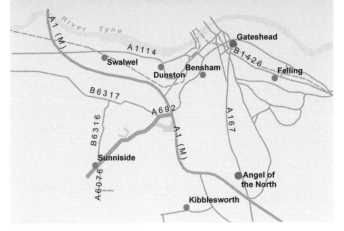

Gateshead

In order to save the area from post-industrial decline, cultural government entities have founded centres for contemporary art and established public art programmes. These have supported the creation of 32 site-specific works throughout the sculptural park along the Tyne by international artists like Gormley (see p. 212), Deacon, Goldsworthy and British artists like Colin Rose and Richard Harris. www.gateshead.gov.uk

Derek Jarman's garden
Prospect Cottage, Dungeness, Kent

This is the title of a highly personal book in which this singular British artist, filmmaker, gardener, and writer expresses his thoughts about his garden, intimate and exceptional in every respect, from the place – a wasteland facing an enormous nuclear plant on the seashore – to the simple fishing house built in 1900, the golden summer light and the tempestuous grey of the other seasons, the extremely sophisticated formal design – the geometric facade out front, the informal back of the house next to the apparently trivial pebbles and small plant and flower thickets, stones in a circle, sculptures made out of fence posts, rusty iron washed onto the shore, and abandoned gardening tools, poppies, lavender, roses, gigantic cabbages, gorse, fennel, lichen, peas, and vegetables. It is an artwork in and of itself, a personal journal that mirrors real life – plants fighting against the wind, Jarman against disease, glorious in its life, melancholy when faced with the fleeting – is there

nothing but mortality? Fragile and renewed each spring, as subtle as a profound poem, a place one does not want to speak about too loudly out of fear that the masses will discover and overrun it. Get lost in the description (read his book), note that there is no lawn – "it goes against nature" he wrote – and that the same harvest yields "beans, cauliflower and cabbage along with peonies and delphinias." He wrote: "Some gardens are paradise. Mine is one of them." The desolate beauty of this radical, living, changing, transitory, isolated, and barely whispered about artwork should be the common, global outcry that at the dawn of this millennium only art created by those working on the margin can save us from old religious fundamentalism and new media dictatorships, consumerism and increasing poverty and the never-ending succession of happy events while the earth is being wounded and humanism decimated. Before dying of AIDS, Jarman only wanted to visit one other garden, Monet's in Giverny.

Irwell Sculpture Trail

Stretching from Salford Quays through Bury into Rossendale and up to the Pennines above Bacup is a 45-km trail with more than 20 sculptures, created since 1997 as part of a programme designed to revitalise the area. Some of the work is by international artists – Ulrich Rückriem in Outwood Colliery, Ringley Road; Michael Farrell in Bacup; Lawrence Weiner; others by British artists like Chris Drury.
Tel.: +44 (0)01612535891
www.irwellsculpturetrail.co.uk

Norton Priory Runcorn

Norton Priory dates back to the 13th c. Located 30 minutes from Manchester by car on the M56, this old monastery now features an archaeological area, a rose garden in the Walled Garden and a sculpture trail with more than twenty sculptures placed within a 15-ha area. The pieces are located at sites throughout the forest chosen by each individual artist. Most of them, like Diane Garvin or Colin Rose, are English. Norton Priory Museum and Gardens, Tudor Road, Manor Park, Runcorn, Cheshire, WA7 1SX Tel.: +44(0)1928569895

Since 1977
Grizedale Forest
Grizedale, Hawkshead, Ambleside
Cumbria, UK LA 22 0QJ
Tel. +44 (0) 3000674495
grizedale@forestry.gsi.gov.uk
www.forestry.gov.uk/grizedale
www.grizedalesculpture.org
www.grizedale.org
Forest Director: Dave Lowe
Arts Development Curator:
Hayley Skipper

Opening hours:
Summer: 10am–5pm
Winter: 10am–4pm
Admission: free
• Access for the disabled
• Pets allowed
• Photographs allowed
• Guided tours
• Educational programmes
• Publications: leaflet, guidemap, books
• Gift shop with affordable artworks and
  some books
• Coffee shop & Snacks
• Picnic area
• Car park: fee charged

How to get there:
• By car: follow Grizedale signs from
  Hawshead / Ambleside or from A590
  M6 motorway to Barrow in Furness
  road
• By bus: infrequent bus / ferry service
  from Windermere
• By train: Windermere Station
• Airport: Manchester

Accommodation & Eating out:
  A tourist area with a wide range of
  hotels, guest houses, B&B, hostels,
  youth hostels, farm cottages, public
  house / Inn's, holiday lets, campsites,
  caravan sites, etc. available in
  Grizedale, Ambleside, Hawkshead,
  Satterthwhite, Coniston, Windermere
  See www.ambleside.u-k.org
  www.cumbria-the-lake-district.co.uk

Grizedale Forest lies in the heart of the Lake District National Park. The surrounding landscape formed by volcanic and glacial activity is celebrated for its natural beauty and gave birth to British Romanticism, a movement of the 18th and 19th c. that rediscovered and passionately exalted nature, heavily influencing how we view both art and nature in the 21st c.

The 2,500-ha forest has beautiful panoramic vistas, waymarked trails, a wide range of outdoor activities, and a collection of around 40 permanent sculptures throughout the forest, hidden deep amongst the trees. The contemporary sculpture created in the forest has roots in the land art movement. In 1968, pioneering forester Bill Grant returned from the US inspired by the combination of art and landscape seen there. Initially focused on the performing arts in the Theatre in the Forest, in 1977 the sculpture programme in Grizedale Forest was founded, the UK's first forest for sculpture, where artists could work directly with the landscape. Historically artists in residence lived and worked for several months as they created temporary and permanent sculpture. Founding principles centred on the forest as a site of production and inspiration, many sculptures being site-specific in nature and artists often sourcing materials and subject matter from the forest itself. Creators of the earliest sculptures included David Nash, and Richard Harris' *Quarry Structure 1977* can still be visited. Made from oak timber hand-cut from windfall trees and slate remnants from the old walled field system, it appears as an extension of this landscape in which wood and stone predominate.

Sculptures constructed from natural materials were always intended to go back to the land, to melt away as other sculptors created new

art for the forest. Nash and Harris were followed by around 90 British and international artists who created many sculptures expressing environmental themes, the heritage of the land and people's relationship with the natural world.

Taking a Wall for a Walk (1990) by Goldsworthy weaves in and out of a line of larch trees, an observation of the nature of the traditional drystone walls that can be seen climbing over the Cumbrian fells and valleys. Sited in 2012, *Concrete Country* by Lucy Tomlins introduces a manufactured construction material into the natural environment in the form of an iconic symbol of the English countryside. Keir Smith was one of the earliest sculptors to work here. Now, two pieces bequeathed after his death, *Last Rays of an English Rose* (1986/87), sited in 2009, and *A Flower in Flower* (1999), sited in 2014, are a legacy of his long relationship with the forest.

Grizedale Forest is cared for by Forestry Commission England and managed sustainably for people, wildlife and timber. This beautiful place is for people to explore and become immersed in the natural world and to view sculpture responding to this unique location. It harbours memories that go beyond history and into the realm of legend. The name comes from Old Norse and means "valley of the pigs." Deforestation for grazing land in the 11th c. and the industrial revolution saw large swathes of the forest cleared. Regeneration began with 70,000 oaks and 1.5 million European larch and other species planted during the 19th c. The use of Grizedale Hall as a prisoner of war camp during World War II was dramatised in the film *The One That Got Away*. Future commissions planned for Grizedale Forest are expected to respond to this unique heritage.

Opposite page:
Lucy Tomlins, *Concrete Country*, 2012

Below, left to right:
Alannah Robins, *Lady of the Water*, 1995
Richard Harris, *Quarry Structure*, 1977

angel of the north

Since 1998
Team Valley, Gateshead
Between A1 motorway and A167 road

Here art makes a no-place of the end of the 20th c. – a highway with some 100,000 vehicles a day – into a landscape with a new identity. The *Angel of the North* is a visual and emotional landmark at the southern entrance to Tyneside, 5 km from Gateshead, and on the edge of the Great Forest of the North.

This gigantic winged work, 20 m high and with a 53 m wingspan, is made of steel with copper so as to resist the wear of the climate. Its author, Antony Gormley, says of it: "The hilltop site is important and has the feeling of being a megalithic mound. When you think of the mining that was done underneath the site, there is a poetic resonance […] The face will not have individual features. The effect of the piece is in the alertness, the awareness of space, and the gesture of the wings – they are not flat, they're about 3.5 degrees forward and give a sense of embrace."

Since 1997
Broomhill Art Hotel & Sculpture Gardens
Muddiford, Barnstaple
Devon EX31 4EX
Tel. +44 (0)1271850262
info@broomhillart.co.uk
www.broomhillart.co.uk
Dir. Rinus van de Sande

Opening hours:
Jan.–Dec.: Wed.–Sun.: 11am–4pm
Jul.–Aug.: Mon.–Sun.: 11am–4pm
20 Dec.–15 Jan.: closed
Admission:
Gallery: free
Sculpture gardens: fee charged
• Access for the disabled
• Pets allowed
• Photographs allowed
• Exhibition hall
• Educational programmes
• Publications
• Bookstore
• Coffee shop
• Restaurant
• Car park

How to get there:
• By car: from Barnstaple take B3230
  to Ilfracombe
• By bus: no. 30 from Barnstaple to
  Lynton
• By train: Barnstaple
• By taxi
• Airport: Exeter or Bristol

Accommodation:
  Broomhill Art Hotel (see address
  above)

Broomhill is located in a valley surrounded by large forests, and consists of three parts; a sculpture garden, a commercial gallery of contemporary art, and a hotel-restaurant.

The four hectares of the once-beautiful but abandoned gardens became the Broomhill Sculpture Gardens, with some 300 sculptures by some 60 artists, under the private initiative of the Van de Sande family, who came here in 1997 from Holland, where they were art dealers. The wooded garden, with birds, a stream, and a trout pond, is particularly splendid in the spring, when bellflowers, daffodils, yellow roses, azaleas, and other flowers bloom.

The sculptures are sited in these surroundings through the search for balance between art and nature. To reach them, visitors walk among serpentine paths between the denser areas of the forest and small fields, between shaded and luminous spaces.

Giles Penny, *Flat Man*, 1997

None of the pieces are on permanent exhibit; rather they change continuously, so that the park is habitually found in renovation. This is because all the works are for sale. They are both figurative and abstract, and made with a diversity of materials such as iron, bronze, and wood. Their authors are mainly lesser-known British figures.

In addition to the park, there is a hall for exhibiting small-format works, drawings and paintings by the different artists related to Broomhill.

The hotel, in a Victorian style, offers seven rooms and a decoration that combines antiquities with pieces from the private collection of contemporary art.

Broomhill Foundation host the NSP, a national yearly sculpture competition for emerging artists. Since 2001, it opens June to next May and changes every year.

Since 1994
Kielder Art and Architecture
Kielder Water and Forest Park
Bellingham, Northumberland, NE 48 28Q
www.kielderartandarchitecture.com
www.visitkielder.co
www.kielderobservatory.org
Curator: Peter Sharpe

Opening hours: permanently
Admisssion: free
• Visitors Centres: Leaplish Waterside
  Park, Tower Knowe, Kielder Castle
• Access for the disabled
• Pets allowed
• Photogrphs allowed
• Itineraries
• Guided tour
• Publications
• Coffee shop
• Restaurant
• Picnic area
• Car park

How to get there:
See visitkielder.com/visit/getting-here
• By car
• By train: nearest station is Hexham
• Airport: Newcastle

Accommodation & Eating out:
  For hotels, inns, guest houses, B&B,
  self catering and caravan / camping,
  events, etc., see www.visitkielder.com

The Kielder Water and Forest Park, in Northumberland, close to the old Scottish border and Hadrian's Wall (122 AD), the ancient Roman limes, is one of the most extensive natural areas (62,000 ha) in Great Britain. Located in the Tyne Valley, it includes an enormous artificial lake, rolling hills (190–600 m) and vast woodlands (80% of the area), *circa* 150 million spruce, pine, and larch trees, rainfall (900–1,200 mm), resulting in a damp, humid landscape with dark skies, illuminated by the pale, northern light, with squirrels, deers and birds that exist alongside an active lumber industry and thousands of visitors seeking out the natural surroundings and outdoor activities. It encompasses a dozen little villages, hamlets, and farms. Bellingham is considered the "capital", and Kielder – "violent water" in ancient Nordic – the name both to the park and the castle (1775).

The visual arts programme was initiated in 1994. In 1999 the first project of the Art and Architecture programme, was realised. The belvedere was designed by the London-based architects Softroom, whose main focus lies with theoretical subjects and fantasy architecture. The belvedere, a term with a long, historical tradition, is reinterpreted here based on the site's characteristics and the object's inherent task. Located on the lake's northern shore, the belvedere's outer layer of curved, polished, stainless steel is a mirror reflecting the surrounding landscape. The circular interior of textured steel has a slightly curved yet rectangular skylight of yellow glass that filters the light, giving it a warm, almost summery quality, even when it is cold and windy outside. James Turrell is one of land art's most ambitious artists. His *skyspaces* deal with interior / exterior

space, light, and the perception of them, the relationship between sky and earth. The *Kielder Skyspace* is one of his most significant European pieces. The site Cat Cairn, a rocky outcrop with spectacular views, is a circular space buried in the earth, accessible only by tunnel, crowned by a ceiling with a circular opening 3 m in diameter. Along the interior walls is a continuous bench, behind that a fibre-optic ring that illuminates the white walls and ceiling. The experience: sitting inside, the spectator sees the sky, framed by the circle, almost as if it were a solid form, and perceives the shifting balance, the relationships between tone, colour, luminosity – born from an array of possibilities as infinite as the changing hours, days, climate, and seasons – and between the artificial interior light and the subdued, delicate shades of natural light outside, particularly nuanced just before sunrise and after sunset.

Minotaur is a labyrinth by the architects Nick Coombe and Shona Kitchen. "The structure plays with the psychology of being lost using discord and asymmetry, interwoven with a series of eccentric devices to challenge the visitor," providing him with deceptive or paradoxical clues that are always symbolic in nature. The labyrinth allows visitors

to experience a state that reaches back in time to the ancient, myth-ical maze of Daedalus, and with it the idea of the rational human being, in command of his space. Kielder Art and Architecture offers much more, from the *Kielder Observatory*, a project won by Charles Barclay in 2005, to the *Kielder Column*, to the *Silvas Capitalis*, to a sculpture by Fiona Curran (2016).

coleford **forest of dean sculpture**

Since 1986
Forest of Dean Sculpture Trail
Beechenhurst Lodge, Forest of Dean
Speach House Road
Coleford, Gloucestershire GL16
Tel. +44 (0)3000674800
www.forestofdean-sculpture.org.uk

Opening hours: permanently
Admission: free
• Car park: fee charged
• Access for the disabled
• Pets allowed
• Photographs allowed
• Guided tours (booking required)
• Publications: map, leaflet, books
• Beechen Hurst Café
• Picnic area
• Car park

How to get there:
• By car: off the B4226 (SO 615 120)
  West of Speech House in the heart of
  the Forest of Dean
• By bus: line 732 from Coleford
• By train: Bristol Temple Meads to
  Lydney Station
• By taxi from Lydney Station
• By bike: National Cycle Network,
  contact Sustrans (Bristol)
• Airport: Bristol

Accommodation & Eating out:
  Visit: www.wyedeantourism.co.uk

Nestled between the valleys of the Severn and Wye rivers, "where England and Wales lie shoulder to shoulder," the Royal Forest of Dean is one of the few Royal Forests left in Great Britain, most having fallen victim to centuries of exploitation as hunting grounds for the monarchy and as sources of charcoal. As early as the Roman Empire, the area's geological innards – coal, iron, stone – were exploited in mines and quarries; later on, the Industrial Revolution crowded the riverbanks with forges and furnaces; 2,000 years as an "explored, exploited and exported" land. And yet, it somehow preserved a unique beauty that has inspired artists, poets and musicians. In 1924 the forest was placed in the care of the government's Forestry Authority, in 1938 it was declared a National Park to protect both its natural treasures and the legacy of its industrial past, and in 1986 the sculptural trail was established. By the year 2016, the park attracted about 300,000 visitors per year. It spreads out across 10,800 ha of gentle hills and undulating valleys with streams, rapids, and local species like the oak and beech, some of which are more than a hun-

dred years old. Within the confines of the so-called "Queen of the Forests," which inspired J.R.R. Tolkien with its aura of magic and mystery, is a 5 km trail with sculptures placed along its course. The artistic commissions are aimed at contributing to the celebration of forest life with artworks that help foster an understanding and appreciation thereof. Therefore, the trail offers both a new way of exploring the forest as well as the enjoyment of about 20 sculptures, located at carefully chosen sites selected by the artists themselves. By 2016 there were 17 sculptures which can be seen on the trail – other 11 works are not longer visible. Some of the pieces, in addition to those pictured here, are *Fire and Water Boots* and *Block Dome* by David Nash (1986), *Grove of Silence* by Ian Hamilton Finlay (1986), *Deer* by Sophie Ryder (1988, 2001), *Hanging Fire* by Cornelia Parker (1986), *In Situ* by Erica Tan (2003), *Echo* by Anni Cattrell (2007), the installation *Hill33*, the outcome of a resarch begun by David Cotterell in 2009, *Yasasin* by Pomona Zipser (2016), two site-specific sculptures by Henry Castle, *Coal Measure Giants* (2016). Temporary projects play an increasingly important role in the Trust's programming like *Sentient Forest* by Andrea Roi (2016–17).

Opposite page:
Kevin Atherton, *Cathedral*, 1986
Keir Smith, *Iron Road*, 1986

This page:
Erika Tan, *In Situ*, 2004
Neville Gabie, *Raw*, 2001

Bonnington House Steadings
Wilkieston, Edinburgh EH27 8BB
Tel. +44 1506889900
www.jupiterartland.org

Jupiter Artland, a sculpture garden and gallery only 19 km west of Edinburgh, is the brainchild of Robert and Nicky Wilson, art collectors. In 1999 they bought Bonnington House, a Jacobean manor house within a 40.5-ha estate, to live in with their family.

The story goes that Nicky, a sculptor herself, deeply influenced by Ian Hamilton Finlay's Little Sparta – see p. 208 – had long dreamed of creating her own sculpture park. Some years later, Jupiter Artland opened to the public. In 2016 it is one of the five finalists for the most important British award in the field, the Art Fund Prize for Museum of the Year, which celebrates museums and galleries across the UK, annually awarding one outstanding winner £100,000.

As an example of outstanding installations, the challenging work of Nathan Coley has settled into the landscape – no less confronting but more at home. The *Cells of Life* landform is by Charles Jencks, architecture historian well known for his postmodernism, and less for his landscape practice and investigations into rocks, cosmology and science.

There is no set route. Clockwise or anticlockwise is your choice. The artworks are landmarks, events, confrontations on a journey of discovery; an open-ended journey. This is the park's concept.

Among artists with permanent works, Anish Kapoor, Antony Gormley, Andy Goldsworthy, Alec Finlay, Sara Barker, Tessa Lynch, Henry Castle, Anya Gallaccio – *The Light Pours Out Of Me,* a sculpture and also part

of a garden – Cornelia Parker, Tania Kovats, Peter Liversidge, Christian Boltanski – *Animitas*, 2016, hundreds of small Japanese bells attached to long stems planted in the ground.

Opposite page:
Charles Jencks, *life mounds*, 2005

Above:
Ian Hamilton Finlay, *XTH Muse*, 2005

Below:
Marc Quinn, *Love Bomb*, 2016
Neville Gabie, *Raw*, 2001

There is a wide range of talks, tours, events, workshops and courses. Temporary exhibitions are held in the indoor gallery. Educational programme for all ages throughout the year; free visits for schools and universities during term times, free educational visits for community groups, etc.

goodwood cass sculpture foundation

Since 1994
Cass Sculpture Foundation
New Barn Hill, Goodwood
West Sussex UK PO18 0QP
Tel. +44 (0)1243538449
info@sculpture.org.uk
www.sculpture.org.uk
Dir. Claire Shea

Opening hours:
Mar.–Nov.: 10.30am–4.30pm
Winter: closed, only visitors with
previous booking
Admission: fee charged
• Access for the disabled
• Pets are not allowed
• Photographs allowed
• Exhibition hall with changing shows
• Publications: yearbooks, books,
  catalogues, leaflets
• Bookshop
• Car park

How to get there:
  See map and website
• Airports: Southhampton, London
  Gatwick

Accommodation & Eating out:
  Contact Chichester Tourist
  Information, Tel. +44 (0)1243775888

Cass Sculpture Foundation is a not-for-profit commissioning and edu-cational organisation that provides a platform for artists to achieve new levels of ambition and share their work with a wider audience. It was established in 1992 by Wilfred and Jeannette Cass. Set within 26 acres of West Sussex countryside, the Foundation is composed of exhibition spaces, an archive, an educational resource and a commis-sioning body. Profoundly committed to fostering new, as well as established talent, the organisation commissions as many as 15 art-works every year. It is consequently home to a constantly evolving display that has included sculptures by Anthony Caro, Eduardo Paolozzi, Rachel Whiteread, Tony Cragg, Antony Gormley, and Sara Barker. All of the works on display are available for sale, with pro-ceeds split equally between the artist and the organisation in order to facilitate new commissions. In the past 23 years, Cass has raised and invested over £10,000,000 into over 250 artists. This policy fos-ters a cycle of creativity, realised on a monumental scale. Each year, the organisation's curatorial team invites a selection of carefully researched artists to submit proposals in the form of drawings and maquettes (small working models) for consideration. These proposals are then incorporated into the archive, an onsite resource that is available to view by appointment. Cass supports its commissioned

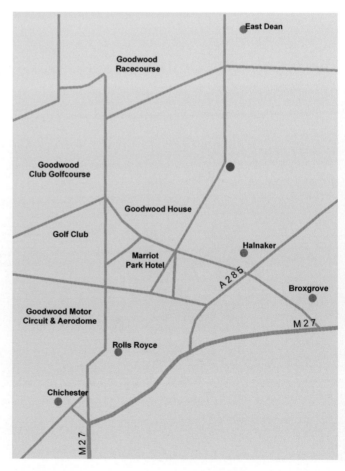

artists at every step of the process, from conception to fabrication and eventually to display. As such, it provides special opportunities for sculptors in the UK as well as internationally, and at varying stages in their careers. The commissioning process established by Cass has become an emulated model. Appealing to corporate companies and public institutions alike, the Foundation has project-managed commissions in London, Hong Kong, and Singapore, and consulted on the establishment of sculpture parks in China, India, and Norway. Cass is committed to developing new opportunities for the display of contemporary sculpture in the public realm. It established the commissioning process and commissioned the first three sculptures on the Fourth Plinth, Trafalgar Square. Most recently, it organised and curated British sculptor Tony Cragg's first large-scale solo exhibition for the London 2012 Festival. The organisation has also partnered with numerous reputable institutions. As motivated by education and the public display of outdoor sculpture as it is by the commissioning process, Cass is open to visitors from April to November and organises ambitious and diverse exhibitions. The result, the Foundation says, is a pioneering not-for-profit organisation that inspires, enables and presents the output of some of the most important figures in contemporary sculpture.

Tony Cragg, *Tongue in Cheek*, 2002

Anthony Abrahams, Ivor Abrahams, Edward Allington, David Annesley, Kenneth Armitage, Zadok Ben-David, Ivan Black, Matt Bodimeade, Willard Boepple, Ralph Brown, Jon Buck, Peter Burke, Anthony Caro, Lynn Chadwick, Robin Connelly, Terence Coventry, Stephen Cox, Tony Cragg, Maggie Cullen, George Cutts, Grenville Davey, John Davies, Richard Deacon, Eva Drewett, Iain Edwards, Nigel Ellis, Garth Evans, Abigail Fallis, Ian Hamilton Finlay, Rose Finn-Kelcey, Mark Firth, Laura Ford, Elisabeth Frink, William Furlong, Bruce Gernand, John Gibbons, Andy Goldsworthy, Antony Gormley, Steven Gregory, Charles Hadcock, Nigel Hall, Alex Hartley, Thomas Heatherwick, Sean Henry, Nicola Hicks, Peter Hide, Shirazeh Houshiary, Jon Isherwood, Allen Jones, Michael Kenny, David King, Phillip King, Bryan Kneale, Kim Lim, Peter Logan, Richard Long, Michael Lyons, David Mach, John Maine, Charlotte Mayer, Bernard Meadows, Cathy de Monchaux, Tim Morgan, David Nash, Paul Neagu, Eilís O'Connell, Ana María Pacheco, Zora Palova, Eduardo Paolozzi, William Pye, Marc Quinn, Wendy Ramshaw, Victoria Rance, Peter Randall-Page, Colin Rose, Sophie Ryder, Andrew Sabin, Michael Sandle, Sophie Smallhorn, Keir Smith, Wendy Taylor, Almuth Tebbenhoff, William Tucker, Gavin Turk, William Turnbull, Jim Unsworth, Glynn Williams, Avril Wilson, Bill Woodrow, David Worthington

Andy Goldsworthy, *Arch at Goodwood*, 2001
Zadok Ben-David
Conversation Piece, 1996
Opposite page:
Above:
Eva Rothschild, *This and This and This*, 2013
Below:
Piotr Lakomy, *Untitled (Every step is moving me up)*, 2015

Since 1977
Henry Moore Studios & Gardens
The Henry Moore Foundation
Dane Tree House, Perry Green,
Much Hadham, Hertfordshire S910 6EE
Tel. +44 (0)1279844194
visits@henry-moore.org
www.henry-moore.org
Dir. Godfrey Worsdale

Opening hours (by appointment only):
1 Jul.–31 Oct.
Wed.–Sun. & public holidays: 11am–5pm
Closed: Monday & Tuesday
Educational visits may be arranged
Wednesdays to Friday
Archive by appointment only
• Access for the disabled
• Pets not allowed
• Photographs allowed outside only
• Guided tours (booking required)
• Exhibition halls with changing shows
• Educational programmes
• Library, by appointment only
• Publications
• Bookshop
• Coffee shop
• Picnic area
• Car park

How to get there:
• By car: take M11 exit 8 and follow
  A120 to Hertford, at the third round
  about follow signs for Much Hadham
  A1(M): take exit 4 to Hertford A414
  A10: take exit marked Harlow,
  Chelmsford, Ware A414 and at the
  second roundabout follow B181 sign
  posted Stanstead Abbotts,
  following B181 marked Roydon
• By train: Liverpool Street Station to
  Bishop's Stortford, 40–60 minutes
  (frequent trains)
• By taxi: from Bishop's Stortford rail
  station (9 km, 15 minutes)
• Airport: London Stansted

Eating out:
Restaurant: The Hoops Inn (next door)

Henry Moore is one of the most important sculptors of the 20th c. From the 1940s until his death in 1986, he was the most celebrated artist in the United Kingdom. It has even been written that "his work," an immense production of close to 6,000 pieces, "had been distributed more widely in the Western world than that of any other sculptor, living or dead" – Peter Fuller, 1988.

During the 1930s he lived in the London neighbourhood of Hampstead, which was also home to Ben Nicholson, Barbara Hepworth, and the critic Herbert Read. Following the outbreak of World War II and the damage his house suffered during a German

bombing raid, he moved to Much Hadham in 1940, a village in Hertfordshire, to the north of what would later become Greater London. Here he lived and worked for the rest of his life and eventually established the Henry Moore Foundation.

The artist created the non-profit foundation in 1977 in order "to advance the education of the public by the promotion of their appreciation of the fine arts and in particular the works of Henry Moore." He generously handed over to the foundation the greater part of the 27-ha grounds and all except one of the buildings of Perry Green, hundreds of sculptures and other works. Perry Green was originally a farm outside the nearby hamlet of Much Hadham, where the Bishops

studios & gardens

of London had their country residence. Moore began with a farm-house, Hoglands – which visitors can view during timed guided tours – and then went on to acquire successively other lands and houses, redesigning the space and structures with care and respect for the environment and the traditional local building style. He transformed the stables into an area for his sculptures and the farm's small shop into a studio for his miniatures. Later on he acquired Bourne cottage and a large parcel of land, which he turned into a sculptural park. The artist built his own world within the confines of this complex and this is where he created some of the most memorable and

Double Oval, 1966

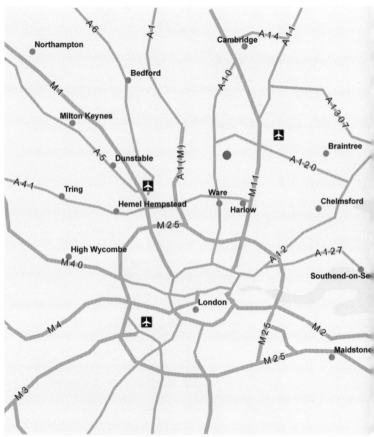

impressive works of his artistic career. Following his death, efforts have been made to preserve the legacy of the foundation exactly as he had wanted, maintaining the halls and studios where he conceived and executed his work in their original state.

The park contains 21 monumental artworks – see map on the following page. The Yellow Brick Studio, built in 1958 on the site of an old pigsty, was where Moore worked on his large-scale pieces. The Bourne Maquette Studio housed all the preparatory work and miniature models for his monumental works. The Aisled Barn houses Henry Moore's tapestries made in collaboration with West Dean College. All these spaces still retain the spirit of the artist who once worked within them.

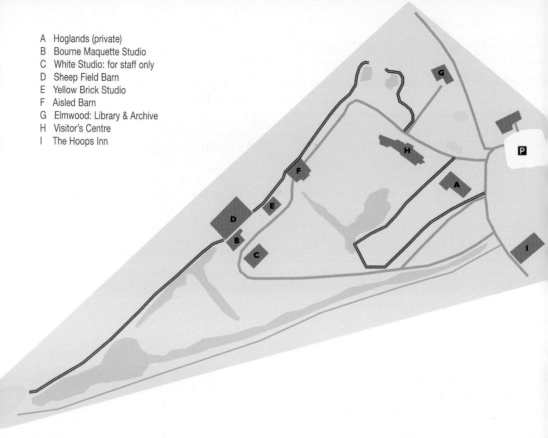

A Hoglands (private)
B Bourne Maquette Studio
C White Studio: for staff only
D Sheep Field Barn
E Yellow Brick Studio
F Aisled Barn
G Elmwood: Library & Archive
H Visitor's Centre
I The Hoops Inn

Opposite page:
The Arch, 1963–69
Three Piece Sculpture: Vertebrae,1968–69

This page: *Sheep Piece*, 1971–72
Large Figure in a Shelter, 1975

ockley hannah peschar sculpture garden

The Hannah Peschar Sculpture Garden
Black and White Cottage
Standon Lane, Ockley
Surrey, UK RH5 5QR
Tel. +44 (0)1306627269
hannahpescharsculpture@gmail.com
www.hannahpescharsculpture.com

Opening hours:
May–Oct.: Fri.–Sat.: 11am–6pm
Sun. and holidays: 2pm–5pm
Tue.–Thur. by appointment only
Nov.–Apr. by appointment only
Admission: fee charged
- School visits
- Studio visits
- Most of sculpture exhibited is for sale
- We do offer group visits with introduction to the garden

How to get there:
- By car, leave the motorway M25 at Junction 9 and take the A24 south signposted Dorking, bypass Dorking and after approx. 6.4 km at the Beare Green roundabout, leave the A24 and take the A29 signposted Bognor Regis and Ockley
- Airports: Heathrow (1 h) and Gatwick (30 minutes)

Broadleaved plants and mature trees support, frame and enhance a changing collection of contemporary sculpture in this stunning garden. Heralded as the first of its kind in the UK, the Hannah Peschar Sculpture Garden has been proudly exhibiting contemporary sculpture in a unique and magical environment for over 30 years. It was the brainchild of owner and curator Hannah Peschar, and has grown from a handful of sculptures to over 150 pieces exhibited every summer in the grounds of the 16th-c. cottage that Hannah and her husband, Anthony Paul, call home. A majority of the work is changed each year, creating a new experience with every visit. Taking retirement in 2016, Peschar has appointed two new curators to bring a new lease on life to the Sculpture Garden. The range of works on display is wide, with styles varying from figurative to highly abstract, innovatively using contemporary metals, wire, glass, ceramics and plastics, as well as the more traditional stone, wood and bronze. Each sculpture is placed in a carefully considered and meaningful relationship with the other featured works within the garden, created by co-curator and award-winning landscape designer Anthony Paul. The result is an inspired combination of peaceful, enclosed harmony and dramatic, surprise vistas in an ever-changing environment.

Ronald van der Meijs, *Sound Architecture 5*, 2014

Ben Barrell, *Swirl' by Stream and New Water Garden*, 2014

st. ives barbara hepworth museum

Since 1980
Barbara Hepworth Museum & Sculpture
Garden
Barnoon Hill, St. Ives
Cornwall TR26 1AD
Tel. +44 (0)1736796226
visiting.stives@tate.org.uk
www.tate.org.uk/stives
Dir. Mark Osterfield

Opening hours:
Mar.–Oct.: 10am–5pm daily
Nov.–Feb.: Tue.–Sun.: 10am–4.30pm
Admission: fee charged
• There are steps and uneven surfaces
  at the Barbara Hepworth Museum
  and Sculpture Garden, which makes
  access difficult. For this reason wheelchair access is by prior appointment only, please call 01736796226
  to arrange.

How to get there:
• By car: take the A30 to St. Ives
• By train: regular train service from
  London Paddington. Change at St.
  Erth for the branch line to St. Ives
• Airport: Newquay, Cornwall

Accommodation & Eating out:
  About ten hotels are available in
  St.Ives. A dozen restaurants are
  available between 10 and 100 m to
  the museum

St. Ives has attracted painters since the 19th c., including Turner and
Whistler. Ben Nicholson discovered it in 1928 and moved here with
Barbara Hepworth at the outbreak of World War II. Along with
Naum Gabo and others, they turned this Cornish town into an out-
post for the abstract avant-garde. The artist, who lived here until her
death in 1975, stipulated in her will that Trewyn, her home and studio, and the adjacent garden, with a selection of her sculptures
placed as she wished, be permanently opened to the public.
The visit to Barbara Hepworth's museum and sculptural garden is an
immersion in the work of one of Britain's most important 20th-c.
artists. Visitors can see about 40 pieces in bronze, wood, plaster,
marble, and brass as well as the many plants, flowers, and trees,
which are beautiful in their own right, but take on a special relevance
when seen in relation to Hepworth's abstract sculptures. The
fascinating relationship between the artworks and the natural forms
that surround them is dealt with in detail in a book by Phillips and
Stephens – see bibliography. The Hepworth Museum, run by the Tate
Gallery since 1980, now forms part of Tate St. Ives and the programmes and services provided by that institution.

View of Barbara Hepworth Sculpture
Garden in spring with *Torso II
(Torcello)*, 1958

salisbury new art centre sculpture park

Since 1994
New Art Centre Sculpture Park &
Gallery
Roche Court, East Winterslow
Salisbury, Wiltshire, UK SP5 1BG
Tel. +44 (0)1980862244
nac@sculpture.uk.com
www.sculpture.uk.com
Dir. Madeleine Bossborough

Opening hours:
Daily: 11am–4pm, closed 23 Dec.–1 Jan.
Admission: free
• Pets not allowed
• Guided tours (booking required)
• Temporary exhibitions
• Car park: free for visitors

How to get there:
• By car from London & Heathrow:
  A mere 90 minutes from London,
  head straight down the M3. Take exit
  8 towards Andover and Stockbridge
  on the A303. Continue through
  Stockbridge on the A30 towards
  Salisbury. After 11 km, turn left
  (Lopcombe Corner) and take the next
  left, signposted Roche Court and
  East Winterslow. Follow the lane to
  the top where you will find another
  sign directing you into the park.
• By car from Salisbury:
  The park is 20 minutes away from
  Salisbury. Take the A30 out of
  Salisbury towards London (ignore the
  signs to the Winterslows). After
  approximately 11 km pass a traffic
  light junction, go up the hill and then
  after the brow turn right, signposted
  Roche Court and East Winterslow.
  Follow the lane to the top, where you
  will find another sign directing you
  into the park.
• By train:
  The gallery is 14 km from Salisbury
  train station and 17 km from Andover
  train station, which run regular services to and from London Waterloo
  (approximately 1 ¼ h). Taxis are
  available at both stations.
• Helipads available, please contact in
  advance

Salisbury has been a pilgrimage destination since ancient times.
Stonehenge has drawn people to it for 3,500 years, and the Gothic
cathedral has attracted visitors for eight centuries. Located just a few
kilometres from Salisbury, the New Art Centre attracts collectors
and visitors with an interest in modern and contemporary art.
The centre comprises a commercial art gallery and sculpture park
which exhibits 20th- and 21st-c. sculpture, paintings, ceramics and
photography. There is a changing exhibition programme of five
to six exhibitions per year, and all artworks are for sale. The centre
specialises in work from 1950 onward, executed in materials such as
bronze, marble, corten steel, fibreglass resin and stainless steel, by
artists such as Anthony Caro, Antony Gormley, Richard Long and
Barbara Hepworth. The centre is, in fact, the sole representative of
Barbara Hepworth's estate.
The New Art Centre has been located at Roche Court, little more
than an hour from London, since 1994. Initially founded in 1957 by
Madeleine Bessborough in the urban setting of Sloane Street in West
London, the centre now covers about 40 ha of parkland surrounding
a 19th-c. house.
The park's landscape is typically English: a lush countryside of wide,
open meadows interrupted by forested areas. The park usually
exhibits approximately 60 artworks at any given time, by renowned
artists such as those mentioned above, as well as other British artists
such as Kenneth Armitage, David Nash, Michael Craig-Martin, Bill
Woodrow, and Edmund de Waal.
The New Art Centre often handles commissions of specific projects
by selected artists, and exhibits annually at Art Brussels art fair.
Previous off-site exhibitions include Caro at Chatsworth, Edmund de
Waal at Waddesdon and Laura Ford at Strawberry Hill House.
The existing house and orangery at Roche Court, built in 1804, have
been physically joined in 1997 by an award-winning gallery space
designed by Stephen Marshall, the well-known architect who also
designed, among others, the Rothschild Foundation archival buildings
in Aylesbury, England. A design of simple lines and natural light, using
frameless glass, wood, and unpolished stone, integrates the building
into its surroundings and provides an ideal space for the changing
exhibition programme. Following the success of the gallery, the New
Art Centre commissioned Stephen Marshall to design a second
building, the Artists' House, a contemporary domestic space for the
display of smaller works of art.
The centre also offers an educational programme through the Roche
Court Educational Trust. Educational visits organised with schools aim
to introduce the students to the rich artistic heritage of the country
through sculpture and other artistic disciplines.

Opposite page: Kim Ling, *Carvings*, 2014

Opposite page, above:
Anthony Caro, *Millbank Steps*, 2004

Right:
Anthoney Gormley, *Another Time XII*, 2010

Below:
Laura Ford, *Days of Judgement, Cats I-VII*, 2012

Since 2005
Mariners Road, Crosby Beach
Borough of Sefton
Liverpool, Merseyside, L23 6SX

Opening hours: permanently
Admission: free

The British artist said: "The idea was to test time and tide, stillness and movement, and somehow engage with the daily life of the beach. This was no exercise in romantic escapism. The sculptures are made from 17 body-casts taken from my body (protected by a thin layer of wrapping plastic). The sculptures are all standing in a similar way, with the lungs more or less inflated and their postures carrying different degrees of tension or relaxation."

How to get there:
• Public transport via three railway stations: Waterloo, Blundellsands, Crosby and a range of bus services as Merseytravel Traveline
  Tel. +44 08712002

Another Place consists of 100 cast-iron, life-size figures spread out along three kilometres of the foreshore, stretching almost one kilometre out to sea. The borough of Sefton consists of a coastal strip of land on the Irish Sea. Crosby Beach is about six miles (9.5 km) north of central Liverpool. It is a non-bathing beach with areas of soft sand and mud, and a risk of changing tides. Visitors should stay within 50 m of the promenade, according to Tourism office.
Before permanent installation here, the project (1995–97) has been seen in Cuxhaven (Germany), Stavanger in Norway, and De Panne in Belgium.

Since 1977
Yorkshire Sculpture Park
West Bretton   Wakefield WF4 4LG
Tel. +44 (0)1924832631
info@ysp.co.uk
www.ysp.co.uk
Dir. Peter Murray OBE

Opening hours: open daily (please
check Christmas closure times)
Summer: Grounds & Centre, 10am–6pm
Galleries: 11am–5pm
Longside Gallery: 11am–4pm
Winter: Grounds & Centre: 10am–5pm
Galleries: 11am–4pm
Longside Gallery: 11am–3pm

Admission: free

• Visitor Centre provides all weather
  facilities, including restaurant, coffee
  bar, shop, resource area
• Access for the disabled
• Dogs on leads at all times in restrict-
  ed areas of the park, no dogs or pets
  in buildings or Formal Garden
• Photographs allowed
• Guided tours (booking required)
• Exhibition halls with changing shows
• Educational programmes
• Library by appointment only
• Archive and Study Centre: large
  collection of images for research
• Publications: about 50 titles
• Picnic area
• Car park: fee charged

How to get there:
• By car: 1.5 km from M1 junction 38,
  following A637 to Huddersfield
• By bus: from Wakefield, Leeds,
  Barnsley, Huddersfield
• By train: Wakefield Westgate (11 km),
  2 h from London King's Cross
• Airports: Leeds, Manchester, London
Accommodation:
  West Bretton: The Old Manor House
  B & B (1km), +44 (0)1924830324
  Near Wakefield: Midgley Lodge Motel
  (2.2 km), +44 (0)1924830069
  Wakefield: Express by Holiday Inn
  (7.5 km), +44 (0)1924830069
  Near Huddersfield: The Three Acres
  (8 km), +44 (0)1484602606

Yorkshire Sculpture Park (YSP) is an art gallery, a museum, and an
independent, non-profit foundation dedicated to modern and contemporary art. YSP lies 29 km from Leeds, 40 km from Sheffield and
60 km from Manchester. Founded in 1977, it was the first park of its
kind in the United Kingdom, and by 2015 it was attracting approximately 400,000 visitors each year. It occupies over 500 hectares of
the Bretton Estate, designed in the 18th and 19th c. with a varied
landscape of modelled hills and valleys, the use of water and thousands of imported exotic trees.

The estate had been divided by the 1940s, then partly reunited by
the YSP and restored as part of a 13-million-pound landscape management plan. The Park endeavours to maintain the spirit of its natural
surroundings and preserve the design of its historic landscape; this
has led to collaborations with architects specialised in sustainable
design, farmers, gardeners, foresters, and artists who intervene at the
site.

YSP pursues activities in different areas: exhibitions by eminent,
acclaimed artists throughout the year; artist residencies, and by commissioning specific projects; a prestigious collection formed by loans
and gifts; and through education, which consists of programmes aimed
at different levels – schools, universities and minority groups, as well
as the general public through tours, workshops, study days and sculpture courses with artists.

The vast parklands and the lay-out of the spaces are best understood by studying the map on page 238. Entrance is from the north

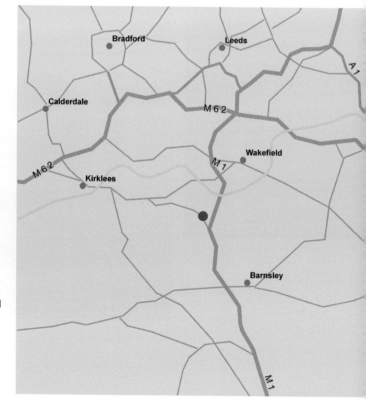

Yorkshire Sculpture Park
Museum of the Year 2014

(by road from West Bretton, Wakefield, or Barnsley). The YSP Centre, a new building inaugurated in 2002, is the gateway to the park and houses the shop and information services and a restaurant offering spectacular views across the Country Park.

East of the Centre is Bothy area with the Bothy and Garden Galleries used for temporary exhibitions of installations, models and films, for example. The Bothy Garden is another open air exhibition space.

Towards the south is the Formal Terrace and Garden from the 18th c. Between the Bothy and this terrace lies the Underground Gallery; an exercise in how to unite a building and the landscape in an imperceptible manner, seamlessly and without interruption; the gallery follows the line of the Formal Terrace and is carved cleanly into the slope of the Bothy Gallery and Garden hillside. This design preserved the view of the park from the Bothy buildings. The roof of the Underground Gallery is made of grass and inside there are three naturally lit halls, which are especially appropriate for exhibiting sculpture.

Since 2005 the Underground Gallery has hosted exhibitions by artists such as William Turnbull, James Turrell, Jaume Plensa, Joan Miró, Henry Moore, Not Vital (2016–17).

Further south are rolling fields, two lakes and the wide open countryside. Everything here changes with the passing hours, days and seasons: bright, frosty mornings, languid summer afternoons, smoky autumn mists. Every moment evokes a different sensory experience of the landscape and the artwork, both equally mercurial in character.

Anthony Caro, *Promenade,* 1996

Artists and works of art shown:
There are usually at least 80 sculptures in the landscape for visitors to see alongside special temporary exhibitons in the galleries. Displays change throughout the year so visitors are advised to call ahead if planning to see something in particular.
Tel. +44 01924832631

Magdalena Abakanowicz, Ai Weiwei, Jonathan Borofsky, Antony Caro, Elisabeth Frink, Andy Goldsworthy, Antony Gormley, Barbara Hepworth, Roger Hiorns, Phillip King, Sol LeWitt, Joan Miró, Henry Moore, David Nash, Julian Opies, Dennis Oppenheim, Sophie Ryder, Serge Spitzer, William Turnbull, James Turrell, Ursula von Rydingsvard, etc.

Opposite page:
David Nash, *Black Steps*

This page, left to right:
Magdalena Abakanovich, *Ten seated Figures* (detail)
KAWS, *Along the Way*, 2013
Elisabeth Frink, *Sitting Man II* (detail),1986

Below:
Barbara Hepworth, *The Family of Man*,1970

The open-air pieces, always at least 80 in total, are placed at different sites — YSP call them the "open-air galleries." Some pieces are grouped together in one area, like the work of Henry Moore in the Country Park. The Access Sculpture Trail designed by sculptor Don Rankin is an interwoven network of paths, plants and sculpture, designed specifically for enjoyment by families and people with disabilities. Sometimes projects are particularly novel, such as a piece by another artist in residence, Simon Whitehead, who came up with *Walks to Illuminate*, inviting visitors to solar or night walks through the park wearing shoes that glow.

The Bretton Estate's 18th-c. chapel — situated in the Country Park — underwent a major restoration in 2013. In May 2014, the newly restored building opened with its inaugural Ai Weiwei exhibition.

Ten minutes from the YSP Centre is the Longside Gallery, a former indoor riding arena converted into an exhibition space with sweeping views onto the park. Shared with the London-based Hayward Gallery, it organises exhibitions from the Arts Council England sculpture collection.

YSP aims to be as family-friendly as possible, at YSP the visitors can touch the sculptures, including such as *Crawling* by Sophie Ryder.

Jonathan Borofsky,
Molecule Man 1+1+1, 1990

Helen Escobedo,
Summer Fields, 2008

Henry Moore, *Reclining figure Arch leg*, 1969–70

variations: socialist realism

After World War II, several countries from the Baltic to the Adriatic Sea came under the hegemony of the USSR and Stalinist communism: the Eastern Bloc or "Stalin's World." The splendid, incandescent, seminal Russian revolutionary avant-garde in architecture, painting, sculpture, graphic and book design, cinema, photography and other arts was eradicated in 1934. Abstraction, futurism, formalism, constructivism and the free expression of the artist were branded as reactionary, a product of the bourgeoisie and capitalism. Forging the "new man" of communism – free and non-alienated – led to the dictatorial imposition of "socialist realism," which was meant to aid this process while providing symbols and models to emulate. It marked a return to an old way of describing the world in real forms, a return to the criteria of eclecticism to educate the working-class masses and glorify party leaders.

lithuania

Gruto Parkas
Near to Druskininkai, 130 km from Vilnius, Lithuania
www.grutoparkas.lt in 5 languages

Admission:
Adults: fee charged
Children: free
• Audioguides
• Museum
• Picture gallery
• Reading club
• Mini-zoo
• Luna park
• Café

For over half a century, Soviet sculpture and visual art in general produced a remarkable number of statues and monuments. The majority were grey, monotonous, kitschy, hagiographic in their praise of leaders, especially Lenin and Stalin, and far removed from the aesthetics and ethics of the modernist movements. Then cracks appeared in the dictatorial centralist system. The fall of the Berlin Wall in 1989 and the rise of Mikhail Gorbachev to the Soviet presidency led to the break-up of the Soviet Union and the end of hegemonic socialist realism. While a backward-looking eclectic postmodernism flourished in the West, Eastern Europe toppled, destroyed, gathered and shut away the statues of communist leaders: a historical paradox or asynchrony unfolding on the global stage.

Not everything, however, was a communist nightmare or even simply bad. In the Slavic world, calls for a re-evaluation appeared as early as the 1970s, with more following in the 1980s. By the 1990s, scattered articles had given way to entire books. An exhibition at the Guggenheim New York (2005), the Stockholm conference in 2012 and several texts put forward a new take on socialist realism. And in several former Eastern Bloc countries, we find artworks in parks, gardens or secluded spots that clearly reflect a historical era, an ideology and political ethos, a culture. Often surprisingly so.

Moving from north to south, our first stop is Grutas Park in Lithuania, also known as "Stalin's World." Along with the Hungarian Szoborpark – or Memento Park – it epitomises Stalinist statuary. When it opened in 2001, the park was met with fierce opposition. 15 years later it remains controversial. Viliumas Malinauskas, a businessman, collected close to 90 sculptures by about 45 artists, that had been removed from the country's public spaces after Lithuania's independence (1990). The 20-ha park recreates scenes from Siberian labour camps and exhibits the sculptures along a 2-km route. The other sections of the park are banal, verging on historical fabrication, and attract both Soviet Nostalgia and Dark Tourism.

The Sculpture Park in Vyšné Ružbachy, a spa and ski town in the Stará Ľubovňa, a district of northern Slovakia, is sited in a former travertine quarry. In 2012, the Tatra Gallery began revitalising the abandoned and dilapidated site with the restoration of works by the Symposium's foun-

slovakia

hungary

Szoborpark / Memento Park
Opened 1993
Budapest, on the outskirts of the city,
Balatoni út / Szabadkai utca corner,
South Buda

www.mementopark.hu (in English)

Right: "Stalin's Boots,"
recreation by Äkos Eleód of what
remained of the original complete work,
demolished by the 1956 Hungarian
Uprising
Below: One of the statues of Lenin

ders, Austrian artist Karl Prantl (1923–2010), France-based Japanese artist Yasuo Mizui, and Slovakian artists Rudolf Uher and Andrej Rudavský. Szoborpark, "statue park" in Hungarian, also known as Memento Park in English for international communication purposes or Memorial Park on certain maps, brochures and public transport signage, is the other significant example of this reassessment or partial defence of Stalinist cultural policy. After the 1949–89 communist period, the authorities removed Soviet-era statues and monuments from the streets and squares of Budapest, but did not destroy them. A public competition in 1991 sought designs for a park to house the pieces, won by the Hungarian architect Ákos Eleöd. In reference to the park Eleöd said, "it is about dictatorship, but it is also about democracy," which allows us to discuss the former.

The park comprises two sections: the first, Statue Park, officially known as "A Sentence About Tyranny," is divided into six oval spaces. It is home to 42 monumental "larger-than-life" statues, which date from the period 1947 to 1989, most of them from the 1950s and 1960s. The majority are well known pieces by recognised Hungarian sculptors in bronze, stone, Mauthausen granite, limestone, marble, steel and concrete. Then

there are 6 anonymous sculptures: artwork as the ultimate collective creation in the Marxist aesthetic, which rejected individualist authorship. The second section is the Witness Square or Neverwas Square, east of the park's main entrance. Admission to this is free. Photography can not convey the full expressive and communicative power, the potent symbolic significance, of many of the artworks. Here one finds statues of Marx and Engels (cubist), Lenin, Dimitrov (à la Rodin), Stalin, his imposing boots on a pedestal; the dynamic diagonal lines of the revolutionary aesthetic of 1919, which inspired Kiss István's grand – in both scale and action – Republic of Councils Monument; or certain heterodox hints in the Hungarian-Soviet Friendship Memorial by Zsigmond Kisfaludi Strobl, a popular Hungarian sculptor. He completed the piece in 1956, the year

Kiss István, *Monument to the Republic of Councils*, inspired by a poster of the revolutionary vanguard, 1919

of the Hungarian Revolution and three years after Nikita Khrushchev, the new First Secretary of the Communist Party, had begun his policy of de-Stalinisation, which provided artistic expression with greater formal freedom. Thus, when examined with rigour and detachment, the supposedly grey, repetitive uniformity of all Stalinist and Soviet art, the so-called socialist realism style – not to be confused with "social realism" from Western countries –, begins to reveal variations, contradictions, and individual resistance, both secret and concealed.

Farther south, and intertwined with ancient Mediterranean culture, lies

Sculptors: Pátzay Pál, Segesdi György, Zsigmond Kisfaludi Strobl, Kiss István, Búza Barna, Mikus Sándor, Kalló Viktor, Megyeri Barna, Szabó Iván, Jordan Kracsmarov, Olcsai-Kiss Zoltán, Herczeg Klára, Farkas Aladár, Gyenes Tamás, Nagy István János, Kiss Nagy András, Baksa Soós György, Marton László, Varga Imre, Szabó György, Makrisz Agamemnon, Ambrózi Sándor / Stöckert Károly, Mészáros Mihály, Kerényi Jen

romania

Parcul Herăstrău
Opened 1936
Bucharest

Romania, named after the Roman Empire, which harbours deviations from socialist realism orthodoxy. Now known as Parcul Herastrau, it was called Parcul Carol II (royal personality cult, 1930–40) when it opened in 1936, then Parcul National, and then Parcul I.V. Stalin. Its current name derives from the lake that stretches across 70 % of the 1.1 km² park. The multi-purpose space houses public activities and over 50 sculptures, interesting in their subject matter: unusual for pieces created at the height of Stalinism and the USSR, they depict architecture, individuals like Beethoven, Bela Bartok, Brâncuși, Chopin, Darwin, Twain, Tolstoy, Romanian myths and legends, and are gentler and softer in form and style.

bulgaria

Museum of Socialist Art
Opened 2011
Sofia
uk Lachozar Stanchov 7, Iztok

How to get there:
It is not the easiest place to find;
metro to GM Dimitrov station and
walk 300 m down the hilá

The big Red Star presiding over the House of the Bulgarian Communist Party (see next page)

Bulgaria was an empire. This remains palpable, even though Old Great Bulgaria lies as far back as the 7th c. The communist regime in Bulgaria after World War II was far more rigid and severe in its doctrinal orthodoxy than the Romanians. This inspired the expression to vote "Bulgarian style," referring to decisions made with disciplined unanimity, often with more votes than voters, as was said to happen during Bulgarian Communist Party meetings.

The era of socialist realism (1944–89) is represented by outdoor sculptures at the Museum of Socialist Art in Sofia. Notable pieces include the giant Red Star, the bust of Lenin, and a sword-wielding lady with an affinity to Stalin and the dynamism of the Italian futurists. Some viewed the museum, with concern when it opened in 2011, others saw it as a satisfying rehabilitation.

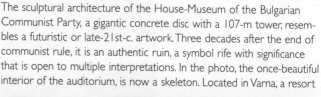

The sculptural architecture of the House-Museum of the Bulgarian Communist Party, a gigantic concrete disc with a 107-m tower, resembles a futuristic or late-21st-c. artwork. Three decades after the end of communist rule, it is an authentic ruin, a symbol rife with significance that is open to multiple interpretations. In the photo, the once-beautiful interior of the auditorium, is now a skeleton. Located in Varna, a resort

town on the Black Sea, 490 km from Sofia, the Park-Monument to the Soviet-Bulgarian Friendship is also interesting, not so much in its entirety as for certain surprising elements: sculptural groups between primitivism and cubism. To find out more, visit: www.atlasobscura.com/places/monument-of-the-bulgarian-soviet-friendship.

Right:
One of the monument's sculptural groups, the *Founding Fathers of the Bulgarian State*

Croatia is across the Adriatic Sea from Italy, with which it shares a maritime boundary. Part of Dalmatia during the Roman Empire, in the 20th c. it belonged to Yugoslavia, set up as a kingdom in 1929, then a Socialist Federal Republic from 1945 until it disintegrated in 1991. The socialist era left the country with two dozen

croatia

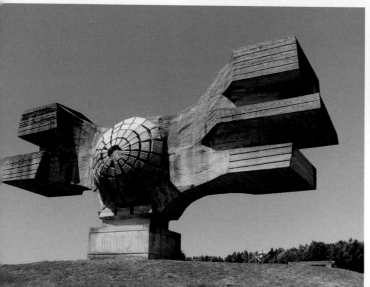

abandoned monuments, which resemble relics from the future, the late 21st c., even later perhaps, beyond *Blade Runner* and cinematic dystopias. Left, see the surprising Monument to the Revolution People of Moldavinas, work from 1967, at the height of

President Tito's rule, by the sculptor Dušan Džamonja (1928–2009). It is located in Podgaric, 100 km east of Zagreb. The morphology of the monument, with a formal plasticity that seeks to express symbolic meaning, moves away from the classic style of the socialist realism imposed by Stalin as a means of propaganda. Džamonja went on to make thoroughly contemporary artworks, as pictured above.

Petrova Gora, Tjentište, Krusevo, Kozara, Jasenovac, Sanski Most, Knin, Nis, Korenica, Makljen, Kolasin, Kadinjaca, Kamenska, Ostra, Sisak, Nicsic, etc. are among the sites with abandoned artworks that are worth exploring in Croatia. You can see them here: www.cracktwo. com/2011/04/25-abandoned-soviet-monuments.

albania

National Gallery of Art
Since 1954
Shëtitorja Murat Toptani, Tiranë 1000
Albania
Tel. 355 42226033
Bulevardi Deshmoret e Kombit,
just in front of Rinia Park

Finally, Albania, perhaps the most obscure and isolated Eastern European country during Soviet rule. The supreme leader (1944–85) was Enver Hoxha, a man of contradictions. He was an iron-fisted ruler and a voracious reader of books that he bought in France. He was radical and violent in eliminating all forms of opposition through executions, long prison sentences, and exiling relatives to tiny police-controlled villages, but he also re-built a country devastated by

Nazi occupation, promoted industrialisation, economic growth, and access to education, which eradicated adult illiteracy. At the same time strict censorship and Marxist-Leninist orthodoxy starved the arts. The National Gallery of Art in Tirana houses a sculpture collection that is representative of this period. The most interesting section is found outdoors, in the backyard: clearly anti-revisionist sculptures that mythologise the leaders – "Uncle Joe," Stalin, and an intriguing later Lenin who is missing his right arm.

* * *

And now, after over 80 years, we come full circle. We once again find ourselves face to face with the same realism, but now it is not rocialist, but capitalist. The first statue in the world to honour the memory of Steve Jobs is a life-size bronze in Budapest, Hungary, erected in 2011.

bibliography

GENERAL

AMIDON, J.; GUSTAFSON, K., *Radical Landscape: Reinventing Outdoor Space*, Thames and Hudson, London 2003

ANDREWS, M., *Landscape and Western Art*, Oxford University, New York 2000

BEARDSLEY, J., *Earthworks and Beyond: Contemporary Art in the Landscape*, Abbeville Press, New York 1998

BERRIZBEITIA, A.; POLLAK, L., *Inside Outside: Between Architecture and Landscape*, Rockport, Gloucester MA 1999

BISHOP, C., *Installation art: a critical history*, TATE Publishing, London 2005

BOETTGER, S., *Earthworks Art and the Landscape of the Sixties*, University of California Press, Berkeley 2002

BONITO OLIVA, A., *Artenatura. 38ª Biennale di Venezia*, Electa, Milano 1978

BROWN, A., *Art & Ecology Now*, Thames and Hudson, London 2014

BROWN, J., *The Modern Garden*, Thames and Hudson, London 2000

COLLINS, J., *Sculpture Today*, Phaidon, London 2007

COOPER, G.; TAYLOR, G. R., *Gardens for the Future: Gestures Against the Wind*, Monacelli Press, New York 2000

CORNER, J., *Recovering Landscape*, Princeton Architectural, New York 1999

CRIMP, D., "Redefining Site Specificity" in *On the Museum's Ruins*, MIT Press, Cambridge MA 1995

DAVIES, S., *The Artful Species*, Oxford Scholarship, Oxford 2012

DAVIES, P.; KNIPE, T. (eds.), *A sense of Place. Sculpture in Landscape*, Ceolfrith Press, Sunderland 1984

DEMPSEY, E., *Destination Art: Land Art, Site-Specific Art · Sculpture Parks*, Thames & Hudson, London 2011

DOMINO, C., *Á ciel ouvert. L'art contemporain à l'échelle du paysage*, Scala, Paris 1999

DUTTON, D., *The art instinct*, Bloomsbury Press, London 2010

ELAM, C., "Lorenzo de' Medici's Sculpture Garden", *Mitteilungen des Kunsthistorischen Institutes in Florenz*, Vol. 36 No. 1/2 (1992), Kunsthistorisches Institut in Florenz, Max-Planck-Institut

EYRES, P., RUSSEL, F., *Sculpture and the Garden*, Ashgate, Farnham 2006

FAGONE, V. (cur.), et al., *Art in Nature. Art works and environment*, Mazzotta, Milano 1996

FANG, W., "Anoixism and its idealistic pursuit" in *Cultura. International Journal of Philosophy of Culture and Axiology*", 12(2):73-80 January 2015

FINLAY, A., HODBY, A., *Avant-garde English Landscape: Some Versions of Landscape*, Yorkshire Sculpture Park, West Bretton 2005

FRANCIS, M.; RANDOLF Jr., T. H., *The Meaning of Gardens: Idea, Place, and Action*, MIT Press, Cambridge MA 1991

FRIED, M., *Art and Objecthood: Essays and Reviews*, University of Chicago Press, Chicago 1998

GARRAUD, C., *L'artiste contemporain et la nature – Parcs et paysages européens*, Hazan, Paris 2007

GRAHAM, Dan," Garden as Theater as museum" in *Rock My Religion*, MIT Press, Cambridge MA 1993

GRANDE, John K., *Balance: Art and Nature*, Black Rose, Montreal 2004

— *Art Nature Dialogues: Interviews with environmental artists*, SUNY University Press, New York 2004

HAMANN, C., *KunstGartenKunst*, Deutsche Verlags-Anstalt, Stuttgart 2015

HARPER, G.; MOYER, T., *Landscapes for art: contemporary sculpture parks*, International Sculpture Center, NJ 2008

HÄUSSER, R.; HONISCH, D., *Kunst Landschaft Architektur. Architekturbezogene Kunst in der Bundesrepublik Deutschland*, Institut für Auslandsbeziehungen 1983

HEAPY, T.; GAMBLE, N., *Outdoor Art*, Oxford University Press, Oxford 2014

HEIDEGGER, Martin, "The origin of the work of art" [1937], in *Poetry, Language, Thought*, HarperCollins, London 2013

HILL, P., *Contemporary History of Garden Design. European Gardens between Art and Architecture*, Birkhäuser, Basel 2004

HOORMANN, A., *Land Art: Kunstprojekte zwischen Landschaft und öffentlichem Raum*, Reimer, Berlin 1996

HUNT, John Dixon, *The Afterlife of Gardens*, University of Pennsylvania Press, Philadelphia 2004

JENCKS, C., *The Universe in the Landscape: Landforms by Charles Jencks*, Frances Lincoln, London 2011

JOHNSON, J.; FRANKEL, F., *Modern Landscape Architecture: Redefining the Garden*, Abbeville, New York 1991

KASSLER, E.B., *Modern gardens and the Landscape*, The Museum of Modern Art, New York 1964, 1984

KASTNER, J.; WALLIS, B., *Land and Environmental Art*, Phaidon, London 2010 — *Nature*, Whitechapel Art Gallery, London 2012

KAYE, N., *Site-specific art. Performance, Place and Documentation*, Routledge, Abingdon 2000

KEMAL, S.; GASKEL, I.; *Landscape, Natural Beauty and the Arts*, Cambridge University Press, Cambridge 1995

KEPES, Gyorgy (ed.), *Arts of the Environment*, Braziller, New York 1972

KRAUSS, Rosalind E., "A voyage on the North Sea": Art in the Age of the Post-Medium Condition, Thames and Hudson, London 2000

— "Sculpture in the Expanded Field" in *The originality of the Avantgarde and other Modernity Myths*, MIT Press, Cambridge, MA 1985

KWON, Miwon, *One Place after Another. Site-Specific Art and Locational Identity*, MIT Press, Cambridge, MA 2002

LANGEN, S., *Outdoor Art: Extraordinary Sculpture Parks and Art in Nature*, Prestel, München 2015

— *Die Kunst liegt in der Natur: Spektakuläre Skulpturenparks und Kunstlandschaften*, Prestel, München 2015

LASSUS, B., "L'obligation de l'invention – Du paysage aux ambiances successives" in *Cinq propositions pour une théorie du paysage*, Éditions Champ Vallon, Seyssel 1994

LAWRENCE, S.; FOY, G. *Music in Stone. Great Sculpture Gardens of the World*, Scala Books, New York 1984

LIPPARD, Lucy R., *On the beaten track. Tourism, art and place*, The New Press, New York 1999

— *Six years: the dematerialisation of the art object*, Praeger, New York 1997

LYALL, S., *Designing the New Landscape*, Thames and Hudson, London 1991

MACDOUGALL, E.B.; JASHEMSKI, W.F, "Greek antecedents of garden sculpture" in *Ancient Roman gardens*, Harvard University, Washington 1981

MADERUELO, J., *El paisaje: génesis de un*

concepto, Abada editores, Madrid 2005
MADERUELO, J. (ed.) et al., *Arte público: Naturaleza y Ciudad*, Fundación César Manrique, Teguise 2001
— vid Maderuelo, under Huesca, *Actas del... 1996, 1997, 1998, 2000*, 2000
MALPAS, W., *Land Art: A Complete Guide to Landscape, Environmental, Earthworks, Nature, Sculpture and Installation Art*, Crescent Moon Publishing, Maidstone, Kent, 2016
— *Land Art, Earthworks, Installations, Environments, Sculpture,* Crescent Moon Publishing, Maidstone, Kent 1998
— *Land Art and Land Artists: Pocket Guide (Sculptors)*, Crescent Moon Publishing, Maidstone, Kent 2013
— *Land Art in Great Britain: A Complete Guide To Landscape, Environmental, Earthworks, Nature, Sculpture and Installation Art in Great Britain*, Crescent Moon Publishing, Maidstone, Kent 2012
MARLAIS, H.; ONORATO, R. J. (eds.), *Blurring the Boundaries: Installation Art 1969-1996,* La Jolla Museum of Contemporary Art, San Diego, CA 1997
MATZNER, F. (ed.), *Public Art - A Reader*, Hatje Cantz, Ostfildern 2004
MASSA, A., *I parchi museo di scultura contemporanea in Italia*, Loggia De' Lanzi, Firenze 1995
MEULEN, M. van der, "Cardinal Loggia De' Lanzi Esi's Antique Sculpture Garden: Notes on a Painting by Hendrick van Cleef III", in *The Burlington Magazine*, Vol.116, No. 850 (Jan. 1974), Burlington Magazine Publications, London
MILLES, M., *Eco-Asthetics,* Bloomsbury Academic, London 2014
MITCHELL, W.J.T., *Art and the Public Sphere,* University of Chicago Press, Chicago 1990
MOORE, C.; MITCHELL, W.; TURNBULL Jr., W., *The Poetics of Gardens*, MIT Press, Cambridge, MA 1993
MORLAND, J., *New Milestones. Sculpture, Community and the Land*, Common Ground, London 1988
MORRIS, Robert, *Continuous Project Altered Daily: The Writings of Robert Morris*, MIT Press, Cambridge MA 19
— "Earthworks: Land Reclamation as Sculpture" in Senie and Webster 1979
— "Notes on Sculpture" in *Artforum*, February 1966
MOSSER, M.; TEYSSOT, G., *The History of Garden Design: The Western Tradition from the Renaissance to the Present*

Day, Thames and Hudson, London 1991
MOYER, T.; HARPER, G., *Landscapes for Art: Contemporary Sculpture Parks*, University of Washington Press 2008
NOLAN, B., *9+1 Young Dutch Landscape Architects*, NAi Publishers, Rotterdam 1999
OLIVEIRA, N. de; OXLEY, N.; PETRY, M., *Installation Art in the New Millenium: The Empire of the Senses,* Thames and Hudson, London 2004
PIGEAT, J. P., *Parcs et Jardins Contemporains*, La Maison Rustique, Paris 1990
RAQUEJO, T., *Land Art*, Nerea, Madrid 1998
REISS, J. H., *From Margin to Center: The Spaces of Installation Art*, MIT Press, Cambridge, MA, reprint 2001
RIDGWAY, B., S., "Greek antecedents of garden sculpture", in *Ancient Roman gardens*, Dumbarton Oaks Trustees for Harvard University, Cambridge 1981
RODRIGUES, J., *Arte, Natureza e a Cidade*, Cooperativa de Actividades Artísticas, Porto 1993
ROGER, A., *Art court traité du paysage*, Gallimard, Paris 1997
ROSENBERG, H., *The De-definition of Art. Action Art to Pop to Earthworks*, University of Chicago Press, New York 1983
— *The Tradition of the New*, Da Capo Press, New York re-issue 1994
ROSENTHAL, M., *Understanding Installation Art: From Duchamp to Holzer,* Prestel, München 2003
SCHAMA, S., *Landscape and Memory*, Alfred P. Knopf, New York 1962, 1996
SCHARDT, H., *Europäischer Skulpturenpark,* Willebadessen 1979
SENIE, H.F.; WEBSTER, S., *Critical Issues in Public Art: Content, Context, and Controversy*, Smithsonian Institute Press, Washington, D.C 1998
SMITHSON, Robert, FLAM J. (ed.), *Robert Smithson: The Collected Writings*, University of California Press, Berkeley reprinted 1996
— *El paisaje entrópico: una retrospectiva. 1960-1973*, IVAM, Valencia 1993
— ed. by N. Holt, *The Writings of Robert Smithson,* New York University Press, New York 1979
— "A Sedimentation of the Mind: Earth Projects" in *Artforum*, September 1968
— "Toward the Development of an Air Terminal Site" in *Artforum*, Summer 1967
SONFIST, A. (ed.), *Art in the Land: A critical anthology of environmental Art*, E.P. Dutton, New York 1972, 1983

STACE, A., *Sculpture Parks and Trails of Britain & Ireland*, A&C Black, London 2013
STRELOW, H., *Ökologische Ästhetik. Theorie und Praxis einer künstlerischen Umweltgestaltung,* Birkhäuser, Basel 2004
STTENBERGEN, C.; REH, W., *Architecture and Landscape. The Design Experiment of the Great European Gardens and Landscapes*, Prestel, München 1996
SUDERBURG, E., *Space, Site, Intervention: Situating Installation Art,* University of Minnesota, Duluth MN 2000
TATARKIEWICZ, W., *A history of Six Ideas* (1976), 1980, Springer 2013
TAYLOR, Marc C., *Double Negative, Sculpture in the Land,* Rizzoli – The Museum of Contemporary Art, New York – Los Angeles, CA 1991
TIBERGHIEN, Gilles A., *La Nature dans l'art*, Actes Sud, Arles 2005
— *Nature, art, paysage*, Actes Sud, Arles 2001
— *Land Art*, Éditions Carré, Paris 1995
— *Sculptures inorganiques. Land Art et Architecture*, Centre Pompidou, Paris 1992
TURNER, T., *Garden History: Philosophy and Design 2000 BC – 2000 AD,* Spon Press, London 2005
VIDLER, A., *Warped Space. Art, Architecture and Anxiety in Modern Culture*, MIT Press, Cambridge MA 2000
VAR. AUTHORS, *Art in the landscape*, The Chinati Foundation, Marfa TX 2000
VAR. AUTHORS, *Artificial natural networks*, Vintage Books, New York 2001
VAR. AUTHORS, *Guía de buenas prácticas. Proyectos de arte contemporáneo en espacios públicos naturales y urbanos,* Fundación NMAC, Cádiz 2002
VAR. AUTHORS, *Dalla natura all'arte, dall'arte alla natura. 38ª Biennale di Venezia,* Electa, Milano 1978
VAR. AUTHORS, *Vision machine*, Musée des beaux-arts de Nantes – Somogy, Nantes – Paris 2000
WARNKE, M., *Political landscape*, *The Art history of Nature*, Reaktion Books, London 1994
WAYMARK, J., *Modern Garden Design Since 1900*, Thames and Hudson, London 2003
WEILACHER, U., *In Gardens: Profiles of Contemporary European Landscape Architecture,* Birkhäuser, Basel 2005
— *Zwischen Landschaftsarchitektur und Land Art / Between Landscape*

Architecture and Land Art, Birkhäuser, Basel 1996

WEILACHER, U.; WULLSCHLEGER, P., *Guide suisse de l'architecture du paysage*, PPUR, Lausanne 2005

WEINTRAUB, L., *To Life!: Eco Art in Pursuit of a Sustainable Planet*, University of California Press, Berkeley 2012

WELLS, R., *Scale in Contemporary Sculpture: Enlargement, Miniaturisation and the Life-Size*, Routledge 2013

WILLIAMS, Richard J., *After modern sculpture: Art in the United States and Europe 1965–70*, Manchester University Press, Manchester 2000

WREDE, S.; ADAMS, W. H. (eds.) *Denatured Visions: Landscape and Culture in the Twentieth Century*, Museum of Modern Art, New York 1991

PARKS & ARTISTS

REECE, Colleen L., *Angel of the North*, Thorndike, Farmington Hills, MI 2005

SIMPSON, David, *Aal Aboot: The Angel of the North*, My World, Houghton-le-Spring 2013

TOREVELL, DAVID, *Liturgy and the Beauty of the Unknown: Another Place*, Routledge, Oxford 2007 Thorndike, Farmington Hills, MI 2005

VAR. AUTHORS, *Guida ad Arte all'arte. 10.*, Associazione Arte Continua, Prato 2005

BONITO OLIVA, A. (cur.); PUTNAM, J., (cur.), et al., *Arte all'arte. 9. La forme delle nuvole*, Associazione Arte Continua, Gli Ori, Pistoia 2004

CRISTIANI, M; GRAZIOLI, E.; HANRU, H., *Arte all'arte. Arte, architettura, paesaggio*, Associazione Arte Continua, Gli Ori, Pistoia 2003

DE CECCO, E. (cur.); TODOLÍ, V., (cur.) et al., *Arte all'arte. 7. Arte, architettura, paesaggio, Miroslaw Balka, Lothar Baumgarten, Tacita Dean, Cildo Meireles, Marisa Merz, Damian Ortega*, Associazione Arte Continua, Gli Ori, San Gimignano 2003

SANS, J. (cur.); TAZZI, P.L., (cur.) et al., *Arte all'arte. 6. Arte, architettura, paesaggio, Marina Abramovic, Cai Guo-Quiang, Jannis Kounellis, Surasi Kusolwong, Pascale Marthine Tayou, Nari Ward, Loris Cecchini, Gianni Motti, Daniel Buren, José A. Hernández Díez, Ottonella Mocellin*, Associazione Arte Continua, Gli Ori, San Gimignano 2002

PINTO, R. (cur.); WILLIAMS, G. (cur.) et al., *Arte all'arte. 5. Arte, architettura, pae-*

saggio, Tania Bruguera, Martin Creed, Wim Delvoye, Alberto garutti, Kendell Geers, Sislej Xhafa, A Constructed Worlds, Associazione Arte Continua, Gli Ori, San Gimignano 2000

MATZNER, F. (cur.); VETTESSE, A. (cur.) et al., *Arte all'arte. 4. Arte, architettura, paesaggio, Daniel Buren, Olafur Eliasson, Joseph Kossuth, Atelier Van Lieshout, Giulio Paolini, Tobias Rehberger*, Associazione Arte Continua, Gli Ori, San Gimignano 1999

MATZNER, F. (cur.); VETTESSE, A. (cur.) et al., *Arte all'arte. 3. Arte, architettura, paesaggio*, Associazione Arte Continua, Gli Ori, San Gimignano 1998

SEVCIK, J.; SANUWAERT, D.; WEIBEL, P., *Art Garden: Austria's Sculpture Park*, Hatje Cantz, Ostfildern 2006

TUIJN, M.; ZEELAND, N. van; BROEKHUIZEN, D., *Museum Beelden aan Zee*, Wbooks, Zwolle 2012

VAR. AUTHORS, *Parade, a choice of the Beelden aan Zee museum*, Museum Beelden aan Zee 2002

SCHROEDER, S., *Skulpturenpark Berlin Zentrum*, Walther König, Köln 2010 Stiftung Blickachsen, *Blickachsen 9: Skulpturen in Bad Homburg und Frankfurt RheinMain*, Wienand 2015

ASSMANN, W.R.; WIESLER, H., *Blickachsen. Skulpturen im Kurpark Bad Homburg v. d. Höhe*, Scheffel, Bad Homburg 1997

VAR. AUTHORS, *Broomhill Sculpture Gardens*, Broomhill Art Hotel, Barnstaple 2003

Cass Sculpture Foundation, *Cass Sculpture Foundation: 20 Years of Commissioning Large Scale Sculpture*, Hatje Cantz, Ostfildern 2012

SHEA, C.; PRATT, K., *Cass Sculpture Foundation: The International Resource for Commissioning, Exhibiting and Selling Monumental Sculpture*, Cass Sculpture Foundation, Goodwood 2012

CASS, W., *The Man Behind the Sculpture: The Autobiography of Wilfred Cass*, Unicorn Press, London 2015

MARCHANT, S.; FLETCHER, J., *Lynn Chadwick the Sculptures at Lypiatt Park*, Blain Southern, London 2014

VAR. AUTHORS, *Cass Sculpture Foundation: The International Resource for Commissioning, Exhibiting and Selling Monumental Sculpture*, Cass Sculpture Foundation, Goodwood 2012

VAR. AUTHORS, *Cass Sculpture Foundation: 20 Years of Commissioning*

Large Scale Sculpture, Hatje Cantz, Berlin 2012

FIZ, A., *Parco internazionale della scultura. Catanzaro*, Silvana, Cinisello Balsamo 2014

VAR. AUTHORS, *The Chianti Sculpure Park*, Parco Sculture del Chianti 2004

VAR. AUTHORS, *Tuscia electa. Arte contemporanea nel Chianti 2002–2003*, Maschietto Editore, Firenze 2003

CAVALLUCCI, F. (cur.), *Tuscia electa 1999*. Hopefulmonster, Torino 1999

— *Tuscia electa 1997. Percosi d'arte contemporanea nel Chianti*, Hopefulmonster, Torino 1997

EZQUIAGA, M., *Museo Chillida Leku*, Chillida Leku, Hernani 2004

GARCÍA MARCOS, Juan A., *Eduardo Chillida*, Txertoa, San Sebastián 2005

HOPPE, W.; KRONSBEIN, S., *Landschaftspark Duisburg-Nord*, Wohlfarth, Duisburg 1999

GORMLEY, A., *Antony Gormley. Exposure*, Gemeente Lelystad, 2011

VAR. AUTHORS, *Skulpturen i naturen, International Skulpturpark Farum*, Farum Municipality Kulturhuset, Farum 1999

ABRIOUX, Y., *Ian Hamilton Finlay. A visual primer*, Reaktion, London 1985– 1992

FINLAY, A. (ed.), *Wood Notes Wild: Essays on the Poetry and Art of Ian Hamilton Finlay*, Polygon, Edinburgh 1995

ZDENEK, F.; SIMIG, P., *Ian Hamilton Finlay: Works in Europe 1972–1995*, Hatje Cantz, Ostfildern 1995

CORDONE, D., *La favola dell'arte e della bellezza. Itinerario a Fiumara d'arte*, Pietro Vittorietti Edizioni, 2010

PETTINEO, A., *Tusa dall'Universitas Civium alla Fiumara d'Arte*, Armando Siciliano Editore, Messina 2012

ELMO, R.; GIOVANNA, *Fiumara d'arte. La rifondazione di un territorio*, Archeoclub d'Italia, Tusa 2008

MARTIN, R., *The Sculpted Forest. Sculptures in the Forest of Dean*, Redcliffe Press, Bristol 1990

FULTON, Hamish, *Walking Passed. Time in the Presence of Nature*, IVAM, Valencia 1992

VAR. AUTHORS, *La Fondation Pierre Gianadda*, Fondation Gianadda, Martigny 1983

MARCHESSEAU, D.; BLANC, Anne-Laure, *Leonard Gianadda: La Sculpture et la Fondation*, Gallery Guy Pieters 2008

VAR. AUTHORS *Skulpturenmuseum Glaskasten Marl: Skulpturen aus dem*

Kunstbesitz, Stadt Marl 2007
MALPAS, W., *Art of Andy Goldsworthy,* Crescent Moon Publishing, Maidstone, Kent 2013
EZIKA, U., *Ready-made und Landschaft,* VDM Verlag, Saarbrücken 2010
GOLDSWORTHY, A., *Andy Goldsworthy: A Collaboration with Nature,* Harry N. Abrams, New York 1990
WARNER, M.; ELLIOT, A., Hat Hill Sculpture Foundation, *Sculpture at Goodwood: British Contemporary Sculpture,* Sculpture at Goodwood, Goodwood 2001
MARLOW, T.; KRENS, T.; MENGHAM, R., *Thinking Big: Concepts for 21st Century British Sculpture,* Sculpture at Goodwood 2002
ELLIOT, A., *Sculpture at Goodwood,* Sculpture at Goodwood, 2000
VAR. AUTHORS, *Sculpture at Goodwood. A vision for twenty-first century British sculpture* Sculpture at Goodwood, Goodwood 2002
BARILLI, R.; *et al.,* Arte Ambientale. La *collezione Gori nella Fattoria di Celle,* Allemandi, Torino 1994
— *Art in Arcadia. The Gori Collection at Celle,* Umberto Allemandi, Torino 1994
CEI, M., *Il parco di Celle a Pistoia,* EDIFIR, Firenze 1994
GORI, G., *Collezione Gori. 30 anni di arte ambientale condivisa. Fattoria di Celle,* Gli Ori, Pistoia 2012
VAR. AUTHORS, *Historia y naturaleza: la Colección Gori,* IVAM, Valencia 2003
VAR. AUTHORS, *Arte ambientale. Fattoria di Celle. Collezione Gori,* Gli Ori, Pistoia 2009
VAR. AUTHORS, *Fattoria di Celle collezione Gori. Un percorso nell'arte ambientale,* Gli Ori, Pistoia 2012
GORMLEY, Antony; HOLBORN, M., *Antony Gormley on Sculpture,* Thames and Hudson, London 2015
— *Land: An exploration of what it means to be human in remote places across the British Isles,* The Landmark Trust, London 2016
— *Horizon Field,* Walther König, Cologne 2010
— *One and Another,* Jonathan Cape, London 2010
— *Making an Angel,* Booth-Clibborn Editons, London 2002
GRANT, B.; HARRIS, P. (eds), *Natural Order. Visual Arts & Crafts in Grizedale Forest Park,* The Grizedale Society, Ambleside 1996

— *The Grizedale Experience. Sculpture, Arts and Theatre in Lakeland Forest,* Canongate Books, Edinburgh 1991
STEPHENS, C.; PHILLIPS, M., *The Barbara Hepworth Sculpture Garden,* Tate Publishing, London 2002
PALLASMAA, J.; REENBERG, H.; HOLL, S., *Steven Holl: Heart – Herning Museum of Contemporary Art,* Hatje Cantz 2009
MADERUELO, J. (dir.) *et al., Huesca: Arte y naturaleza. Actas del V Curso: Arte público,* Diputación de Huesca 2000
— *Huesca: Arte y naturaleza. Actas del IV Curso: Desde la ciudad,* Diputación de Huesca, Huesca 2000
— *Huesca: Arte y naturaleza. Actas del III Curso: El Jardín como arte,* Diputación de Huesca, Huesca 1998
— *Huesca: Arte y naturaleza. Actas del II Curso: El Paisaje,* Diputación de Huesca, Huesca 1997
— *Huesca: Arte y naturaleza. Actas del I Curso,* Diputación de Huesca, Huesca 1996
MADERUELO, J., *Fernando Casas, Natur-geist,* Diputación de Huesca 1997
MOURE, G., *Richard Long. Spanish Stones,* Diputación de Huesca – Polígrafa, Huesca – Barcelona 1999
CHILLIDA, A.; LEBRERO, J., *Ulrich Rückriem,* Huesca 1995, Diputación de Huesca 1995
VAR. AUTHORS, "National Identity After Communism: Hungary's Statue Park," in *Advances in the History of Rhetoric,* Vol.18, Supp.1, 2015
VAR. AUTHORS, *El bosque de Agustín Ibarrola,* Diputación de Bizkaia, Bilbao 1987
BLÖMEKE, K., *Museum Insel Hombroich. Die begehbaren Skulpturen Erwin Heerichs,* Hatje Cantz, Berlin 2009
CASTRO, X.A, *Isla de las Esculturas,* Illa da Xunqueira do Lérez – Pontevedra Diputación de Pontevedra 1999
JOHNSTON, P., *Visiter les jardins de l'ima-ginaire,* Sud Ouest, Bordeaux 2004
PEAKE, Tony, *Derek Jarman,* Overlook Press, New York 2002
JARMAN, D.; SOOLEY H., *Derek Jarman's Garden,* Thames and Hudson, London 1995

On Jupiter Artland:
JENCKS, C., *The Garden of Cosmic Speculation,* Frances Lincon, London 2005
JACOBI, F., *Dani Karavan: Retrospektive,* Wasmuth, Tubinga 2008
KARAVAN, D., *Dani Karavan,* Benteli

Verlag, Bern 2003
— *Dani Karavan,* Maschietto, Siena 1999
VAR. AUTHORS, *Domaine 1994,* Domaine de Kerguéhennec, Bignan 1995
VAR. AUTHORS, *Le Domaine de Kerguéhennec,* Inventaire général, Parcours du Patrimoine, Rennes 1988
KIENAST, D., *Dieter Kienast. Die Poetik des Gartens,* Birkhäuser, Basel 2000
— *Kienast Gardens,* Birkhäuser, Basel 1997
KIENAST, D.; VOGT, G., *Kienast Vogt. Friedhöfe und Parks / Parks and Cemeteries,* Birkhäuser, Basel 2001
— *Kienast Vogt. Außenräume / Open Spaces,* Birkhäuser, Basel 2000
DAHL, C., J., *Kistefos-museet,* Labyrinth Press, Oslo 2000
GRAHAM, Dan, *Skulpturenpark Köln. Köln Skulptur 4. 10 Jahre: 10 Years Skulpturenpark Köln 1997–2007,* Walther König, Köln 2007
VAR. AUTHORS, *KölnSkulptur 1.Zeit-genössische Bildhauer im Skulpturenpark Köln,* Wienand Verlag, Köln 1997
TRUMMER, Th.D., *KölnSkulptur #8,* Waltherkönig 2015
TRUMMER, Th.D., *KölnSkulptur #6,* Waltherkönig 2011
VAR. AUTHORS, *Sculpture in the Rijks-museum Kröller-Müller,* Enschede, Haarlem 1992
VAR. AUTHORS, *Kröller-Müller. The First 100 Years,* Enschede, Haarlem 1989
VAR. AUTHORS, *Kroller-Müller Museum,* J. Enschede, Haarlem 1978
ANDELA, G., *Sculpture Garden Kröller-Mutler Museum,* Nai 010 Publishers, Rotterdam 2009
— *Beeldentuin Kröller-Müller,* NAI Uitgevers, Rotterdam 2007
BLOEMHEUVEL, M., *Kröller-Müller Museum: The History of a Sculpture Garden,* NAI Publishers, Rotterdam 2007
VAR. AUTHORS, *Kunstwegen. Das Reisebuch,* Vechtetalroute mit Kunstwegen 2005
VILKS, Lars, *Myndigheterna som konst-närligt material. Den långa historien om Nimis, Arx, Omfalos och Ladonien,* Ladonia 2003
— *Nimis och Arx,* Ladonia 1994
KARNELL, G.W.G., Prof. Em., Stock-holm School of Economics, "Artistic eccentricity – a societal dilemma for rights bureaucracy," a contribution to the discussion about law and the arts
BROCKHAUS, C., *Wilhem Lehmbruck*

Museum Duisburg, Prestel, München 2001

LEHMBRUCK, W,; SCHUBERT, D., *Wilhelm Lehmbruck Catalogue Raisonné der Skulpturen*, Wernersche Verlagsges. Worms 2001

WILHELM-LEHMBRUCK-MUSEUM DUISBURG, *Europäische Skulptur der Zweiten Moderne, Programm und Perspektive: Kurzführer*, 1990

SHEELER, J.; GILLANDERS, R., *Little Sparta: A Guide to the Garden of Ian Hamilton Finlay*, Birlinn 2015

SHEELER, J.; LAWSON, A. (Photo), *Little Sparta: The Garden of Ian Hamilton Finlay*, Frances Lincoln, London 2003

GILLANDERS, R., *Little Sparta. A Portrait of a Garden*, National Galleries of Scotland, Edinburgh 1998

VAR. AUTHORS, *Parque de Esculturas Tierras Altas Lomas de Oro*, Ayuntamiento de Villoslada de Cameros 2000

LONG, R., MOORHOUSE, P., HOOKER, D., *Walking the Line*, Thames and Hudson, London 2005

KULTURMANN, U., *The Art of Richard Long*, Crescent Moon Publishing, Maidstone, Kent 2011

LAIRD, M.; PALMER, H. (Photographer), *The Formal Garden: Traditions of Art and Nature*, Thames and Hudson, London 1992

TOJNER, E.T.; CRENZIEN, H.; WAMBER, J., *The Louisiana Sculpture Park*, Louisiana Museum of Modern Art, Humlebæk 2010

VAR. AUTHORS, *Louisiana, the collection and buildings*, Louisiana Museum of Modern Art, Humlebæk 1995

VAR. AUTHORS, *La Fondation Marguerite et Aimé Maeght*, Adrien Maeght, 2000

MARCHÁN, S., *Fundación César Manrique*, Lanzarote, Axel Menges, Stuttgart 1996

BORSICH, W., *Lanzarote & César Manrique*, Mariar, Madrid 1994

BENTEIN-STOELEN, M.R., *Collection Catalogue of Middelheim Open-Air Sculpture Museum*, Middelheim Museum, Antwerpen 1993

CASSIMAN, B., *Catalogue New Sculptures*, Middelheim Museum, Antwerpen 1993

VAR. AUTHORS, *New Sculptures, Open-Air Museum of Sculpture Middelheim*, Middelheim Museum, Antwerpen 1993

VAR. AUTHORS, *Acquisitions 1994–1997*, Middelheim Museum, Antwerpen 1997

OHMAN, N., *Moderna Museet, Stockholm*, Scala 1998

PHEBY, H., *Henry Moore: Back to a Land*, Yorkshire Sculpture Park, West Bretton 2015

VAR. AUTHORS, *Henry Moore at Perry Green (Henry Moore Foundation)*, Scala Publishers, London 2011

KOSINKI, Dorothy M. (ed.), *Henry Moore: Sculpting the Twentieth Century*, Yale University Press, London and New Haven, CT 2001

MITCHINSON, D., *Celebrating Moore: Works from the Collection of The Henry Moore Foundation*, Lund Humphries, Aldershot, Hampshire 2006

BUSSMANN, K.; KÖNIG, K. (dir.); MATZNER, F. (ed.), *Skulptur.Projekte in Münster 1987, Westfälisches Landesmuseum für Kunst und Kulturgeschichte à Münster*, DuMont Verlag, Köln 1987

— *Sculpture. Projects in Münster 1997*, Gerd Hatje, Stuttgart 1997

VAR. AUTHORS, *Skulptur-Projekte in Münster 1987*, Du Mont, Köln 1987

VENET, B., *L'experience du Muy*, Somogy, Paris 2009

WILKINSON, A., *Within the landscape*, New Art Centre, Salisbury 2003

VAR. AUTHORS, *Fundación NMAC 2002 / 2003. Montenmedio Arte Contemporáneo*, Fundación NMAC, Vejer de la Frontera 2003

VAR. AUTHORS, *Arte y naturaleza. Montenmedio Arte Contemporáneo*, Fundación NMAC, Vejer de la Frontera 2001

VAR. AUTHORS, *Skulpturlandskap Nordland = Artscape Nordland*, Geelmuyden Kiese 1999

VAR. AUTHORS, *Artscape Nordland 1994, Report from Seminarium in Bødo and Henningsvaer*, Artscape Nordland, Bødo 1994

VAR. AUTHORS, *Centre of Polish Scultpure in Oronsko*, Oronsko 2002

SEVCIK, J.; SNAUWAERT, D.; WEIBEL, P., et al., *Art Garden – Austria's Sculpture Park (Österreichischer Skulpturenpark)* Hatje Cantz, Ostfildern 2006

VAR. AUTHORS, *The Panza Collection*, Skira, Milano 2002

VAR. AUTHORS, *Villa Menafoglio Litta Panza and the Panza di Biumo Collection*, Skira, Milano 2001

ELÓSEGUI ITXASO, M., *El Peine del Viento de Chillida: ingeniería de su colocación por José María Elósegui*, Colegio de Ingenieros de Caminos, Canales y Puertos, Madrid 2008

GIANELLI, I., *Il giardino delle sculture*

fluide di Penone, Allemandi, Torino 2008

GOLDSWORTHY, A., *Refuges d'art*, Fage Editions, Lyon 2008

LANDESBETRIEB WALD und HOLZ NRW, *Rheinelbe - Art in Nature: Der Skulpturenpark von Herman Prigann*, Klartext, Essen 2010

FUCHS, R. H. (ed.), *Ulrich Rückriem. Estela & Granero*, Ministerio de Cultura, Madrid 1989

VAR. AUTHORS, *Guía del Parque Municipal García Sanabria*, Excelentísimo Ayuntamiento de Santa Cruz de Tenerife 1994

VAR. AUTHORS, *Santa Cruz de Tenerife. Esculturas en la calle*, Gobierno de Canarias. Consejería de Cultura, Santa Cruz de Tenerife 1985

VAR. AUTHORS, *2° Simposio Internacional de escultura de Santo Tirso '93*, cat. expo., Santo Tirso 1993

MORLIN, Diego, *Sentiero del Silenzio*, Editori Vari 2014

GERMEN, S., *La Mormaire, Richard Serra*, Richter, Düsseldorf 1997

KRAUSS, R., *Richard Serra / Sculpture*, Museum of Modern Art, New York 1986

VAR. AUTHORS, *Serralves: the Foundation, the House and the Park, the Museum, the Architect, the Collection, the Landscape*, Serralves Fundaçao, Porto 2002

PARMIGGIANI, S. (cur.), *Daniel Spoerri. La messa in scena degli oggetti*, Skira, Milano 2004

MAZZANTI, A. (cur.), *Il Giardino di Daniel Spoerri*, Gli Ori, Pistoia 2004

VAR. AUTHORS, *Il Giardino di Daniel Spoerri, Piccolo gabinetto delle curiosità degli artista del Giardino di Daniel Spoerri*, Kunsthaus, Crenchen 2004

BUSCH, C., et al., *Many Happy Returns. Kunstverein Springhornhof, Neuenkirchen 2003*, Cristoph Keller, Berlin 2003

VAR. AUTHORS, *Kunst-Landschaft 1967–2000*, Kunstverein Stiftung Springhornhof, Falazik 2001

AGOSTINI, L., *Il giardino dei Tarocchi*, Lulu.com, Morrisville NC 2007

SAINT PHALLE, N. de, with JILL JOHNSTON, and G. PIETROMARCHI (photographs), *Niki de Saint Phalle Mythos Tarot-Garten*, Benteli Verlag, Bern 2005

MAZZANTI, A. (ed.); RESTANY, P.; CRISPOLTI, E., *Niki de Saint Phalle. Il Giardino dei tarocchi*, Charta, Milano 1998

VAR. AUTHORS, *Trilogy. Kunst – Natur – Videnskab, Tickon*, Danmark 1996

VAR. AUTHORS, *Umedalen Skulptur 1994–2004*, Galerie Stefan Andersson,

Sweden 2004

VAR. AUTHORS, *Le Vent des Forêts. Catalogue ouvres 1997–2003*, Vent des Forêts, Fresnes-au-Mont 2003

VAR. AUTHORS, *Le Vent des Forêts, Catalogue thématique des ouvres 2004*, Vent des Forêts, Fresnes-au-Mont 2004

ARNOUX, R. et al., *La Fondation Bernar Venet*, Bernard Chauveau éditeur, Suresnes 2014

LAUBE, Lucy M., *Vigeland Sculpture Park Oslo: Definitely One of Oslo's Highlights and a Unique Experience*, Calvendo Verlag 2014

WIKBORG, T., *Gustav Vigeland: his art and sculpture park*, s/c 1990

PERALTO, F.; PERALTO MORENO, R., *Typical Spanish: performance en los alrededores del Museo Vostell Malpartida*, Corona del Sur, Málaga 2011

— *Visita de riguroso incógnito al Museo Vostell Malpartida*, Corona del Sur, Málaga 2011

VAR. AUTHORS, *Museo Vostell Malpartida*, Editora Regional Extremadura, Mérida 2003

VAR. AUTHORS, *Vostell en las Colecciones Malpartideñas*, Editora Regional de Extremadura y Ayuntamiento de Malpartida, Mérida, Malpartida 2001

KLEMENT, C., *Der Skulpturenpark Waldfrieden*, Skulpturenpark Waldfrieden, Wuppertal 2012

MAHLBERG, Hermann J., *Vom Haus Waldfrieden zum Skulpturenpark*, Verlag Muller und Busmann 2011

VAR. AUTHORS, *Wanås 2005 – Contemporary Nordic Sculpture 1980–2005*, Wanås Foundation, Knislinge 2005

VAR. AUTHORS, *The History of Wanås*, Wanås Foundation, Knislinge 2004

LIN, MAYA, *Wanås 2004–Maya Lin*, Wanas Foundation, Knislinge 2004

VAR. AUTHORS, *Risk of Maturing – Vision and choices*, Wanås Seminar, Wanås Foundation, Knislinge 2003

VAR. AUTHORS, *Wanås 2003–4 Swedes*, Wanås Foundation, Knislinge 2003

VAR. AUTHORS, *Wanås catalogues 1989–2002*, Wanås Foundation, Knislinge 1989–2002

VAR. AUTHORS, *Art at Wanås*, Wanås Foundation, Knislinge 2000

VAR. AUTHORS, *Wanås 2000*, Wanås Foundation, Knislinge 2000

VAR. AUTHORS, *Malmö Artmuseum at Wanås*, Wanås Foundation, Knislinge 1999

VAR. AUTHORS, *Wanås 1998*, Wanås

Foundation, Knislinge 1998

VAR. AUTHORS, *Wanås Exhibitions 1987–1997*, Wanås Foundation, Knislinge 1997

VAR. AUTHORS, *Wanås the art, the park, the castle*, Wanås Foundation, Knislinge 1994

CORTS, Udo, et al., *Skulpturenpark. Wiesbadener Kunstsommer 2004*, Galerie Hubert Winter, Wien 2004

MOTTO, A.; MOTTO, J.L., *The Woodland Outdoor Sculptures: Installations from 1974–2009*, ATM Productions 2009

MAGNER, D., *Devil's Glen. Sculpture in Woodland*, Sculpture in Woodland 2004

COULSON, Sarah, *KAWS Catalogue at Yorkshire Sculpture Park*, Yorkshire Sculpture Park, West Bretton 2016

VAR. AUTHORS, *Yorkshire Sculpture Park: A Guide To Works in the Open Air*, York-shire Sculpture Park, West Bretton 2015

COULSON, S., *Miró: Sculptor: Yorkshire Sculpture Park*, Yorkshire Sculpture Park, West Bretton 2012

GOLDSWORTHY, A.; FISKE, T., *Andy Goldsworthy at Yorkshire Sculpture Park*, Yorkshire Sculpture Park, West Bretton 2007

GREEN, L.; MURRAY, P.; ARMITAGE, S., *Yorkshire Sculpture Park: Landscape for Art*, Yorkshire Sculpture Park, West Bretton 2008

LILLEY, C.; PHEBY, H., *Miró: Sculptor: Yorkshire Sculpture Park 17 March 2012 to 6 January 2013*, Yorkshire Sculpture Park, West Bretton 2012

— *Peter Randall-Page at Yorkshire Sculpture Park: Exhibition Guide*, York-shire Sculpture Park, West Bretton 2009

LILLEY, C.; HODBY, A., *Yorkshire Sculpture Park: Essential Sculpture Guide*, Yorkshire Sculpture Park, West Bretton 2009

MURRAY, P.; LILLEY, C.; PLENSA, J., *Jaume Plensa*, Yorkshire Sculpture Park, West Bretton 2011

NASH, D.; PROULX, A.; MURRAY, P., *David Nash at Yorkshire Sculpture Park*, York-shire Sculpture Park, West Bretton 2010

PHEBY, H.; NASH, D.; LILLEY, C.; COULSON, S., *David Nash at Yorkshire Sculpture Park*, Yorkshire Sculpture Park, West Bretton 2010

VAR. AUTHORS, *Henry Moore in Bretton Country Park*, Yorkshire Sculpture Park, West Bretton 1994

SOCIALIST REALISM

AUCOUTURIER, M. et DEPRETTO, C., "Le 'Réalisme Socialiste' dans La littérature et l'art des Pays Slaves," *Cahiers Slaves*, No. 8, Université de Paris-Sorbonne, Paris 2004

BANKS, M., ed., *The Aesthetic Arsenal: Socialist Realism Under Stalin*. The Institute for Contemporary Art, P.S. 1 Museum, New York 1993

BAUDIN, A., *Le realisme Socialiste Sovietique de la periode Jdanovienne (1947–1953)*, Peter Lang, Bern 1997

BOWN, M. Cullerne; TAYLOR, B. (eds.), *Art of the Soviets: Painting, Sculpture and Architecture in a One-Party State, 1917–1992*. Manchester University 1993

DOBRENKO, E., *The Landscape of Stalinism. The Art and Ideology of Soviet Space*, University of Washington 2003

DOBRENKO, E.; SAVAGE, Jesse M., *Political Economy of Socialist Realism*, Yale University Press, New Haven 2007

EAGLES, DEPARTMENT OF; GERVEN, Vincent van, *Workers Leaving the Studio: Looking Away from Socialist Realism*, Punctum Books, Poole, Dorset 2015

GROYS, Boris, *The Total Art of Stalinism: Avant-garde, Aesthetic Dictatorship and Beyond*. Princeton University 1992

— *The Total Art of Stalinism*, Verso, London 2011

FITZPATRICK, S., "Culture and Politics under Stalin: A Reappraisal" in *Slavic Review*, Vol. 35, No.2 (Jun.,1976)

GUTKIN, I., *The Cultural Origins of the Socialist Realist Aesthetic*, Northwestern University Press, Evanston IL 1999

ICOMOS DEUTSCHLAND, *Sozialistischer Realismus und Sozialistische Moderne. Welterbevorschläge aus Mittel- und Osteuropa. Hefte des Deutschen Nationalkomitees*, Hendrik Bäßler, Freiburg 2014

LAHUSEN, T.; et al., *Socialist Realism without Shores*, Duke University 1997

PETROV, M., *Automatic for the masses: the death of the author and the birth of socialist realism*, University of Toronto Press, Toronto 2015

ROBIN, R., *Socialist Realism: An Impossible Aesthetics*, Stanford University Press, 1992

SCHMULÉVITH, E., *Réalisme socialiste*, Champs visueles, L'Harmattan 2000

VAR. AUTHORS, *Socialist Realist Art: Production, Compsumption, Aesthetics*, Centre for Baltic and East European Studies, Södertörn University, Moderna Museet, Stockholm 2012

sources, credits and acknowledgements

131 above, 131 down Cortesía de la Associazione Arte Continua, San Gimignano

132–133, 134, 136, 137 above, 137 down Gori Collection, Fattoria di Celle, Photo: Aurelio Amendola.

139, 141 left, 141 above, 141 down Il Giardino de Daniel Spoerri, Photo: Barbara Räderscheidt, Colonia

142–143, 144 above, 144 down ©Arte Sella, Photo: Giacomo Bianchi

145 Art Park, Cortesía Elena Carlini / Carlini & Valle architetti

147 Open-Air Art Museum at Pedvale, Photo: Ojars Feldbergs

148, 149 above, 149 down Europos Parkas, Photo: Gintaras Karosas

150–151 Courtesy of Jeppe Hein

153 left Courtesy of Annet Gelink Gallery, Amsterdam ©Photo: René van der Hulst, 153 right The I Company

154 Gemeentemuseum Den Haag

155, 156, 157 Flevoland: Konstruierte Natur

159 ©Kröller-Müller Museum, 160 above, 160 down, 162 ©Kröller-Müller Museum, Photo: Walter Herfst

161 ©Kröller-Müller Museum, Photo: Cary Markerink

163 Museum Beelden Aan Zee, Photo: Rob Verhagen

164 Beeldenpark Een Zee van Staal

165 Open Air museum Drechtoevers

168 a 171 Skulpturlandskap Norland, Photo: Vegard Moen

172 Kistefos Museum

173 Ekebergparken

174 Photo: Artur Starewicz

175 Embajada de Polonia, Photo: Piotr Grden

176, 177 Centrum Rzezby Polskiej, Photo: Jan Gaworski

179 Fundaçao Calouste Gulbenkian,

180 Fundaçao de Serralves, Photo: Attilio Maranzano

181 Fundaçao de Serralves, Photo: Rita Burmester

182, 183 above, 183 down Museu Internacional de Escultura Contemporânea de Santo Tirso, Photo: Luis Ferreira Alves

185, 187, 188 above, 188 down, 190c, 191 The Wanås Foundation Photo: Anders Norrsell; 190a The Wanås Foundation, 190b The Wanås Foundation Photo: Thibault Jeanson

192 left, 192 right Lars Vilks, Photo: Mats Svensson

193 above, 193 down Lars Vilks, Photo: Lars Vilks

194–195 down, 195 above Moderna Museet, Stockholm

195 centre ©Yayoi Kusama, Photo: Asa Lundén

196, 197 Umedalen Skulptur

198 Archivo documenta artes

199 Kienast Vogt Partner, Zurich (today Vogt Landscape Architects, Zurich / Munich) ©Christian Vogt

200 Stiftung Sculpture Schöenthal

201 down, 201 above Courtesy of John Schmid, The Sculpture at Schoenthal Foundation, Photo: Heiner Grieder

202–205 ©Fondation Pierre Gianadda, Martigny, Suisse

208 Robin Gillanders, Photo: Robin Gillanders

209 Howard Sooley ©Howard Sooley

210, 211 left, 211 right Grizedale Forestry Commission Sculptures ©Forestry Commission

212 Courtesy Antony Gormley and Jay Jopling / White Cube ©Antony Gormley

213 Broomhill Art Hotel & Sculpture Garden

214, 215 above Art and Architecture at Kielder, Photo: Peter Sharpe

215 down Art and Architecture at Kielder, Photo: Cat Cairn

216, 217 Forest of Dean Sculpture Trail

218, 219 above Jupiter Artland, 219 down photo: Keith Hunter

221, 222 Cass Sculpture Foundation

223 Photo: Barnaby Hindle ©Cass Sculpture Foundation

224, 227 above The Henry Moore Foundation, Photo: Michael Phipps

226 left The Henry Moore Foundation, Photo: Julian Stallabrass

226 right, 227 down The Henry Moore Foundation, Photo: Michael Furze

228 above, 228 down Courtesy of Hannah Peschar Sculpture Garden, Photo: Hannah Peschar

229 Barbara Hepworth Museum and Sculpture Garden ©Bowness, the Hepworth Estate, Photo Marcus Leith and Andrew Dunkley ©Tate 2004

231, 232a, 232b, 232c, 233 New Art Centre Sculpture Park and Gallery

234, 235 Another place

237, 238, 239, 240, 241 ©Yorkshire Sculpture Park and the artists, Photo: Jouty Wilde

242 Gruto parkas

243, 244 Memento Park

245 above Parcul Herastrau

245 down, 246 above Museo de Arte Socialista

246 down, 247 above Croatia

247 down Galeria Nacional de Arte

256 Dani Karavan

acknowledgements:

Joao Almeida
Stefan Andersson
Stefanie Baumann
Thomas Bendix
Andreas Benedict
Sofia Bertilsson
Giacomo Bianchi
Lies Boelrijk
Gianni Bolongaro
Kerry Chase
Olivier Delavallade
Coralie Desmurs
Bettina v. Dziembowski
Miriam Ekwurtzel
Ojars Feldbergs
Ellie Field
Piero Giadrossi
Fabio Guerzoni
Camilla Gustavson
Marie-Céline Henry
Gintaras Karosas
Tressa Lapham-Green
Vikki Leedham
Rafaelle Lelievre
Teresa Luesma
Miranda MacPhail
Susana Martin
Gianfranco Molino
Diego Morlin
Susanne Mortensen
Thomas Niemeyer
Alice O'Connor
Miguel Mª Otamendi
Roberto Pajares
Hannah Peschar
Ilaria Pigliafreddo
Bisi Quevedo
Jane Richardson
Christian Rogge
Hayley Skipper
Estela Solana
Chris Sullivan
Rinus van de Sande
Lars Vilks
Stephan Wolters

Dani Karavan, *Passages. Homage to Walter Benjamin,*1990–1994, Port Bou, Gerona, Spain
The tittle of the work is a direct reference to Benjamin´s book in 2 vols. collecting the unfinished Arcades Project, or Passagen-Work, 1927–1940